Creative Country Construction

Building & Living in Harmony with Nature

Robert Inwood
& Christian Bruyère

Sterling Publishing Co., Inc.

New York

Library of Congress Cataloging-in-Publication Data

Inwood, Robert.
    Creative country construction : building & living in harmony with nature / Robert Inwood
    & Christian Bruyère.
        p. cm.
    Includes index.
    ISBN 0-8069-7115-0
    1. House construction—Amateurs' manuals. I. Bruyère, Christian. II. Title.
TH4815.I56 2000
690'.837—dc21   99-086650

Drawings by Robert Inwood
Photos by Robert Inwood and Christian Bruyère,
except on pages 7, 8, and 9 by R. Neumann
pages 261, 266, 267, 268, 272, 273 by James Woodward
Designed by Judy Morgan
Edited by Rodman Neumann

1 3 5 7 9 10 8 6 4 2

Published by Sterling Publishing Company, Inc.
387 Park Avenue South, New York, N.Y. 10016
© 2000 by Robert Inwood & Christian Bruyère
Distributed in Canada by Sterling Publishing
c/o Canadian Manda Group, One Atlantic Avenue, Suite 105
Toronto, Ontario, Canada M6K 3E7
Distributed in Great Britain and Europe by Cassell PLC
Wellington House, 125 Strand, London WC2R 0BB, England
Distributed in Australia by Capricorn Link (Australia) Pty Ltd.
P.O. Box 6651, Baulkham Hills, Business Centre, NSW 2153, Australia
Manufactured in the United States of America
All rights reserved

Sterling ISBN 0-8069-7115-0

CONTENTS

PREFACE   4

INTRODUCTION   6

1 STONE FOUNDATIONS, WALLS & WINDOWS   10
Stone Masonry 10 ● Arched Windows in a Stone Wall 27

2 CHIMNEY CONSTRUCTION, FIREPLACES & HEATING   32
The Fireplace 32 ● A Central Fireplace 49 ● If You Heat with Wood,
This Is the Heater 57

3 WOOD-FRAME HOUSE   66
Spaces and Relationships

4 LOG HOUSE, VERTICAL STYLE   80
From Many Creeks Flows a River

5 LOG HOUSE, SADDLE-NOTCH STYLE   100
Doing What Comes Naturally

6 LOG HOUSE, CHINKLESS (SWEDISH) STYLE   120
An Author Builds—Christian Bruyère

7 LOG CONSTRUCTION, DOVETAIL-NOTCH STYLE   140
Overcoming Difficulty through the Help of Others

8 POST & BEAM, WITH STUCCO & "MASONRY" INFILL   158
Wood-Fired Sauna—Robert Inwood

9 POST & BEAM, WITH LOG & CORDWOOD INFILL   172
Gathering Together

10 POST & BEAM, WITH HALF-TIMBERING   190
As the Surroundings; So Shall It Be

11 LOG POST & BEAM, WITH HAND-MILLED PLANKS   206
In Accord with the Time

12 LOG POST & BEAM, WITH CURVED-POLE ROOF   226
A Sheltering Arch

13 OUTBUILDINGS, ADAPTED TO THEIR CALLING   234
Wood-Frame Greenhouse 234 ● Sunken Greenhouse 244 ● Cedar Log Root
Cellar (by Kathryn Woodward) 254 ● Gambrel-Roofed Root Cellar 274

METRIC CONVERSION   284

INDEX   285

PREFACE

Creative Country Construction is a documentary on owner-built homes and building techniques which emphasize individual creativity and problem solving. The best parts of the two classics *In Harmony with Nature* and *Country Comforts*,. by the author/illustrator team of Christian Bruyère and Robert Inwood, are combined with the emphasis on portraying a variety of different building styles; thus each chapter presents a home or structure that utilizes a specific building technique.

The content of the book originally was inspired by Inwood & Bruyère's investigations into information to help them plan and build their own homes. In the course of meeting and talking with a variety of local homesteaders and builders, a wealth of knowledge began to emerge on the techniques and skills needed to build and live in the ultimate country house.

The underlying theme which tied all of the building ideas together was the fact that these were all techniques and projects which were accomplished by "average" men and women, many of whom had little or no previous experience in the building trades.

Armed with a portable tape recorder, camera, and sketch book, the authors approached the many individuals who had crafted the buildings and were nearly always met with an enthusiastic response.

In order to try to capture the often colorful flavor of the individuals, many of the notes were transcribed directly from the taped interviews. This allowed us to recount first person descriptions, telling the stories behind the choice of approach that suited their needs and personalities, and conveying speech patterns and local terminology. The drawings were done using visual notes made on site; the major renderings were completed on location.

This focus on the lives of the people and projects they initiated weaves together the tales of various properties, emphasizing the nature of the people who undertook them, and the importance of adapting to the ongoing evolution inherent in all aspects of life. In the decades since the publication of their two books, the authors have made return site visits; their observations give closure, here, to the stories of each chapter.

The authors have undergone their own transformations. Chris Bruyère has moved to a more urban environment and is a successful writer and producer for film and television. Robert Inwood has gone from a fairly free-styled illustrator to a specialist in architectural design and heritage restoration—he still lives on his homestead in the country in a passive-solar/earth-sheltered building of his own design and construction. It is the authors' hope that this volume may prove an inspiration to others who are still in the planning and dreaming stages of making a move to a more simple country way of living, as well as a source of ideas for those who are currently involved in building those dreams into a reality.

—— Robert Inwood
Illustrator/co-author

INTRODUCTION

INWOOD 19

Driven by a need to create our own dwellings, we learned the skills necessary, and like pioneers of previous generations, ultimately derived great satisfaction from directly shaping our own environments.

It is this sense of the love and struggle, and personal accomplishment, that we wish to convey in a way that demystifies the building process. By showing the evolution of how each structure was created, and using nonarchitectural-styled illustrations, the various building procedures are shown to be very do-able. The first two chapters present stonework techniques necessary for foundations and chimneys. Then each chapter presents a home or structure that utilizes a specific building technique.

The underlying theme which ties all of the building ideas together is that the construction methods have been adapted through trial and error, as a means of solving problems as they

Detail of flat notched wall, circa 1750.

arose. The same diversity of appoaches and adaptation of methods is evident in homesteads of previous generations. The stories in this documentary capture the spirit of people forging their own special abode out of natural materials in unspoiled countryside, to live in harmony with nature

Log house, using a flat-notched style of log wall construcion at the Walnut Grove Plantation, circa 1750, Spartanburg, South Carolina.

Creative Country Construction is part of a long tradition of books designed to aid the homesteader. In 1872, C.P. Dwyer published a small book originally titled *The Immigrant Builder* (New York: Claxton, Remson & Haffelfinger). Still in print and retitled *The Homestead Builder: Practical Hints for Handymen*, Dwyer's small book is still useful. The style and original information from *In Harmony with Nature* and *Country Comforts*, first published over 20 years ago, is of the same enduring nature as Dwyer's, while told from the individual builder's point of view. All of the information in this new book, *Creative Country Construction*, is just as relevant and useful to "homesteaders" in the new millennium as it was to those folks back in the 1970s who made the decision to shift their lifestyles to a mode which gives the individual a greater connection to the land and their own domicile.

Creative Country Construction—not exhaustive in it's exploration of particular building styles—offers a broad overview, and much practical information, on the principal variations of log and timber-frame construction methods. There is also a variety of creative ideas dreamed up by the builders to work affordably with recycled materials.

Most of the log houses in *Creative Country Constuction* are built to feature the beauty of the log construction. The builders didn't cover their outside walls with clapboarding. Some houses, such as the wood-frame house of Chapter 3 and those in Chapters 6 and 9, do use clapboarding. Many pioneering log houses were not left with the logs exposed directly to the weather, but were covered with clapboarding. When the Big House of the Walnut Grove Plantation was renovated in the 1960s the workers found a log plank dovetail-notched subwall behind the clapboards. The subwall

Log building, using the saddle-notch style of log wall construction at the Walnut Grove Plantation, circa 1750, Spartanburg, South Carolina.

Log house, using the dovetail-notch style of log wall construction at the Walnut Grove Plantation, circa 1750, Spartanburg, South Carolina.

had been cut and fitted carefully but no mortar or chinking was used. The massive dovetail-notched walls were shaped to present a flat surface for the house to be covered with clapboarding.

Over the intervening decades, the homesteaders who tell their stories in *Creative Country Constuction* were revisited. These site visits are highlighted at the end of each chapter. Our observations offer some insights into how the structures had been holding up and the changes that had been made. Some of the buildings were in better shape than their builders, many of whom had experienced personal relationship issues which caused them to have to leave their properties. Nevertheless each of the structures is still someone's home and the owners were always happy to share their observations about the pros and cons of some of the decisions that were previously made in their structures.

Exposed corner of the Big House at the Walnut Grove Plantation, using the dovetail-notch style of log wall construction with no chinking, circa 1750, Spartanburg, South Carolina.

The Big House, at the Walnut Grove Plantation, covered in clapboarding, was renovated in the 1960s. The original circa 1750 main house was also covered in clapboarding. The renovation had exposed a subwall made entirely of dovetail-notched log planks with no chinking. Spartanburg, South Carolina.

CHAPTER 1

STONE FOUNDATIONS, WALLS & WINDOWS

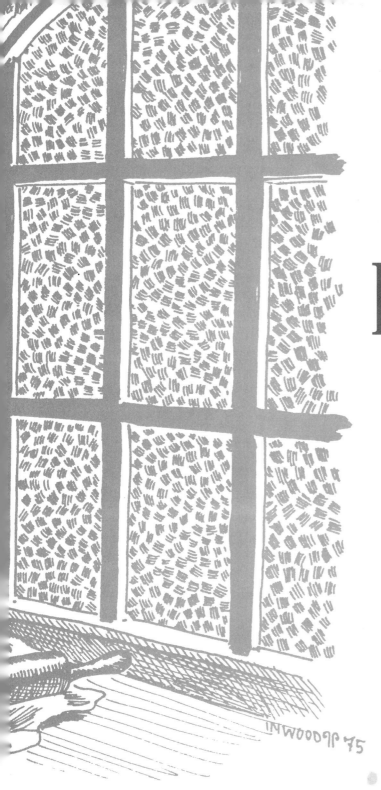

INWOOD '75

Stone Masonry

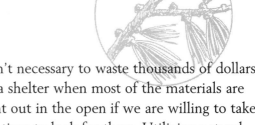

I t isn't necessary to waste thousands of dollars on a shelter when most of the materials are right out in the open if we are willing to take the time to look for them. Utilizing natural timber and local stones, we can bypass the enormous expense of prepared lumber and volumes of concrete.

After working with logs for a while, both of us, Bob and Chris, couldn't even consider dimensional lumber as a main material for a shelter. We found it too limiting—and expensive—and although it is a "green" product it still requires a huge commitment of resources. There have to be fallers to fell the trees, skidders to take them to the trucks, and the trucks in turn drive them to the mill where the timbers are sawed into right-angled boards, wasting much of what remains. This process employs thousands of people, but demands a huge amount of machinery and an enormous expenditure of energies.

Another Way to Go

An alternative to using all of these resources would be to find a piece of wooded land, and build with what you have at hand after you thin out a few of the trees. Sure, there is a lot of labor involved, but at least you'd be working for yourself with materials that don't need such an amount of external preparation as does dimensional lumber. We find that the rigidity of this material tends to hinder creativity because the straight lines and right angles do not allow the building process to flow with the natural shapes and contours of raw timber.

And rock . . . so few people even notice the beauty and potential of this extraordinary and omnipresent material. And few realize how permanent and maintenance-free a stone foundation or wall can be if done right. But then again, stonework isn't for everyone, the same way as finding a wooded lot and working with logs and natural timber isn't for everyone.

1-1 Building the log walls on the stone foundation.

Working with Stone

Stone work requires a dedication. One must really get into working with it and not worry about how long it takes to accomplish one's goal. But we should enjoy the act of creating beauty. People should be able to sit back and appreciate their efforts and not worry about spending too much time on a project. A friend needed help building his stone foundation for his home. It took us two years of working on it when we felt like it, and we never regret the time spent (1-1).

We apprenticed with limestone—but give us the strength and finish of granite any day. It is the least affected by the weather, whereas limestone and sandstone are the most affected because they are so porous and the cement holding the grains together can be easily dissolved. Granite is not at all porous; in fact it is a crystalline igneous rock, which is a way of saying that the rock probably solidified at some depth from molten material to give an internal fabric

of interlocking crystals. This fabric makes it very difficult to split properly. Even with subsequently developed irregular veins, granite does not tend to split well. So when working with it take this into consideration and always try to find the most square and angular rocks you can. If you are fortunate enough to be working in an area underlain with metamorphic rocks, such as schist or gneiss, then you may have better luck finding well-shaped rocks or being able to shape those you have.

The durability of any stone wall will be determined by the quality of the joints between the stones and the climate. Incas, Egyptians, Greeks, and peoples of other ancient civilizations used dry-fit mason work of incredible precision. Many of their structures still stand. A variety of elements can attack stone, largely depending on the climate. In colder climates water can seep between the joints or into cracks, freeze, then expand and cause even huge rocks to shift or break. This is the most important factor to be conscious of in stone wall building. If you do not prevent this, your wall will not last the first winter. Wind can erode stone over very long periods of exposure, but most of the process of alteration of rock and erosion in general is directly the result of running or dripping water.

Selecting a Building Site

Before we got into figuring out the design and materials needed for my friend's house we chose a building site. Actually, the first site chosen was in a small clearing of usable soil. We soon decided against it since there was so little cleared area on his land. Why waste the part that has some topsoil when there was a huge hunk of bedrock nearby which couldn't be used? Besides, with bedrock we are guaranteed against shifting and erosion. What more natural complement to the bedrock could we offer but a foundation of granite stone? Our decision was simple.

Before You Work in Stone

Learn to select rocks as you go on trips to town, outings, or on visits to friends' homesteads. Be constantly on the lookout for possible rocks.

Again, in choosing a rock, make sure it has at least two flat or nearly flat sides. Try to figure out the face, the broad surface which will be seen after the rock is set in; the seat or bottom that will adhere to the mortar below; and the top, the resting

brick, but there aren't many of those around; besides, if there were you would become limited in the design. The next best rock would be one whose top slopes slightly back with sides angling into the backing.

Here are some of the names we devised for usable rock shapes (one can create one's own nomenclature):

Bricks—very square, right-angled rocks which are a dream to work with.

piece of cheese

wedgeback

bula

brutus

brick

place for the seat above. If the top slopes outward, forget it, because there is no possible way you can secure a rock above it and expect it to hold the immense weight of the structure it will be supporting. If the top slopes inward, fine—the space left can be filled with smaller pieces to provide a flat ledge for the rock above. Of course, the ideal rock to work with would be a square or rectangular right-angled

Brutus—big rocks.

Bulas—smaller pieces of any usable shape (bula means "hard bread" in Jamaican).

Piece of cheese—wedge-shaped rocks with a broad face, flat top and bottom, and sides which slant inward, meeting at the rear.

Wedgeback—a flat face, top, sides, and bottom, with a back that slopes away very steeply.

1-2 Using the right tools for stonework.

Getting Started

We trucked in several loads of beautiful, multi-colored, granite rocks of all sizes and shapes. As we began working with them we soon realized the solidness of this material. We attempted shaping and splitting possible beauties with a two-pound mason's hammer (1-2). There are other tools that would be useful in cutting stone. The stone chisel is excellent for scoring and cracking. With it one should have a sledgehammer light enough so it could be swung often without getting the builder overly tired.

First we chipped a line across the section we wanted to cut and went back over that line several times patiently, with the sharp end of the hammer, then trying to knock off the unwanted piece with the blunt end (1-3). The more you chip at the line the better chance your rock will split at that point.

This is a process that works well with softer stone but was just too unpredictable with granite. We ended up breaking several lovely rocks into small chunks which were later used only to fill in behind the facing. But we did have a few rocks with small protruding knobs that were usually quite easy to knock off in this manner.

Needless to say, we became more selective, gathering rocks that we did not have to shape. We searched for large rocks with at least two flat sides, preferably with a long flat face and a flat seat that was no more

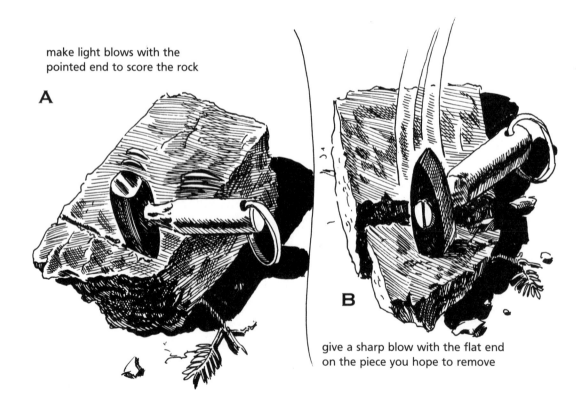

make light blows with the pointed end to score the rock

A

give a sharp blow with the flat end on the piece you hope to remove

B

1-3 Breaking off an unwanted piece of rock.

than 9" in depth to fit our design specifications. We needed good-sized rocks but none heavier than what the two of us could lift. It was important to maintain a personal thing between us and the rocks without the interference of machines and tools to lift.

We found many rocks from a nearby construction site where they were blasting in a new road. Most of these rocks were exceptionally angular and proved to be ideal for the foundation walls; in fact they enabled us to build incredibly smooth, flat-faced walls that we could never have made without such material. When planning a wall or foundation it is best to try to avoid having openings and sharp corners as much as possible. Corners take five times as much attention because cornerstones are special, brick-like shapes which should alternately "tie back" into both walls and keep the walls from falling out under a load (1-4). Corners should be planned so securely that they could stand free to create the total support of the building above.

We got into precision straightness because we were finding rocks that expressed that style. We'd never suggest this design unless there were optimum materials at the builder's disposal . . . and plenty of time.

Seeing the Project Through

This project took about 150 six-hour days to complete. Six hours is a full day of masonry work. Gathering took us about 50 percent of the actual working time. Sometimes a simple trip up the road would take us hours but would reward us with several usable pieces. This is all part of the organic process of development . . . nature is never in a hurry—only people are.

We used 50 tons of material that was handled at least three times. Some rocks went through the whole history of the building without being used. So be wise and select the proper rocks in the beginning. It will make your job so much easier.

1-4 Corners take a lot of planning.

Planning the Foundation

Before beginning to set up the foundation walls, get to know the individual rocks as you would pieces of a jigsaw puzzle. Lay them flat on the ground, attempt to create designs with them . . . mix larger ones with smaller ones, triangular with square . . . visualize what they would look like on the wall . . . see which ones complement others. Once you mortar them in place they are permanent . . . there is no changing them around. After you are satisfied with a section, try setting it up as a dry wall to see how it stands. When you are pleased with how each rock sets and balances among the others, take that section down, making certain not to disturb the positioning, and mortar them together.

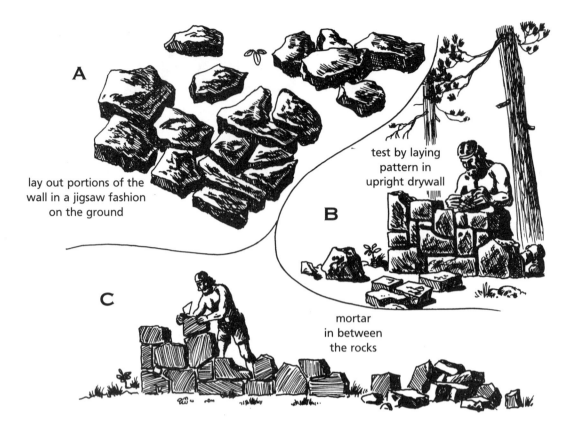

A lay out portions of the wall in a jigsaw fashion on the ground

B test by laying pattern in upright drywall

C mortar in between the rocks

1-5 Take your time to work out the composition of your stone wall.

Remember, never hurry—be extremely patient. Sometimes it takes a long time for the ancient wisdom of these rocks to communicate, for they have been silent since long before any of us have been around. But in time, they will express their own design that most complements them (1-5).

At this time, before actually setting up much of the first wall, be sure to figure out all the openings, vents, electrical holes, drains, water pipe positions, etc. It would be a near impossible task to install these necessities as an afterthought—when the walls are set up. We're sure we wouldn't want to attempt it.

Starting the First Course

Starting anywhere along the wall with the first course of stone, we worked toward the corners. This is because the cornerstones are usually the hardest to stand up freely. Having the wall next to the corner already complete aids in supporting the cornerstones. However it is often necessary to "juggle" (curse and coax) the penultimate rock that fits next to the cornerstone because the corner is a fixed point and can only go in one position (refer to 1-4).

The outer dimensions of the foundation are 20' × 26'. To figure out the rectangle we simply made a scale drawing and found the length of the diagonals from opposing corners. That length was converted to actual size. The exact center was marked and the crossing diagonal was also staked. A 20' side was measured and the stakes were adjusted accordingly. A right-angling 26' side was then checked and a string was placed around the perimeter. The corners could be confirmed by running a 6' line along one side and an 8' line along the intersecting side. If the diagonal of those two lines is 10', then the corner is a right-angled square corner.

Mixing the Mortar

If you are not using a small cement mixer it is a good idea to make a mixing pad of some sort before you begin setting up the walls. We created a 2" to 3"-thick pad made of hardened Portland cement from a 1.5 mixture. It is 6' in diameter, poured right on the ground. On this we mixed the mortar.

The mortar is a mixture of 1 part masonry cement to 4 parts sand. The sand should consist of ⅔ fine river sand and ⅓ coarser sand. Since the adhesion of mortar to sand is critical, you should make a test before mixing the whole batch to make sure the sand is clean enough to use. Fill a quart jar ⅔ full with sand, then add water to fill the jar. Shake it up and leave it for a few hours. If more than ⅛ inch of silt settles atop the sand, then it is too dirty to use without first washing—an arduous job requiring a large flow of water and hand turning of the dirty sand.

We first mixed the mortar and sand dry in the center of the slab, making certain that it all had a consistent mortar-gray color. Then it was spread out over the slab, drilled with a fine spray of water, and was all brought back to the center and worked, gradually adding more water, until it had the desirable sticky, clinging (cloy) consistency.

Do not add any more lime to the mixture to achieve the desired stickiness. Masonry cement has enough lime already mixed in with it—any more will weaken the strength of the mortar. Also, be sure that the mortar is never richer than the 1.4 mixture. The more excessively rich the mixture is, the larger the coefficient of expansion; thus the greater will be the chance that the setting cement will crack and shrink.

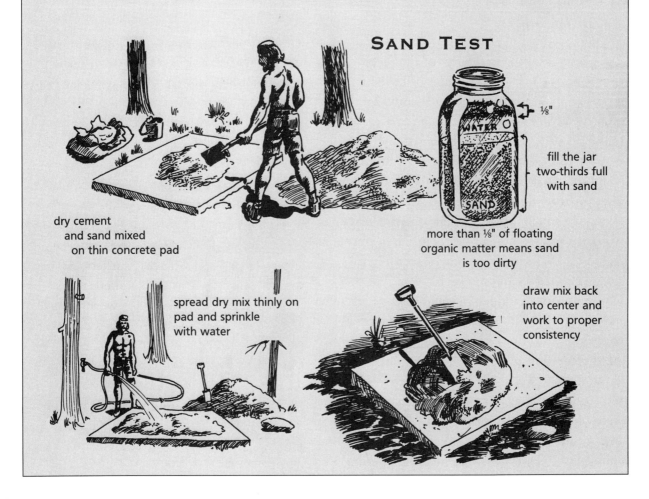

SAND TEST

dry cement and sand mixed on thin concrete pad

⅛"

fill the jar two-thirds full with sand

more than ⅛" of floating organic matter means sand is too dirty

spread dry mix thinly on pad and sprinkle with water

draw mix back into center and work to proper consistency

1-6 *String guide systems.*

Using Templates

Once we found the perimeter of the rectangle we set up the vertical templates or upright guides to make certain our walls would be plumb and straight. We used two template frames at each corner, which consisted of two parallel vertical boards spaced the width of the wall (18") apart and were put in a couple feet directly beyond the end of each wall face to allow us enough space to maneuver the heavy stone without colliding into them. They were rested on the ground and braced securely to stakes, stumps, or trees in such a way that they would remain exactly in place in case we bumped or fell into them. We even left some trees around to brace these posts. After they were secured in place, two horizontal strings, about 2' apart vertically, were extended from template to opposing template. The strings were both plumb above the face of the wall they guided and could be moved up as the courses were laid. The templates and lines

were a headache to work with because we were always becoming entangled with them as we were struggling with the heavier stones. But never attempt a structural support such as this foundation without such guides because you can't do it (1-6 and 1-7).

DETAIL OF STRING LEVEL

1-7 *Corner overlap of string level.*

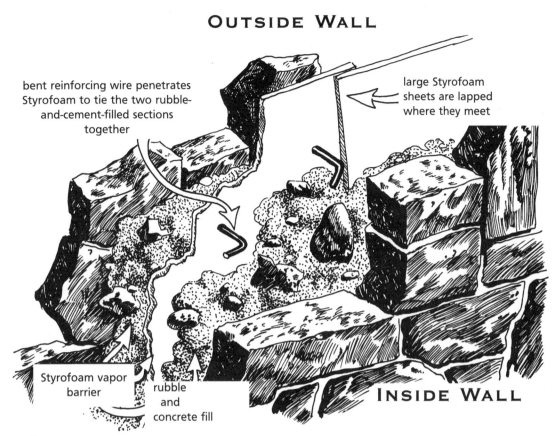

OUTSIDE WALL

bent reinforcing wire penetrates Styrofoam to tie the two rubble-and-cement-filled sections together

large Styrofoam sheets are lapped where they meet

Styrofoam vapor barrier

rubble and concrete fill

INSIDE WALL

1-8 Wall structure.

The Structure of the Walls

The foundation walls are 18" thick all around, consisting of an outer face of no more than 9", a Portland cement and "bula" backing, a vapor barrier of ½" Styrofoam, an inner wall backing, and an inside wall face. The two faces were set up first. The Styrofoam was then placed in the trench created by the opposing faces and pieces of heavy gauge wire were poked through the Styrofoam on approximately a 2' grid. Each bent end was sunk into the fresh cement backing between the inside and outside face, creating a tie for the two walls. The backing mixture was poured on either side of the lapped Styrofoam sheets before the surrounding masonry had a chance to completely set up, allowing it all to "monolithically" tie together, usually about one hour after doing the faces (1-8).

Styrofoam insulation is brittle and cracks quite easily but has proven to be an excellent thermal and vapor barrier. This vapor barrier

Excessive Moisture

On rainy or very humid, damp days it takes as much as three times as long for mortar to set up, depending on the moisture content in the air. Be extremely careful when attempting to lay stone during a light rain because the heavy moisture content will cause the mortar to sag and droop under the weight of the stone.

prevents the movement of warmth and humidity from inside to outside. If this is not prevented, the warmth will meet the snow, ice, or frost on the outer wall which would then seep back into the wall, possibly refreezing and causing the wall to crack.

If moisture were allowed to penetrate through the walls, splitting and cracking of the mortar would also eventually occur. We installed the Styrofoam mainly as a thermal insulation because stone has a very low R factor (18" of rock provides less insulation then 3½" of fiberglass). But even with the thermal barrier some cold still manages to come through the walls during the winter. So ½" of Styrofoam did not prove to adequately solve this problem. If we'd used 1" of Styrofoam I think this chill factor would have been greatly reduced. Besides being thicker, that size is much easier to handle and it wouldn't have cracked so readily as we worked with it. We are not advocating the use of Styrofoam. You can use anything that proves to be a good vapor barrier with insulative value. You can even fill garbage bags with old cardboard or waxed cartons for this purpose.

Take a Break to Clean Up

Before going on to the next course of stone be sure to clean off with a steel brush the rocks which were just set in place and point up the mortar. If you wait much longer than within 2 or 4 hours afterwards, the mortar will have set up on the faces, thus making it necessary to employ an acid chemical (muriatic acid) to remove the dry mortar. This chemical is a costly, odorous, and unpleasant alternative to taking time as you go to clean off your stone. Besides, the cleaning process will give you a little time between courses to sit back and appreciate your work. Many such breaks are imperative when indulging in any creative endeavor, especially one that will be so permanent.

A Problem in Masonry

To the layperson the hardest part of working with rocks is interlocking the pieces. If you are not good at putting together jigsaw puzzles don't attempt rock masonry.

Here is a test for those interested in checking their skill of visualizing in three dimensions. If you can figure out this problem, you are ready to work with stone. If not, then you should take the time to familiarize yourself more with this media before attempting to build any supporting structure out of it.

You have up to three cuts to shape a 1" round rod of any length so that it will pass through a 1" square, a circle with a 1" diameter, and an isosceles triangle with a 1" base and a height of 1". The rod has to pass through each of these flat geometric designs perfectly, leaving no excess spaces and without destroying the shapes and designs in any way. You can practice on doweling or other material.

You can find the answer to the problem at the end of this chapter on page 31. But try to answer it yourself before you look at the answer.

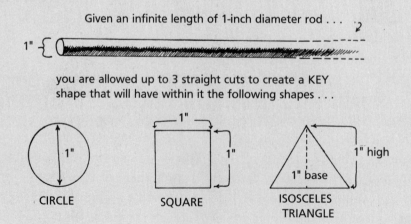

Given an infinite length of 1-inch diameter rod . . .

1"

you are allowed up to 3 straight cuts to create a KEY shape that will have within it the following shapes . . .

1"

CIRCLE

1"

1"

SQUARE

1" high

1" base

ISOSCELES TRIANGLE

1-9 *Construction got better with experience.*

There is a noticeable difference between the lower portion of the north wall where we started and the upper area of that wall. It looks much more raggedy and rough than the others. We got progressively better with experience, concentrating more on the finish as we felt more comfortable with the mortaring (1-9).

Before taking the corners up again we reinforced them with twisted strapping bands. These bands were 5' in length, extending at right angles 2½' in either side from the corner, one on each side of the Styrofoam. They were laid in at vertical intervals of about 18". The twisting provided them with much more bonding strength, making them immovable within the concrete (1-10).

Pointing

The best time to do the pointing or cutting back is just before the mortar completely sets up. Pointing is the process of trimming the excess mortar that sticks out between the joints of stone.

There are several styles of pointing. Some masons prefer a deeper look. This provides rich, full-shadowed joints and is best for contrasting the dimensions of the rocks. It also weatherproofs the mortar by cutting it back, shielding it with overhanging stone.

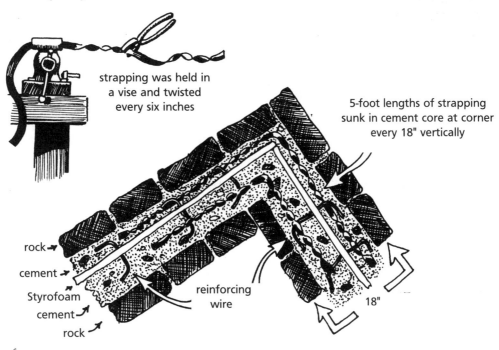

strapping was held in a vise and twisted every six inches

5-foot lengths of strapping sunk in cement core at corner every 18" vertically

rock
cement
Styrofoam
cement
rock

reinforcing wire

18"

1-10 *Top view of corner.*

1-11 The joists and flooring with the bedrock below.

We searched through several building supply and hardware stores to find a material for this purpose, but everything was so outrageously expensive it was prohibitive to use. Outside of one store we found a pile of scrap-metal shipping bands. We were told we could have them. We searched for more in other places, including the local mill, and soon brought home all we needed for free.

Height of the Walls

Be sure to plan all openings before you begin construction because there is no way to accommodate them once the walls have set up. The walls went up to about the 3½" level where we inserted the floor joists, cellar vent openings, and door frames. This height was chosen because the high point of the bedrock extended 3' higher than the low point (1-11 and 1-12) and we wanted to allow another 6" to bring the joists above the ground. The joists were spaced at 24" intervals, extending from a short distance out past the front wall to 8' beyond the rear wall as supports for an outside porch area (1-13 and 1-14). These longer ends will be sheltered from the direct weather by the porch, but the short stubs in the front, east wall have no protection; they were left exposed (1-15). If we were to put them in again we would just extend the front ends to meet the Styrofoam; this way they would have a vapor barrier protection and still have plenty of support from the 9" inner wall section.

There is no creosote or other preservative around the joists where they come in contact with the mortar and concrete. We didn't feel it necessary since they are of durable cedar and we don't have to worry about getting capillary action from the soil beneath because we have a floor of bedrock. But even if the joist ends rot in time, which they are bound to do anyway, our children or grandchildren or whoever will be around then can just pound them out and insert replacements, trimming them where they meet the walls for proper fit.

Below the floor level we put in a 6" vent on the east and west walls to allow the warm air to escape from below the floor. These vents

1-12 Bedrock under the foundations and floor area.

1-13 *Floor joists.*

1-14 *Joists extend to support a porch.*

were formed with 6" stovepipe pieces that were left in. Earlier we put in openings at the bottom of these walls to allow the cold air to come in and circulate through the basement. This airflow provides proper ventilation and prevents mildew and vapor buildup (1-15).

This will probably be a great root cellar once we complete the house.

Setting the Door Frames

The door jambs were also put in at this level. We used uncreosoted railroad ties for this purpose because they were durable and available. They have spikes driven and bolts drilled into their sides to tie into the masonry and

1-15 *Short joist stubs exposed to the weather.*

join them to the wall logs. These frames were made plumb and they acted as a guide for the new inside corners of the rockwork (1-16 and 1-17).

1-16 *Setting the door frames.*

1-17 *Inside view of the door frame.*

1-19 *Stone walls allow for the notched sills.*

1-18 *Water pipe.*

After the frames came the water pipe opening. This was put in above the floor, in the west wall. For this we simply sank a piece of ½" galvanized pipe which we could later deal with (1-18).

We slowly raised the walls a bit higher, carefully considering the design of each as we went. By now we got emotionally involved with some of the rocks, we handled them so much. But many of them just didn't seem to fit anywhere. Up to this point we could use

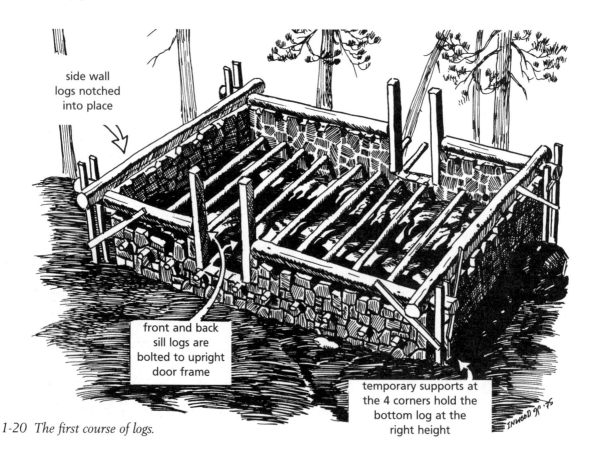

side wall logs notched into place

front and back sill logs are bolted to upright door frame

temporary supports at the 4 corners hold the bottom log at the right height

1-20 *The first course of logs.*

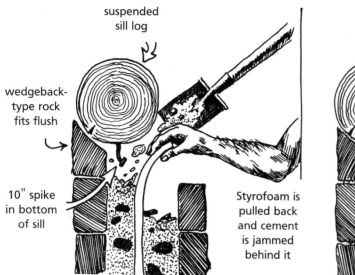

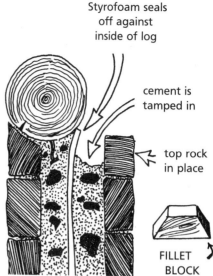

1-21 Providing a solid seat for the sill logs.

whatever size rock we could lift into place, the larger the better, but now we had to prepare for the sill logs, which meant narrowing down our supply to the special shapes needed, without disturbing our design.

The long sill logs which rested above the east and west walls were set in place on the center of the wall and held there with braced uprights. The shorter side logs were round-notched onto them. This meant that the two long walls had to be raised to one height and the side walls had to extend a few inches higher to accommodate the sills above them (1-19).

The Last Courses of Stone

It was a difficult, painstaking operation to fit the last courses under the logs. But at least we had a permanent horizontal line to work up to instead of an estimated line that could not duplicate the exact contour of the log. The Styrofoam barriers were set in so they touched the bottom center of the sills, then we experimented with several rocks until we could find the right combination for the first outer wall. We set up the outer walls first, then filled in the backing from inside. This was a tricky maneuver, which I'll explain in turn. After we figured roughly out the last course of an outer wall, spikes were driven into the bottom of the

sill that rested over it. We were careful to position the spikes so they would not interfere with the last course of rocks, but would extend out into the mortar and cement instead (1-20). The outer wall rocks were then mortared into place. Now the tricky part. The Styrofoam was bent back, which sometimes broke it, and the rubble and concrete for the outer wall facing was shoveled in and tamped hard around the sill log to provide a solid seat for it (1-21 and 1-22).

1-22 The sill logs sit solidly on the stone foundation.

The Styrofoam was then bent into vertical position, and the last courses of the inner face were carefully dry fitted. The spikes were driven in and a few of the top-course rocks were mortared. The rubble and cement backing was then tamped in behind the face and a few more rocks were set in. This process continued until the last rock was placed. Then on to the next wall.

Before finishing the ledges above the inner walls, we sunk "fillets," or small wedge-shaped pieces of wood, into the mortar to provide nailing blocks for the wood pieces which would cover them (1-23 and 1-24). These wooden ledge covers would be useful caps, providing needed shelf space. They would also shadow the very top of the inner stone wall and give it a contrast of timber with stone.

1-23 Interior wall.

A Foundation Worth the Effort

As you can see, our careful, meditative approach proved to be not in vain. We have succeeded in constructing not only a useful, strong foundation, but an aesthetically beautiful monument that should still be standing long after we are all dead and gone. I wish you could see the richness and array of colors in these rocks. They are so pleasing to look at that we can sit for hours observing them, and we do just that sometimes. This is the feeling I want every time I complete a project. How about you?

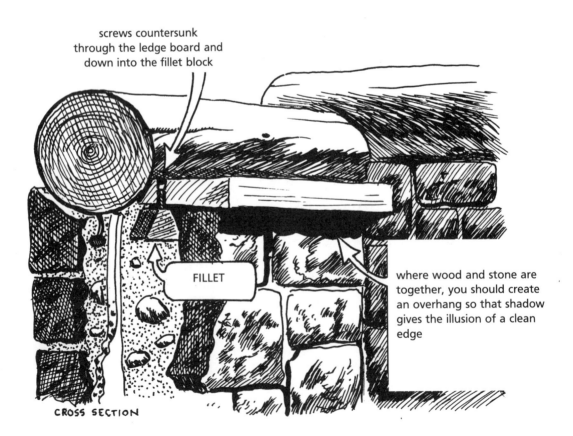

screws countersunk through the ledge board and down into the fillet block

FILLET

where wood and stone are together, you should create an overhang so that shadow gives the illusion of a clean edge

1-24 CROSS SECTION

Arched Windows in a Stone Wall

Along the tiny unpaved roads that surround our little bakery there are many dwellings and homesteads which have been carefully constructed out of the available materials that we are so lucky to be endowed with in this area. Some make good use of the forest, some make good use of the stone, some combine the two materials to put a bit of beauty around them. So we wanted to contribute to this beauty by adding a little of our own heritage into the bakery. And what more Scottish building material is there than stone.

A Dream of Round Windows

We had a design in mind for a dream house in the round, built out of stone. We made a little model of that round house and put in a few round windows. We still haven't made it a reality and probably won't for a while, so I decided to give the bakery a touch of my dreams by making the kitchen front out of rock with arched windows (1-25).

Basic Post & Beam to Start

We constructed the building, using a post-and-beam style, leaving the front kitchen wall open between the 6' spanning posts. We wanted to give a contrast to the logs and stuccoed exposed beams which comprise the rest of the face, and we wanted this contrast to be stone. Because the building is post and beam, none of the structural weight is on the rock wall, it is all on the outlining posts. This gave us freedom to experiment with the windows. A fondness for round and oval architecture inspired us to devise a way to put arched windows into the front wall.

1-25 Arched windows in a stone wall.

Lower Stone Wall

Though we hadn't really worked much with stone, we knew enough to get started. First, we made sure the bottom course was the thickest and wide enough to support the weight that was to be put on it. Second, we made certain that the outside face was very straight and plumb. We knew the upright posts were plumb so we nailed 1 × 6 boards across the posts, all the way up the front. This was the outside form. We then collected as many of the straight, flat-face rocks as we thought we needed. This was quite easy since the nearby lake shore is full of such angular and extremely colorful rocks.

We piled the rocks jigsaw-puzzle-style on top of each other, making sure the flattest side faced the front and the bigger rocks were at the bottom. We tried the rock that fitted in best, then mortared it in, giving each course a chance to set a bit by going along the whole wall before beginning another course. For this

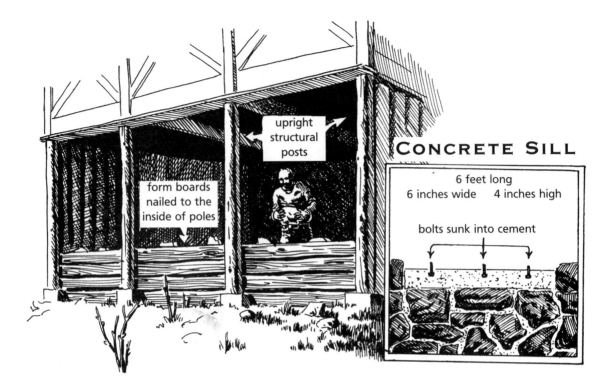

upright structural posts

form boards nailed to the inside of poles

CONCRETE SILL

6 feet long
6 inches wide   4 inches high

bolts sunk into cement

1-26 Setting up a concrete sill.

purpose we made our own mixture of Portland cement and lime. Premixed cement is like cake mixes—if you want to buy it premixed you have to pay for it. I mixed two parts lime to one part Portland cement and added nine parts of sand. This made a good workable mortar. Be careful when you use the lime because it burns your fingers. We worked with rubber gloves to prevent the lime from burning.

The stone wall was built in this manner for about 30" in height. At that point we wanted to put in the windows. To prepare a sill for them, the mortar was formed and flattened above the rocks. This way bolts to hold the sill boards in place could be sunk into the mortar instead of into the rocks. It is much easier to sink bolts into wet mortar than into granite rocks (1-26).

The Trouble with Forms

The problem with using forms that cannot be easily removed before the mortar has a chance to set is that mortar, no matter how careful your are, builds up around the rock. This leaves ugly clumps in the joints that cannot be cleaned off because the mortar has already hardened by the time the form is taken off. If a person were to use removable forms here this problem could be remedied.

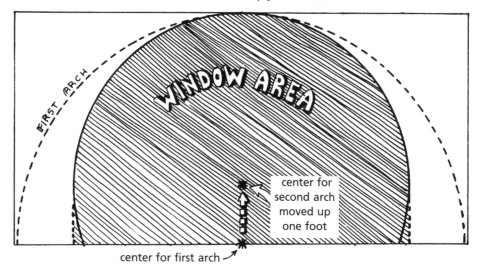

cut from 4' × 8', ½" plywood sheet

FIRST ARCH

WINDOW AREA

center for
second arch
moved up
one foot

center for first arch

1-27 *Designing the form of the arched windows.*

A Method for Arched Windows

This method actually worked quite well. First we took a sheet of 4' × 8', ½" plywood and laid it on the floor. We found the exact center along the length and drove a nail in at that point. Then we attached one end of a 4' piece of string to that nail and the other end to a pencil. we drew an arch, starting from one corner, to the middle of the side opposite the nail, and down to the other corner. We didn't like that shape because it was too wide at the ends, but the height was just fine. The nail was moved 1' closer to the apex of the arch and the string was shortened to 3'. We drew that

arch and left the bottom foot beyond the nail on either side straight, to make an elliptical arch instead of a half round (1-27).

After the shape was figured out we cut it out with a Skilsaw™ and finished the edges with a hand plane. We then took a thin strip of 3"-wide veneer and tacked it along the edge of the half-oval form, off-centering it to one side to affix the window framing to it. We felt it wise to make the framing now and attach it to the form and casing. This would give the form, casing, and frame additional strength, tying it all together as one interlocking unit to hold it all in place (1-28).

saber saw

veneer is tacked to the
edge of the window frame

1-28 *Cutting out the form.*

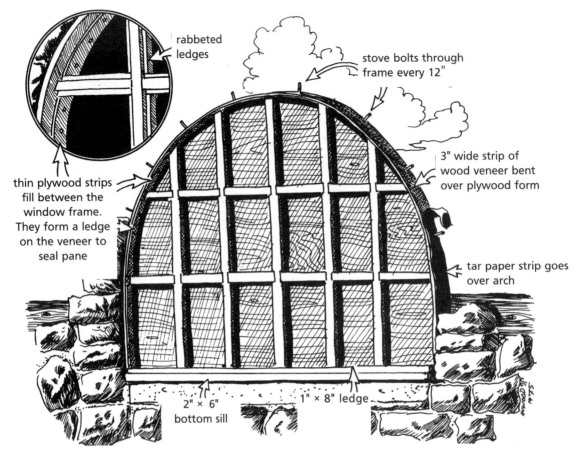

rabbeted ledges

stove bolts through frame every 12"

3" wide strip of wood veneer bent over plywood form

tar paper strip goes over arch

thin plywood strips fill between the window frame. They form a ledge on the veneer to seal pane

2" × 6" bottom sill

1" × 8" ledge

1-29 Arched window seen from inside the building.

Making Window Frames

Wood strips 1" × 1" were used for the window frames. This framework is comprised of five upright pieces of varying lengths following the arch. The outside edges of these uprights were dadoed ¼" on either side to provide laps for the 12" × 16" window panes, leaving about a ½" tongue in the center to hold the panes in place. There were also grooved strips that interlocked with them to frame the panes. These 12" horizontal strips were rabbeted on the outside edge and a sill strip was nailed in place across the bottoms of the upright pieces. Holes were drilled 1' apart around the veneer border for stove bolts which would be sunk into the setting mortar to hold the strips in place around the window frame. The spring tension of the bent strips would aid to keep it in place after the form was removed. Each of these three window forms was made ready before going any further (1-29 and 1-30).

The 2 × 6 sills were bolted over the formed mortar seats below the window opening and the completed window forms were placed above them, with the plywood facing the inside. A few temporary nails were then attached to the outside form to keep them in place and the rockwork was mortared around the arches all the way up to the 2 × 6 wall plate above. The only tricky part of this whole operation was slanting the rocks above the arches and still making the design blend in with the other stones. It all worked to our satisfaction.

Removing the Forms

After the mortar set for a while the plywood window forms were removed. Care was taken not to disturb the veneer and 1 × 1 window frames. The outside forms were also taken off at this point and we got to see the mortar-clumped rocks. Oh well, at least we didn't have to look at that face all day. We were very careful to trim the mortar between the

1-30 *Interlocking frame of windows.*

1-31 *Interior of bakery.*

inside rocks and clean them off, leaving a nice finish on them. After all, we would be looking at them several hours each day as we prepared the baked goods for the upstairs bakery (1-31).

We used opaque, corrugated plastic instead of glass for the windows to keep out the glare and because we didn't want to go through the trouble of cutting a rounded edge on glass. It is hard enough to cut a straight edge on glass, let alone getting fancy with it.

These windows were held on the inside with curved slats that followed the arch. They were nailed along the veneer strip, which covered the bolts and holes (see 1-30). The windows were puttied on the outside. Putty did not work so well because it did not properly adhere to the plastic.

A question might come up about the insulative value of this rock wall in a cold area such as this. We realize that stone is not a good insulator but we haven't been uncomfortably chilly at all. Once the ovens are going, the kitchen remains quite warm and what little heat that might escape through the stone is welcome to do so.

Solution to Problem

The problem is on page 20. First cut is angled from dead center of circle, 1" long, until it meets either side. Second cut begins at same dead-center spot and angles out to other side, also being 1" long. Third cut severs angled end from remaining rod.

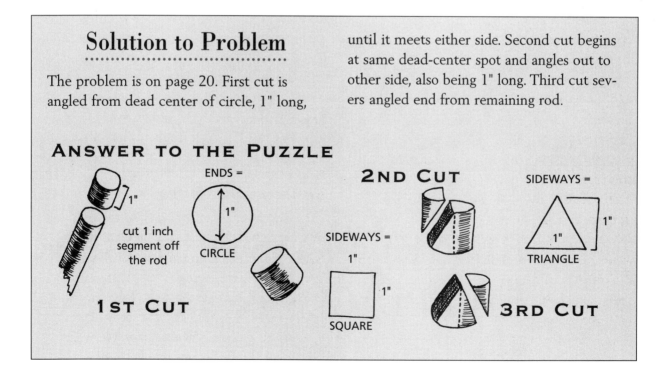

ANSWER TO THE PUZZLE

1"

cut 1 inch segment off the rod

1ST CUT

ENDS =

1"

CIRCLE

SIDEWAYS =

1"

1"

SQUARE

2ND CUT

SIDEWAYS =

1"

1"

TRIANGLE

1"

3RD CUT

CHAPTER 2

CHIMNEY CONSTRUCTION, FIREPLACES & HEATING

The Fireplace

We were already familiar with the warm, earthy presence of an aesthetically beautiful fireplace and its natural attraction to people like ourselves who enjoy intimate get-togethers with friends. Such a fireplace is a must in our home and became the major consideration in the design. We wanted a fireplace with which we could participate while eating, while conversing with friends and also while working in the kitchen. It is important for us to have as much exposure to its warmth and nourishment as possible.

A Question of How to Proceed

Upon designing the house we figured out the size and location of the fireplace but had no idea of what the finished product would look like until after gathering the materials. We began working with the materials—and let the process flow. Soon the project began to take on its own energy and to determine its own form.

Our accumulation of stone consisted of several shallow, flat-faced pieces and a whole lot of rough, square ones. We knew a plain straight fireplace would not be the natural outcome, so we experimented with the stones. We laid them out on a flat surface and played with them as one would a jigsaw puzzle. The flat stones seemed to want to gather together in the center section, leaving the square stones at the ends. We stacked the center stones flat-ways, so only their edges were revealed. This produced a horizontal feeling in the center which protruded out beyond the receding sides. It emphasized

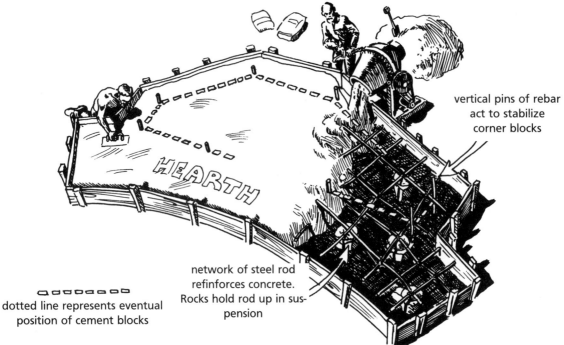

vertical pins of rebar act to stabilize corner blocks

network of steel rod reinforces concrete. Rocks hold rod up in suspension

dotted line represents eventual position of cement blocks

2-1 Fireplace hearth and foundation.

contrast and a third dimension. Then we put in a few niches here and a little shelf there, where some of our things and plants could go. We did what felt right as we worked with the materials.

Allowing for a Hearth

When laying the slab be sure to take the hearth into consideration, though there is not a great deal of weight on it. We have built hearths on the floor joists and mortared the facing onto a constructed wood box frame. The frame was prepared with paper to absorb expansion and reinforced with a wire for support. This works well if the rocks are not too thick or too big. But with this method you usually get a crack between the hearth masonry and the fireplace proper because the floor joists are bound to shrink and the whole thing is built on them. The hearth of this fireplace is built on the slab foundation.

There is a popular material that can be purchased for the fireplace. It is a rough, rustic-looking rock that is quite sharp around the edges and is precut to produce a clean effect without exposing much mortar or many joints. But this material is fairly expensive, whereas the type of stone we used is just sitting there waiting to be picked up. The commercial product may make some things easier and have an aesthetic appeal to some, but it takes away the chance to be freely creative with the design because of its uniform thickness and lack of dimension.

The Chimney's Foundation

We began the actual construction of the fireplace by pouring a very adequate slab for the heavy structure. This slab should not be less than 10" thick and should be reinforced with a ½" reinforcing rod, crisscrossed throughout it, especially on the two sides where most of the structural weight is going to be supported. A vertical anchor of ⅜" rebar, coming out to meet the corner concrete blocks framing the firebox, should also be included. This slab must extend at least 12" beyond the perimeter of the fireplace in all directions and could also be the base for the hearth, depending on design.

You want a strong slab so you need to make a mixture one part Portland cement to five parts sand. The adhesive strength should not be broken up with too many plumbs (large rocks) or else the whole slab will be weakened. Large rocks do not provide enough tiny surfaces for the concrete to adhere to and cement together (2-1). Remember, if you are going to go through the trouble of building anything with masonry—masonry being permanent, expensive, and very difficult to alter—build it with the proper materials. Do not skimp—especially do not skimp on the slab. It is the foundation for a very heavy, permanent structure. If the slab cracks or crumbles, so does the fireplace.

The Firebox Design

Once the slab has been poured you can begin laying out the fireplace in terms of firebox preference. The two most popular alternatives are the double-jacketed metal heatalaters or heatforms and the traditional handmade firebrick box (2-2).

Heatalaters or heatforms are supposedly the more efficient route. They allow quick emission of hot air into the living area, whereas it takes firebrick longer to heat up before it radiates. The heatalater is easy to install and comes as a whole unit. Firebricks have to be set up, shaped, and adhered together. This usually becomes a long, involved process, but is a very satisfying and creative one.

We prefer to build the firebox out of firebrick. It is cheaper than buying the metal unit; is more aesthetically pleasing; and it can be shaped to optimum efficiency. Though firebrick takes longer to heat up than the metal form does, it retains heat much longer. The bricks stay warm several hours after the fire has gone out completely, thus they keep out the chill factor much longer than the metal form does. Firebrick will also last more than 20 or 30 years.

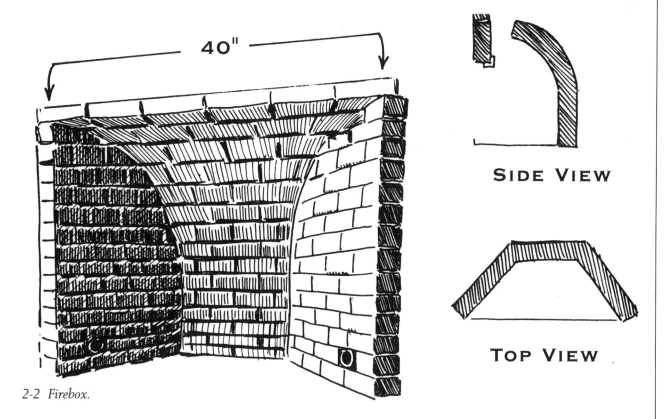

SIDE VIEW

TOP VIEW

2-2 Firebox.

Our main argument for firebrick is that one can form it to a desired shape. At the rear, we angle the firebox side walls deliberately toward the center along the lines of the classic "Rumford" fireplace. Though there is a 40" opening in the width of the front, the back side is only about 16" to 17" in width.

The "Rumford" Fireplace

Sir Benjamin Thompson, known by the title Count Rumford, set out principles of efficient fireplace design in the late 17th century. He did pioneering work on heat production, radiant heat, and practical work on ventilators, stoves, flues, and fireplace design. It is the high, shallow firebox that characterizes the "Rumford" fireplace.

There are several reasons for this design. The reflected heat from this firebox is far greater than from a deeper, conventional one. Thus a small fire in this box will work just as well as a larger one. This is a major fuel-conserving factor, if nothing else. It takes a larger fire to fit a conventional box or heat-formed box because the backsides are deeper. There is far less reflective heat coming into the room from the deeper boxes, consequently there is less heat economy. The deeper the firebox, the more the reflective heat rises into the throat and dissipates up the chimney instead of coming into the living area. With a shallow firebox, the reflective area is closer to the living area, thus more rising, reflective heat enters it.

The rate of smoke emission increases proportionately with the depth of the firebox, especially in early stages of the fire, because there is more room for air to circulate around a deep box.

We tend to make the lintel higher than what many people are used to. This provides more of a view of the fire. From the hearth up to the lintel our firebox is 32" high.

Air Circulation

Before actual construction of the firebox we designed a vent system, enabling oxygen to enter in from the exterior, flow under the firebox, and come out the sides to supply the fire. A standard fireplace will utilize a huge amount of room oxygen, consequently depleting the living area of air. This causes its inhabitants to feel weary and fatigued. Also, without the exterior air supply, chilling foot drafts occur as the fire draws oxygen. A well-known formula explains that a standard fireplace will cause the displacement of over twice the amount of room air required for optimum ventilation; therefore at least half the amount of oxygen for the fire should be drawn directly from the outside and not be permitted to pass through the room to the fireplace.

The air is brought in from the outside through a 3" opening formed by a juice can that goes from the exterior bottom and comes in from directly underneath the firebox, between it and the slab. I allowed an opening for it there the width of the firebox and 2½" in height. The air intake is located at the lower right of the stonework masonry exterior (2-3).

2-3 Stonework exterior.

One outlet comes through near the right front side of the firebox and the other travels beneath it, coming out on the left side opposite the first (2-4).

Starting Construction

The construction of this air intake system was tricky. The first course of brick around the sides and back of the firebox was mortared directly to the slab, leaving 3" spaces near the front of either side as air channels. A piece of sheet metal was placed over this bottom course. It acted as a form for the 2" secondary slab which the firebrick bottom of the firebox rests on. Rebar was distributed throughout the area above the sheet metal and a second course of brick was mortared in place around it. This second course also acted as the side form for the 2" of concrete which was then poured over the sheet metal. After the concrete dried, the bottom firebricks were put in over it.

This secondary slab construction created a 2½" plenum over the slab for an air chamber which would allow the passage of air from the exterior air intake through the bottom plenum, out to either side of the firebox. Two 3" juice cans were used as forms on the lower sides and another course of firebrick was

2-4 *The firebox with angled sidewalls.*

adhered around the firebox. An archway of brick was then mortared around the vent openings to protect them from the later rubble and concrete fill that will be put in between the firebox and the surrounding concrete block (2-5).

If we were able to redo this vent system we would bring both of the outlet vents 2" forward, more to the front of the box. As it comes in now, the air hits the fire from the sides, blowing it a bit toward the hearth. If the vents were nearer to the front the incoming air would blow the fire to the back where it could more efficiently warm the bricks and radiate its heat.

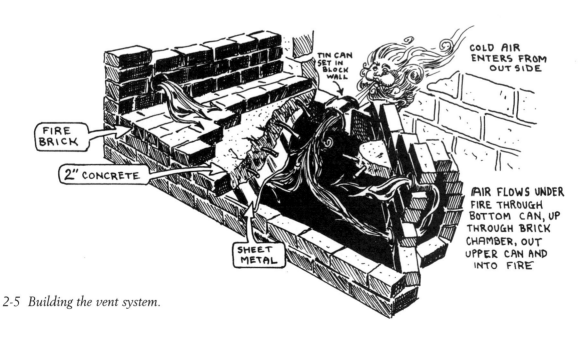

2-5 *Building the vent system.*

The sides of the firebox were then laid. The overall dimensions of this area are very crucial but one is free to choose from several designs depending on one's own needs. We used a bell-shaped curve at the back. The mason from whom we learned prefers this design, and so do we. It provides more of a gradual flow in the back of the firebox, allowing the fire to follow a gentle curve. To establish this curve you put a little bit more fire clay between the backs of the firebricks, then between the fronts. This tilts the top of the brick face slightly toward the front of the fireplace.

When setting the firebrick a commercial fire clay should be used. You want only a small amount between each brick because it is the firebrick not the clay that radiates the heat. In volume the clay will eventually crumble. It takes only about 25 pounds to do a standard firebox.

Corbeling

Corbeling is a popular method of obtaining a tapered slant. The bricks lie flat instead of gradually sloping to the front as in the bell-shaped curve. Each tier of bricks is stepped up half a brick's width until the 60-degree angle reaches the desired height. The courses of brick are alternated; one course consists of a double thickness of brick with the side of the bricks as face, the next with the end of the front brick as face. The smoke chamber should be constructed with this double thickness of brick to prevent smoke seepage in case one layer of brick begins to crack. The local building code usually requires this precaution. We're dealing with something that can never be repaired, so it must be done right in the beginning.

Fire clay is mixed with water to a consistency of heavy cream. The firebricks must first be submerged in water for a minute or two until they almost quit bubbling. This enables the clay to stick on the brick like glue. If the bricks are left in the water too long they have to be dried out a bit before the fire clay will stick. The bricks are then raised straight on the back and sides of the firebox for 9".

Shaping the Form of the Firebox

Now we made a template form, shaping the end of a piece of ¾" fiberboard to the bell-shaped curve. The bricks were then laid to follow the gradual curve. We periodically used this pattern as one would a level, to make sure the curve was true. This curve must be a gradual one to prevent any humps from occurring as the brick courses are raised (2-6).

To narrow the surface of the back of the firebox as it curved forward, the sides were also splined inward at a good angle. Then the back was soon angled outward again above the center so that the back plane would widen almost to the traditional angle at the throat to prevent smoking. This design improved the radiant efficiency.

In other words, when you decrease the width of the side walls by splining or corbeling them, the back wall has to come forward. And since the side walls are angled outward the back also gradually becomes wider. Corbeling or splining is the process of creating a taper or angle by overlapping each course above it, thus forming an angled or herringbone shaped intersection. There is an added complication in my firebox design: the splined sides also meet the back at various angles depending on the bell-shaped curve, causing the crossing bricks to overlap. This made it necessary to trim the exposed face of every other brick with a forked-head type chisel, blending it with the others. The backs did not have to be dealt with because they would be covered with the rubble-concrete backing behind the firebox.

FORK CHISEL

BEGIN LAYING WALLS OF FIREBOX

TIN CAN VENT

SOAK BRICKS UNTIL THEY ALMOST STOP BUBBLING

TAP TAP

2-6 Shaping bricks.

To chisel these faces you first mark off the portion you want eliminated, and softly hit the chisel repeatedly on that line until it gouges a groove all around the brick. Keep going around until you make a clean break. Practice this on a few discards before trying it on the actual bricks you will be using. Remember it's a gradual process and patience must be exercised to make proper breaks.

To begin shaping the form of the firebox flare, we start setting the brick back a bit just before the halfway point of the back side. This is a simple process. we just use less clay on the back side of the bricks until they gradually curve outward. This widens out the back of the firebox directly above the firebox, where the maximum radiation occurs (2-7).

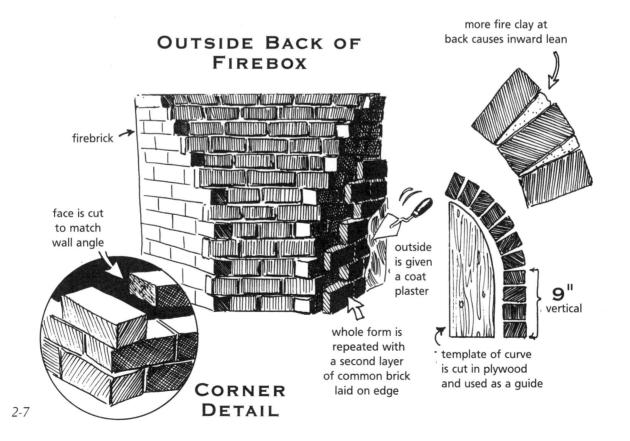

OUTSIDE BACK OF FIREBOX

more fire clay at back causes inward lean

firebrick

face is cut to match wall angle

outside is given a coat plaster

whole form is repeated with a second layer of common brick laid on edge

9" vertical

template of curve is cut in plywood and used as a guide

CORNER DETAIL

2-7

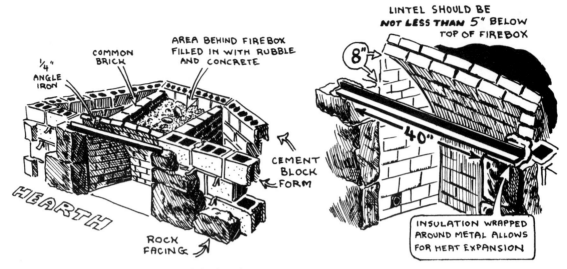

2-8 *Fireplace raised up to positioning of the lintel.*

We took great pains to make certain the opening at the throat was the proper width in proportion with the smoke chamber and flue area. If it were too narrow there would be tight spots at either end of the lintel, thus causing the smoke to come back into the room instead of going up the throat. If it were too wide there would be an unnecessary loss of heat.

Building the Damper and Flue

The firebrick ends at the throat of the fireplace. This is the area where the smoke escapes pass the damper and flows into the smoke chamber. Here we put in a reinforced shelf of 3½" × 4½"-thick angle iron. This shelf extends 4' supported on either side by the concrete block and rockwork face. It absorbs the weight of the lintel, mantel, and chimney face, taking any structural weight off the firebox. When iron gets hot it expands far more than the rocks; therefore the expansion must be allowed for. For this purpose a small amount of fiberglass insulation was put in at either end of the iron shelf. This provides an air space at the ends into which the expansion of the iron could take place. This shelf is located toward the backside of the fireplace at the beginning of the throat (2-8).

The throat is about 8" to 10" above the lintel. This is where the damper is located. You have a choice of building your own damper, having one made to fit the throat area, or buying a commercial damper arrangement. Though the commercial ones are foolproof, they are far deeper than they need to be and fit into a wider throat than the one on my fireplace. Our throat is 4" deep from the back of the lintel to the top of the firebox, and is 40" in width. We wanted a wide firebox area for viewing purposes. Because this opening is so wide the throat could be as shallow as 4" and still be efficient. The throat opening must have at least the same area as the flue opening, and it would be if it were even a bit larger. In other words, if a flue were 12 × 12, its opening would be 144 square inches; so the throat area would have to be at least that. The throat on this fireplace has an opening of 40" × 4", which equals 160 sq. in.; this is more than sufficient.

We chose to make our own damper. It consists of a long rod with a flat 4" piece of iron welded to one side of it and a control rod attachment which is hidden in the stone face of the fireplace. At the end of this control rod there is a kinked or bent handle which maneuvers the damper flap. When the damper is flopped down

Working with Mortar

Here are a few hints on using mortar. Make sure the mortar (mud) is of a consistency that when placed on a trowel and flipped a bit, it spreads across the tool and the excess moisture comes to the surface. Don't have it so wet that it just slops over the edge or so dry that moisture doesn't come to the surface when the mud is worked. If it is of a nice, sticky consistency it will hang onto your trowel as you turn it over onto the block. You then spread a large amount on the top edges of the block already in place and the sides of the block you are setting. Be generous with the mud. You can always clean off the excess later.

If the block you have set is lower than the others on that course, lift it and slap on more mud. If it is higher, tap it with the trowel handle until it is the same height as the others. If the back is low, tap the front down to compensate, and vice versa. There are no real secrets to successful block laying; just be patient and remember to use as much mud as possible. It is easier to wipe off the excess mud than to lift the heavy blocks several times.

CONCRETE BLOCKS

PLUMB LINE

PUT MORTAR ON END OF BLOCK TO BE PLACED

SPREAD MORTAR ON TOP OF BOTTOM BLOCK

UNEVEN MORTAR CAUSES BLOCK TO LEAN OUT OF TRUE...

MORTAR SHOULD BE ½" THICK

TAP WITH TROWEL HANDLE TILL MUD REDISTRIBUTES

CHECK LEVEL

DAMPER 4" × 40"
CLOSES ON LEDGE
CREATED BY LINTEL STONE

LINTEL STONE

DAMPER CONTROL ROD COMES OUT THROUGH MASONRY WALL

4" WIDE BY 40" LONG

2-9 Install a damper in the throat of the chimney.

it is closed; when it is flopped up it is open. The damper should be of a size that when it expands from heat it still opens and closes without touching the throat. Also, during construction, be sure to work the damper daily to free it of mud (mortar) that may have fallen from above. We advise installing a damper in, because when you are not using the fireplace you can close it off in cold weather and the room heat will not go up the chimney (2-9).

Directly above the throat is the smoke chamber. It extends between the long, narrow throat to the 12" × 12" flue opening and is the area in which the sizes of openings are converted. Because of this conversion a smoke shelf is created. This smoke shelf stops downdrafts. When the downdraft hits it, it curls back up the chimney. It is located directly above the sloping firebox back, which also helps form it.

The smoke chamber and smoke shelf are built with normal brick because these areas do not get hot enough to warrant the use of firebrick. The sides and front of the smoke chamber are gradually corbeled at about a 60-degree angle until they outline the 12" × 12" flue opening. The backside remains pretty much straight up and down.

We plastered both sides of the smoke chamber to prevent any creosote seepage through the mortar. The inside, being corbeled, consequently has a series of rough, stepped-up edges. It is a difficult job but this surface has to be made smooth so that the smoke can travel up without any hindrances. The plastering should be done as the smoke chamber is being built. We used a flat trowel and made the plaster good and fat (sticky) so it would adhere well to the joints. Then we plastered the outside, making certain it was sealed thoroughly. You can't be overly precautious when it comes to preventing unsightly creosote seepage (2-10).

Instaling the Flue Liner

The size of the flue depends on the size of the opening of the firebox proper, and the height of the chimney. If the chimney height is 12' or less you must make the cross section of the flue at least ⅛ of the total cross section of the area of the firebox opening. If the chimney is 15' or thereabouts, the flue opening should be ⅒ of that area; if the chimney is 25' or over, it can be 1⁄12 that area. In other words, the higher the chimney, the smaller the flue liner needs to be because the length supplies the necessary area for proper draft pull.

The flue liner can be set on a reinforced shelf of angle iron. This shelf is supported between the stone or block work that surrounds the flue liner. It is located in front, directly above the smoke chamber and carries a lot of the structural weight of the masonry and brick front of the fireplace.

The flue lining should be raised with the concrete blocks and the outer stonework. To minimize confusion, We'll explain each process separately.

A fireplace should not be built without a flue liner. No building inspector will pass one without it.

We put mortar between each flue lining joint as we stacked them. An architect looked at one of the flues we happened to be constructing and he wanted to know why we were mortaring the joints. He said that within two years after it was built the mortar would crack anyway. We maintained that it all depended on how you did it.

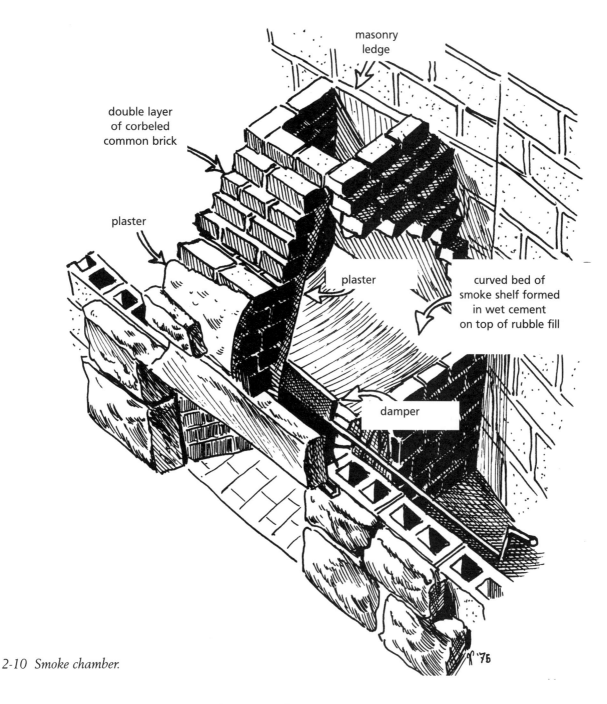

2-10 Smoke chamber.

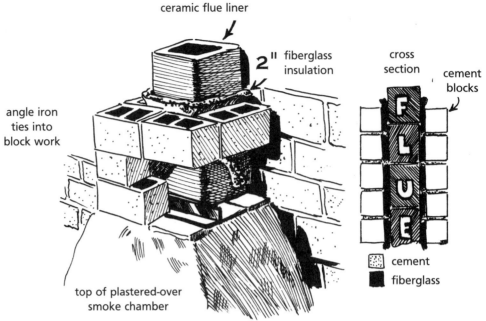

ceramic flue liner

2" fiberglass insulation

cross section

cement blocks

angle iron ties into block work

F L U E

cement

fiberglass

top of plastered-over smoke chamber

2-11 Start of the chimney flue.

Normally your flue is going to have stonework, concrete blocks, or brick around it. There should be a space allowed for expansion between the flue liner and this masonry. We always insulate this space with no less than 2" of fiberglass insulation—sometimes even more. This insulation also cuts down the creosote problem.

We brought the insulation up to within 1" of the top of the flue liner we were working with. Then we put the mortar on top of the insulation and on top of the joint. The mud was well packed all the way around it, sealing it in. Above all that we put in more insulation and climb right up with the stack. What we end up with is virtually a well-insulated and mortared flue stack held in place partially by the insulation. It is only tied to the exterior very tenuously by a bit of mud around each joint.

With this method we supply an area for the flue to expand and contract without cracking anything. If it were made solid, sure as mischief it would expand and crack (2-11). If you want to bypass the insulation process you should at least put a couple of layers of paper or something equally porous around the flue liner to create an air space to absorb the expansion.

The flue liner must have at least 12" of stone, concrete block, or brick around it, or a combination of any of these three materials. For economy, aesthetic creativity, and structural soundness I chose to use a combination of multi-colored, multi-textured stone for the face and an inner structural base of concrete block. The concrete block frames the flue and the firebox. It provides the facing stone with a flat surface for stacking and it is a structural necessity when constructing large, wide fireplaces. Concrete block is far easier and faster to construct than mortared stone and it is an excellent base for the textured stone.

Since the concrete blocks are uniform in size they can be laid very quickly around the flue and firebox. We suspended a string from an overhanging board at each corner of the area to be covered with the block. A plumb bob hangs from the strings to maintain the true vertical line; then that line is held taut with a bottom brace.

When constructing around a narrow area such as a fireplace or a flue, it is not necessary to have a network of horizontal guides. The blocks can be eyeballed in place horizontally. Care must be taken though to make certain that there is a uniform thickness of ½" of mud between each layer to make certain the blocks will stack properly. The vertical string guides have to be constantly checked to ensure that the blocks are true. Also, it is a good idea to tie in every third course of block with a binding wire grid to secure the tall, narrow stack in place.

The concrete blocks were raised along with the firebrick in the firebox. Ties must be set into the mortar between the blocks to secure the facing material to them. A commercial flat metal tie can be purchased for this job or strips of rough-surfaced, perforated sheet metal can be used. Also, we filled in the blocks with Zonite insulation for added thermal protection of the flue (2-12).

METAL STRIPS PLACED IN CEMENT BETWEEN BLOCKS GIVES ANCHOR FOR ROCK FACING

2-12

Setting Up the Stone Facing

When setting up the stone facing you can eyeball it if you want to, but we found that after raising the stones 4' or 5', eyeballing becomes too inaccurate so we use string guides.

The proper way to build up stone is to begin at one corner and go up 2' or say 30", depending on the rocks you are using. If you have two rocks and they fit in really easy— great. Then you move around the whole structure, and by the time you are back at the corner you started at, it is all set up. Sure, its green and you have to be careful not to bang into it, but you shouldn't have any difficulty. We've gone up as much as 4' at a time. We just started going on a corner and kept right on going. Everything kept falling into place just like a chess game. Every move we made was just beautiful. We always had backup for it. When you get into that kind of mood, just let her go . . . flow with it. You have to be extremely careful though if you are attempting to go 4' at a time. Your rocks can't be too big or too heavy. It's better to stick within 2'.

Before pointing or striking the joints—that is, before digging the mortar out—make sure it has set a good 4 to 8 hours, depending on the weather (longer if it's damper). The pointing process gets rid of the excess mortar which squeezes out between the stones as they are set in place. Striking helps reveal the rocks and gives them a more rustic, three-dimensional feeling. We use a simple screwdriver for this operation.

Good Stonework

The thing about stonework that makes it a good piece of work is how clean you can keep the face of the rocks, rather than leaving them covered with mortar. At the end of a day or half way through the day, depending on how fast the mortar is setting up, we clean off the freshly laid stones with a sponge. We making certain to remove all traces of mortar on the faces and pointing where necessary.

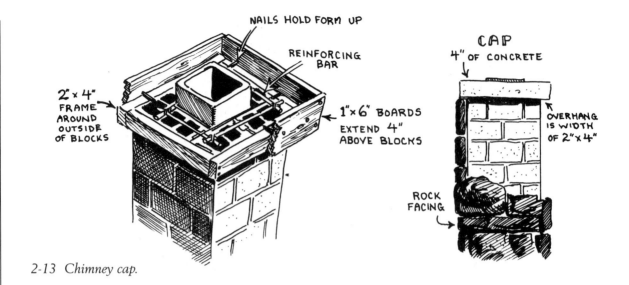

CAP
4" OF CONCRETE

NAILS HOLD FORM UP

REINFORCING BAR

2" x 4" FRAME AROUND OUTSIDE OF BLOCKS

1" x 6" BOARDS EXTEND 4" ABOVE BLOCKS

OVERHANG IS WIDTH OF 2" x 4"

ROCK FACING

2-13 Chimney cap.

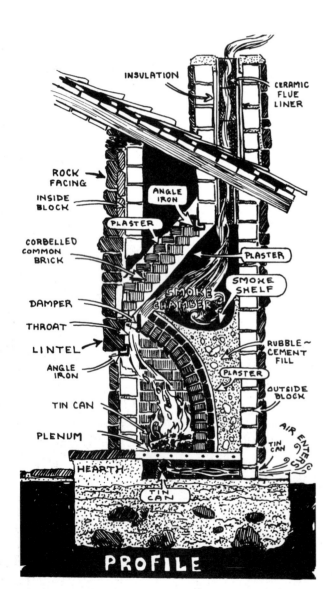

INSULATION

CERAMIC FLUE LINER

ROCK FACING

INSIDE BLOCK

ANGLE IRON

PLASTER

CORBELLED COMMON BRICK

PLASTER

SMOKE CHAMBER

SMOKE SHELF

DAMPER

THROAT

LINTEL

ANGLE IRON

TIN CAN

PLENUM

RUBBLE ~ CEMENT FILL

PLASTER

OUTSIDE BLOCK

AIR ENTERS

TIN CAN

HEARTH

TIN CAN

PROFILE

2-14 Cross section of the fireplace and chimney.

Installing the Chimney Cap

The chimney should be capped off with 4" of concrete. It is best to cap it with concrete instead of mortar because concrete doesn't have as great a tendency to crack in mass as mortar does. But concrete will crack in mass—that's why expansion joints are used in car ports, etc.—but in a small place above the chimney such a precaution is not necessary.

If the chimney was made of concrete blocks, a form for the cap could be built quite simply. You take 2 × 4s and put them around the top of the chimney. Nail 1 × 6s around the exterior of the top of the 2 × 4s, letting them extend up 4", then just let the frame hang on nails over the chimney top. This way the cap overlaps the exterior side of the concrete blocks by 1½", the width of the 2 × 4s. Be sure to leave 4" of the flue liner exposed as an inside form.

We bring the insulation right up to within a couple inches of the top and lay reinforcing rod around the poured cap.

A similar type form can be used above stone, but care must be taken to shape the top of the chimney stack so it will support such a form (2-13).

The face and firebox were built simultaneously and everything was taken up at once except the exterior wall. That was constructed later. It took a helper and 17 or 18 days to do

2-15 Cleaning the stone face.

the entire interior area, except for the hearth, which was also added later (2-14).

Cleaning Up

After we finished the stone face, we cleaned off the joints with a solution of 50 percent muriatic acid, 50 percent water. You can use a steel brush or a stiff bristle brush to take the cement stains off the face of the rock. This is a messy job that should be done with gloves. When all the unsightly cement stains are gone, wash the face down thoroughly to remove the acid residue, then let it dry. Now, we'll let you in on a secret: Take a bottle of Coca-Cola™, put it in a pan, and wet down a sponge with it. Then go over the rocks with the sponge. A mason told us this one. We thought the guy was off his rocker, but it really works. It gives the stones a nice clean feeling (2-15).

The Final Details

As we finished the interior of the fireplace the weather began to get real nasty, so we didn't start the exterior facing until the following spring. We used the same principles as were used in the interior face (2-16) and it turned out just as beautiful, adding a rustic monument to the entrance of the house (2-17).

We are indeed happy with our fireplace. It has become the central point where people gather around and communicate, especially in winter. In that season we swing the divan to the middle of the living area to create a semicircular continuation of the hearth, thus making the area around the warm fireplace snug and cozy.

2-16 The finished fireplace, indoors.

2-17 The view outdoors.

A Central Fireplace

The fireplace is the structural, aesthetic, and functional axis of the house. It is the center of strength in its dominant form.

Structurally, it is the point where the two roofs join together; aesthetically it is where the design contrasts blend to epitomize the flow of the spaces and relationships within the house; functionally it is the gathering place which provides warmth and nourishment to all who join together around it. It joins everything in the same way that mortar joins stone, nails join wood, and real communication joins people. If care and patient awareness are utilized throughout the development of the fireplace, it will carry on the flow . . . doing its part in bringing it all together.

Initially we had thought a fireplace would be a bit extravagant but, after all, we were building a house that we planned to live in for a long time, so we might as well include all the luxuries we wanted as we constructed it instead of adding them on later as expensive afterthoughts. This is one decision we never regretted. We just love watching the open fire in winter. It keeps the house totally warm and is an excellent social center.

The Central Idea

We planned this fireplace to be in the center of the house, dividing the kitchen and living room areas. Sure it takes up a lot of space but it is much more efficient, being entirely indoors. It is surrounded by its own warmth instead of located on a weather exposed outer wall. It retains its own heat, radiating it back into the house through the rock face and upstairs red brick (2-18). None of the radiant heat dissipates out of the cold side of an exposed chimney. This also reduces the problem of smoke condensing into creosote because it doesn't get quickly cooled off by the outside weather.

Since we had to build a huge chimney for the fireplace we decided to incorporate as much as possible in the one central stack so we didn't have to deal with several expensive and tedious chimney stacks. We designed this complex so it would include within its 2½' × 6' main base a chimney flue for the basement furnace, a fireplace and flue, a flue for the kitchen cook stove, and as an afterthought a small built-in oven. We didn't really decide on the oven until the basement block foundation was built. There was only a limited space between the heatform unit and the exterior wall. Consequently, the largest possible oven we could have was 20" wide (2-19 and 2-20, on the following page).

2-18 *The central fireplace takes up space, but it is surrounded by its own warmth, radiating the heat back into the house rather to the outside.*

2-19 *Kitchen woodstove and oven vented into the central chimney.*

2-20 *Wood-fired furnace in the basement, to be vented into the central chimney.*

Pouring the Slab

We began construction by pouring a 4"-thick slab that extends 6" beyond the base of the chimney complex on all sides, approximately 5' × 7'. A mixture of 2 parts sand, 2 parts gravel and 1 part Portland cement was used. No large rocks were put in for volume. When you want a solid foundation under a structure that is going to be carrying a tremendous amount of weight it would be best to not break up the slab with large rocks but make it of continuous small aggregate. We did not put any rebar in the slab because it was set on bedrock and hard-packed gravel. It is usually wise to reinforce the slab with rebar on square centers, a little below the middle of the pour.

Above the slab we began the block enclosure around the perimeter of the base, allowing for the necessary flue and ash pit open-

ings as the courses were raised. A 8" × 16" column was left hollow from the slab to the top of the base (floor joist level) to save on blocks at the right side; then we put in a column of blocks and left another space 2' long by 16" wide in the center for an ash pit. This ash pit also extends from slab to floor level. A clean-out slot was allowed in the bottom block at the center of the ash pit at the front wall. On the left, the blocks were stacked solid to a height of approximately 5½' where the furnace's thimble pipe intersects it (see 2-20). At that point the 8 × 8 furnace flue stack was started. A hole in the bottom flue tile was cut out to accommodate the intersecting furnace pipe. The flue linings were stacked and mortared together to beyond floor level, creating an inner form for the main floor slab. So at the main floor level, just below the

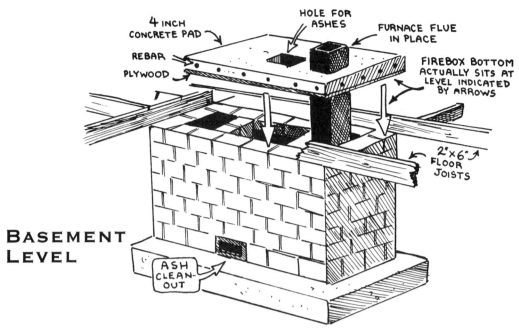

4 INCH CONCRETE PAD

REBAR

PLYWOOD

HOLE FOR ASHES

FURNACE FLUE IN PLACE

FIREBOX BOTTOM ACTUALLY SITS AT LEVEL INDICATED BY ARROWS

2"x6" FLOOR JOISTS

BASEMENT LEVEL

ASH CLEAN-OUT

2-21 Chimney foundation.

floor joists, two spaces were cut into the plywood bottom form: one for the furnace flue and one for the ash pit. Since the main floor had already been laid and a 4' × 6' hole was framed between the floor joists, the surrounding 2 × 6 joists and headers were used as the side forms for the 6" slab which we then poured. The slab was reinforced with rebar placed on 12" centers wherever possible (2-21). The plywood was buried forever.

Building the Hearth

The blocks for the hearth were placed across the front of the already set-up slab, allowing 4" on the three outer sides for the stone face. The top was then finished with flat sheets of commercial slate. The perimeter of the block structure was laid out with a few

courses of block, 4" in from the surrounding edge to allow for the rock face.

The Metal Firebox

Next came the firebox unit (2-22). We used a metal heatform firebox for several reasons, mainly because it was easy to install and created a nice air circulation flow through its double walls. The cool air enters through two low intake vents and circulates around the fire in the space between the walls. After it heats up

HOT AIR FLOWS INTO ROOM

OUTER FORM

INNER FORM

VENT FOR COLD AIR

COLD AIR ENTERS

2-22 Metal firebox.

it rises by convection, goes out the upper vents, and flows through the room as an auxiliary heat source. Heatforms also make it easier to construct the fireplace and chimney because they provide an inner form for the surrounding masonry (see 2-22).

On top of the slab, between it and the above heatform firebox, a layer of 4" firebrick was laid. The unit was then set on the firebrick. The heatform is a double-jacketed steel unit consisting of firebox, throat, smoke shelf, and damper assembly. Its double-walled construction allows it to take in cool air from the low air inlet vents, circulate it through the space between the walls of the firebox, and expel it as warm air out the round air flues in the throat. Once this unit was set in place it was lined with insulation wherever it came in contact with masonry, to allow for metal expansion and contraction. Since the firebox

2-23 *Details of the central fireplace.*

and throat area were shaped by the heatform, the smoke shelf masonry was an easy chore using rough filler brick between the metal and the outside block work to form the curved shelf. After the insulation and necessary block was put around the heatform, a piece of angle iron was set into the block work on either side, above the throat. This angle iron supports the 12" × 12" flue linings and the surrounding chimney masonry.

Meanwhile, the masonry around the furnace flue was also raised and our afterthought oven was allotted for on the other side of the fireplace. Since the heatform took so much space, 46" overall width in front, 33" in back, there was little room left for an oven. In fact even to have an oven that had only 16" × 18" inside dimensions at the opening we had to steal space from the side of the fireplace, eliminating the bricks that should be between the two structures. There is only 2" of firebrick and a thickness of fiberglass insulation between the oven and the heatform. Actually this does provide the advantage of the oven unit being heated by the fireplace as well as by its own firebox. And there is no problem with the oven burning out since it is constructed of firebrick.

Installing the Flue

The 8" × 8" flue opening for the oven and cookstove was started about 3' up from the floor, just level with the oven's firebox. This flue opening is located deep into the chimney structure from the kitchen side to allow the oven to have a depth of 24" in front of the flue. This is a dual-purpose flue for the oven and for a cookstove. (2-23 and 2-24). Just under this oven there are two small-

2-24 *Stonework around firebox.*

er compartments, a 10" × 10" firebox that extends 32" in depth to the back of the flue opening and a shallower ash pit below. The doors to these three compartments are old iron furnace doors mounted on steel plates that were embedded in the masonry. The oven and firebox are surrounded by a lining of 4" of firebrick. The top bricks are held up with a series of 2" steel straps which go across the top of the oven box. These straps and the ¼" rebar grate bottom of the firebox are also embedded in the surrounding masonry (2-25).

FLUE

OVEN

FIREBOX

ASH BOX

FIREBRICK WALLS

METAL BARS SIT ON TOP OF WALL BRICKS SUPPORTING OVEN ROOF AND FLOOR

RODS FORM FIRE GRATE

CEMENT BLOCK

2-25. *The position of the flue in relation to the oven, firebox, and ash box.*

The air from the oven fire comes in through the ash pit door's air control and goes through the ¼" rebar grills which the fire fuel sits on. The fire then heats the oven from underneath and from behind as it goes up the flue. It burns terrific. The long chimney pulls the smoke out just beautifully. It heats up great, except it can't be damped down to build up a good, continuous heat in the oven for proper baking.

One remedy for this problem would be to put a damper inside the flue above the oven. This would keep the heat close to the oven and cut down flue drafts. One damper would regulate both the cookstove and oven if it were placed above where the cookstove pipe intersects the flue. Right now if we close down all the mechanisms of the cookstove and then open the fire door to the oven, the cookstove would damp down even more because the draft would be sucked into the fire door opening, reducing the amount coming down from the flue. Also, to circulate the heat around the oven to the utmost efficiency we suggest planning the oven so it would include air channels around the sides. This would provide an even heat around the oven instead of only heating the bottom and back of it.

The Rock Face

The inside block and masonry were continued up until the top of the main floor, then the rock face was started. Remember to insert quite a number of corrugated tin ties in between the concrete blocks so the stone face will hold securely to this inner concrete form. We wanted a cobblestone finish on this fireplace, so we searched the nearby creek and river beds for this kind of round rock. You don't have to worry about such rocks exploding from heat because none of them will be in direct contact with the fire.

The mortar mixture was the standard mix with one additional part Portland cement. A ¼" mesh screen was used to screen the sand. We prefer using coarse sand when mortaring rocks together because this material provides more adhesiveness. It has more angles that grip each other and interlock than does the finer sand.

Early Afterthoughts

FIREBOX—Even with all the metal heat-form firebox's advantages we still sometimes have second thoughts about a firebrick firebox because the thin sheet metal construction of the heatform cools off much faster than firebrick. So when using a heatform the fireplace is warming up rapidly and cooling off rapidly after the fire is out, as opposed to 4" of firebrick taking a while to heat up but retaining heat long enough after you put the last log in at night to keep the house warm until morning. And with a little effort and ingenuity an air-circulating unit can be made with firebrick, having both the advantages of retaining heat and giving off extra heat through convection. All you have to do is back the firebrick with a ⅛" thick double-walled sheet metal jacket with air ducts so you can draw the cold air in from below and bring it out through the upper outlet vents. Then back the outer layer of sheet metal with the necessary 4" of clay brick.

HEARTH—If we were to rebuild the hearth we would make it slightly wider for aesthetic reasons. This would also make it more comfortable for people to sit on. As it is now, its 16" width is too narrow for a person to sit on and be far enough from the direct fire. Also a wider hearth would help prevent soot and debris from spilling out on the floor.

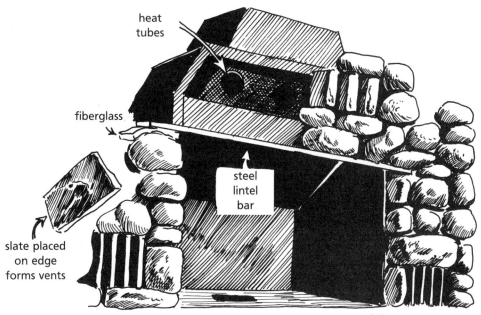

heat tubes

fiberglass

steel lintel bar

slate placed on edge forms vents

2-26 *Structural details.*

HEARTH

The round stone facing went relatively quickly—about 25 sq. ft. or 2' all around the structure in a single day with two of us working steadily (2-26). Actually you could go as high as you want with any single course until the mortar and already seated stones can't carry any more weight without slumping or falling out. We tried to get each stone to fit so it wasn't dependant on mortar to hold it on top of the stone below it (2-27 and 2-28). If it was put in a precarious position so we had to hope that the mortar would hold it, it was taken off and altered by either tilting it until it was secure or trimming it with a stonemason's hammer.

Placing the Iron Lintel Bar

The stone face surrounds all the concrete block and the outer edges of the heatform (see 2-26). An iron lintel bar was placed across the front of the firebox, a few inches below the steel frame of the heatform. It overlaps the sides of the firebox opening by 2" on either side so it could be embedded in the mortar face (40" long across 36" opening). Fiberglass was put around the iron lintel where it comes in contact with the masonry to compensate for expansion. This bar was set below the top of the firebox opening to shorten its height because there are doors on either side of the

2-27 *Lower air intake vent.*

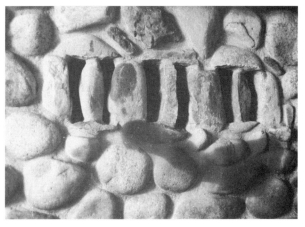

2-28 *Warmed air outlet vent.*

fireplace which bring in drafts that sweep the smoke out into the room. The lower lintel keeps the smoke from rolling out of the firebox. This fireplace burns fuel beautifully even without a grate. When you don't have a grate the coals go into the ashes, radiating their heat longer than if they were suspended over a draft. Being on the firebrick instead of on an open grate, wood burns slowly and more efficiently, thus saving on fuel.

The low intake openings on either side of the firebox were covered with thin layers of slate on end, spaced far enough apart to not interfere with the incoming air (see 2-27 and 2-28, on the previous page). The outlet vent above the box was also dealt with in the same manner with flat stones on edge, allowing an aesthetic contrast between the round cobblestones and the flat materials.

2-29 Red brick facing of upstairs area.

Completing the Chimney

The concrete blocks were continued above the main floor, around the three flues, but were slightly recessed so the red brick facing would be above the main floor blocks. This portion of the stack was designed this way so the heavy red bricks would not be directly above the lower cobblestone facing, but be raised on the more solid concrete block foundation.

The red bricks were stacked almost to the ceiling where they were replaced with a couple of concrete blocks for contrast and strength (2-29). The facing was continued out beyond the roof with alternating red and beige bricks. Then the whole chimney structure was capped with 1½" of concrete and a lip extending 2" beyond the stack all the way around it.

Later Afterthoughts

AIR—If we were to design the fireplace over we'd figure out some way to run a duct or channel from the firebox to the outside of the house so it would not deplete the oxygen inside the room.

FIREPLACE—If this fireplace were to be reconstructed we would make it 16" narrower at the base (one block shorter) to have more basement space and save on expensive materials and labor. The basement concrete work could then be corbeled out near the main floor to accommodate the cantilevered hearth instead of supporting it with such a massive foundation.

SHELVING—Also as an afterthought I would have put in bolts or hinges for shelving above the cook stove so kitchen implements would be in a handy place above it.

If You Heat with Wood, This Is the Heater

The fireplace can certainly be the aesthetic and functional center of the house. But if you are seeking efficiency and dependable warmth, then you are likely to be attracted to some sort of conventional woodstove or masonry heater.

Where we live, wood for heating is abundant. It is indeed wise to use the cheapest, most available resource to heat our house, but we didn't want to deal with the hardships of cutting and splitting small rounds for a conventional woodstove or small heater (2-30). Also, we have no desire to be constantly sweeping up wood debris and washing down soot-covered walls.

2-30 Our solution to heating with wood.

2-31 *Details of the heater system.*

Looking for What Works

When visiting friends who heat with wood we usually notice a premature drowsiness which comes over the group until someone takes the initiative to open a window or two. The fatigue is caused by the lack of oxygen in the room. As wood burns it uses up the same oxygen we breathe. But opening the windows of course allows cold air in. The stove then has to be adjusted to put out more heat, thus using up a greater amount of fuel.

After much thought, solutions to each of these problems came to us. To prevent pollution of debris and soot, the ideal wood-burning stove should have an outdoor loading chute and must be airtight, having no leaks to the interior. To prevent oxygen depletion, this stove must draw its oxygen from other areas instead of the area which is being heated. To save physical energy, the stove should be able to take large pieces of wood so one does not have to split short rounds. I soon developed a workable design for the ideal wood-burning heater.

Since there is a basement in our house, we decided to locate the damper there instead of exposing it to the variables of the sometimes severe weather. The oxygen comes up from this area to feed the fire. For convenience we knew that we would also have to devise some method of working the damper from the living area so whoever was enjoying the comfort of the warm living area did not have to leave it to adjust the air intake.

Designing the Heater

All of these considerations went into figuring out the workable dimensions for the wood heater. Since the only real constant was the size of the open 45-gallon-drum heat-exchanger unit, we had to first do the necessary welding on it. This consisted of cutting through from end to end and opening it up to a half oval shape. After achieving that shape, we set the open drum on the floor and estimated the outer dimensions of the brick enclosure that would house it. The size of the hole would be the area of the drum plus 6" air space around the drum plus the width of the surrounding brick enclosure. The 39" × 39" opening was then cut out (2-31). These steps allowed us to figure out and construct the concrete slab.

Laying the Slab

The operation of laying the concrete slab which is located less than 2' below the floor followed from cutting the hole. By cutting the hole first, we had plenty of room to stand as we built the forms and poured the slab. Its thickness is irrelevant as long as it can support the weight above it; 6" to 8" is adequate. The slab is made up of an inexpensive mixture of sand, Portland cement, and a large quantity of rock for volume. The perimeter of the slab is the same as the perimeter of the hole in the floor because the slab will be supporting the base and the brick enclosure (2-32).

After the slab set up, a few courses of brick were mortared inside its perimeter. An inner lining of firebrick was then stacked along the inside surface of the red brick and was cemented together with a commercial fire clay. Mortared rock could substitute for the outer brick but because rocks have a greater tendency than red brick to crack by expansion and contraction, they should not be used in direct contact with fire.

Installing the Damper

Below the floor, low enough so the entire firebox would be in the basement area, we installed a four-holed, manifold-type damper system. We tried to locate an old truck manifold for the job but could not find one the proper size so we had one made up. This manifold had to be mortared into the brick base in

BRICK FIRE CHAMBER

2-32 *The fire chamber.*

2-33 *Baement section.*

such a way that instead of any structural weight being on it, all the weight was carried on the bricks between the four tubes.

Bolted onto the damper and sealed with an asbestos gasket is a commercial air intake vent. This vent has a tongue which protrudes above a pivot pin. When the tongue is depressed by the vent rod, the vent opens and allows oxygen in. When pressure is removed, gravity automatically shuts the vent. We prefer utilizing gravity in closing the damper to prevent the damper from being left open by accident.

On the outside of the basement, below the loading door space, we installed a clean-out slot to collect the accumulating ashes. This slot can be any size as long as it can be easily covered. It should be located just under the level of the damper to prevent clogging. This clean-out hole has a removable cover that is held on by two wing nuts and sealed with an asbestos gasket (2-33 and 2-34).

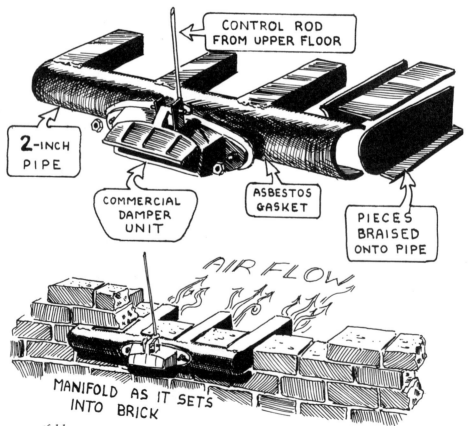

2-34 *Installing a maifold.*

Placing the Brick

After the manifold damper was installed the red bricks and firebricks were set up to floor level. At this point the firebrick was completed and two ¾" angle iron ledges were welded on the bottom ends of the drum so it would fit directly over the firebox. Care was taken to make certain the inside diameter of the firebrick agreed with the inside diameter of the drum ledges. The outer red bricks were then extended up into the living-room area. Having the firebox below the floor gives the house a warm basement and a warm floor area.

Preparing the Drum

The heat exchanger drum (2-35) was at this point made ready for installation. After the ledges were welded on, an 8" hole was taken out of the top front of the drum. A thick-walled length of pipe, 8" in diameter by 10" long, was welded above the hole. A commercial 8" damper was then set into the flue support pipe, and square base of 1" angle iron was welded to the top of it. This angle-iron base allowed the flue liner to temporarily be supported by the heat exchanger until the bricks were mortared around it.

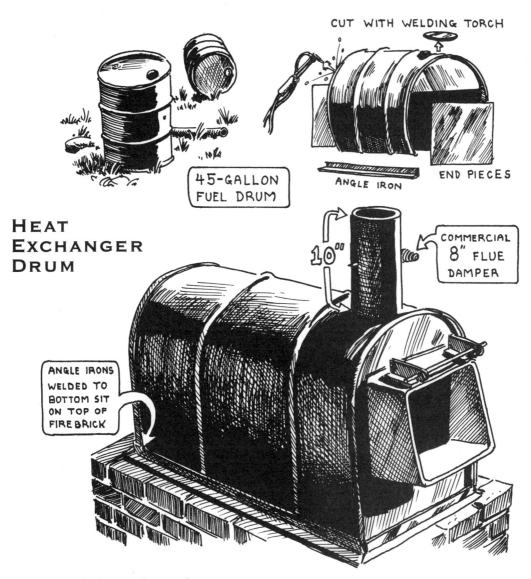

CUT WITH WELDING TORCH

45-GALLON FUEL DRUM

ANGLE IRON

END PIECES

HEAT EXCHANGER DRUM

10"

COMMERCIAL 8" FLUE DAMPER

ANGLE IRONS WELDED TO BOTTOM SIT ON TOP OF FIREBRICK

2-35 Preparing the heat exchanger drum.

Using a Proper Flue

A word of caution to those who do not want to foot the price of a commercial flue liner. If you build your own flue, make sure it is smooth inside and out and is of an equal diameter top and bottom for proper draw and easy clean-out.

Creosote sticks in crevices and can be very difficult to remove from a rough surface. Also, if you don't use a ceramic or stacked oil-can flue liner, there is danger of the liquified creosote seeping into the mortar and discoloring your bricks or rockwork.

Creosote is made up of very small molecules and can seep into the tiniest cracks. Because of this characteristic it is an excellent wood preservative. This is one place to definitely not chance a shortcut.

In our opinion, the safest and easiest chimney to deal with is one that is straight up and down. A straight chimney allows creosote to drop into the firebox instead of collecting in angled areas. To check for creosote buildup, I simply open the door, stick my head into the furnace, and look up. If I can see the sky I don't clean the chimney.

A heavy ¼" iron frame was then welded onto the front of the drum to support the salvaged boiler loading door and a 14" by 16" hole was cut out for it. A lip was added around the 14" by 16" opening to enclose the door and two rod supports were attached above the opening for it to hang from (see 2-35).

Because the door is held tightly shut by its own weight working with gravity, it keeps the wood burner airtight and free from draft (2-36). The gravity closing feature is also a safety factor. When loading dry branches into the firebox, the existing fire sometimes explodes and leaps out. If I had to take time to

2-36 *Details of the loading door.*

DOOR PLACEMENT ON FRONT OF DRUM

BRICKS ARE STEPPED IN TO EQUAL SLANT OF LOADING DOOR

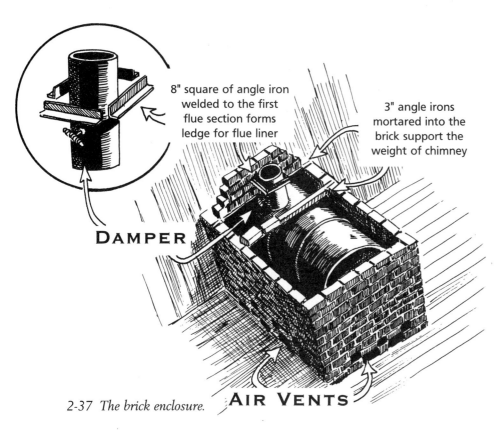

8" square of angle iron welded to the first flue section forms ledge for flue liner

3" angle irons mortared into the brick support the weight of chimney

DAMPER

AIR VENTS

2-37 The brick enclosure.

stop and think about shutting the door when such an explosion occurs, there'd be a good chance we might be singed before being able to do this. With gravity, the door shuts when we let go of it.

The original thought was to make the heat exchanger out of brick instead of a 45-gallon drum, but we later realized that brick takes much longer to heat up than the drum. When you come in from the cold you want to be able to open the damper and get immediate warmth instead of waiting ½ hour before the bricks get hot. True, bricks would last almost indefinitely but so will the drum, if it is not allowed to get red hot. Since the drum is only a heat circulator it does not come in contact with the actual charcoals; thus it will not burn out from contact with fire.

The Brick Enclosure & Chimney

The ornamental brick enclosure around the heat exchanger drum and the chimney were then continued up from the base. We wanted adequate air circulation around the heat exchanger so I allowed 2" of air space between

the drum and the bricks. This air circulation factor allows for maximum heat circulation throughout the living area. Before raising the brick enclosure, I made sure to allow several openings between the bottom bricks to draw in cold air from the floor, which would prevent draft problems. Without this precaution the cold air would creep up to the top and get heated without properly circulating.

The brick enclosure and chimney were then raised and a tapered (for aesthetic purposes) chimney front was built above them. This front rests on a heavy 3" angle-iron support that extends from outside enclosure brick on the opposite side. When completed the enclosure was high enough to easily sit on. Directly above the drum, a heavy-gauge mesh screen was fitted in. It is a safety screen and sometimes seconds as a drying rack for clothing and other items . . . but by no means should the air circulation space around the heat exchanger be interfered with for obvious fire reasons.

This brick enclosure is the favorite spot in winter for our friends. First thing they do is come in and set their cold bottoms on the bricks; then after everybody thaws out a bit, the conversations begin (2-37).

The flue lining was then stacked above the support and the chimney bricks were mortared in the usual alternating tier method. The chimney was raised to a height of 10" above the peak of the roof for safety.

Keeping the Chimney Clean

Creosote can become a problem in any wood-burning heater. I have had little success with

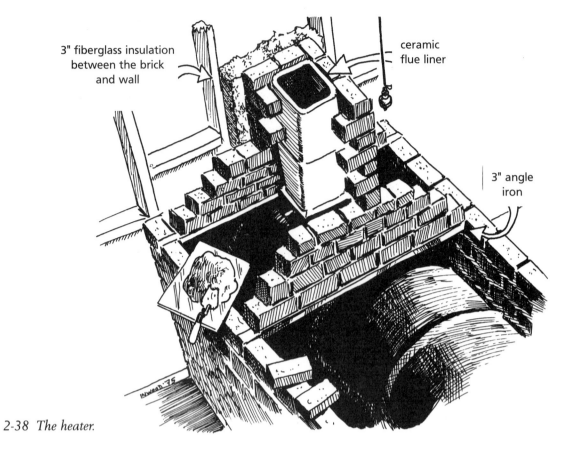

3" fiberglass insulation between the brick and wall

ceramic flue liner

3" angle iron

2-38 *The heater.*

2-39 *The chimney is well insulated.*

burning creosote out of chimneys. It is a waste of fuel and it is bad for the heat exchanger to get the furnace hot enough to liquify the residue. Even if you do get the furnace hot enough, you never get all of the creosote. The residue that remains crystalizes and becomes part of the flue. This buildup eventually disturbs the draw and must be removed. For clean-out I use a 20' long 1" × 1" stick with a flat scraper on the end.

Even though this heater is designed to burn wood slowly, I have to clean out the flue only every six weeks because the chimney is well insulated (2-38 and 2-39). There is 3" of insulation between it and the outside wall to slow down the condensation of smoke. Creosote is condensed smoke. If the chimney is kept warm your creosote problem is cut in half.

The width and length of a chimney are not critical with this heater design as long as the opening is uniform, top and bottom, for draw. A friend of ours has a similar setup with a 3' × 6' chimney in which he built a smoke chute. He put in a large airtight door enabling him to walk into the stack and he installed grates for hanging bacon and sausages for smoking. This proved to be an excellent smokehouse because creosote smoke is cool and does not cook the meat. The draw is not interfered with either.

Smoke curls out of the heat exchanger drum and curls through the huge opening.

The Outdoor Loading Door

As a final touch to protect the loading door from the weather and to ensure that it is air-tight, an outer door was added. This painted plywood door encloses the loading door and its inside is lined with aluminum foil to reflect any escaping heat back into the heat exchanger (2-40).

Firing Up the Heater

The heater was then ready for the big test. Before lighting the first fire, we protected the bottom cement slab with a 4" layer of sand for the charcoals to rest on. With the sand there is no need for a grate. We used any type of wood that was available: cedar, fir, birch, larch, etc. Cedar burns fastest but not hottest and birch is excellent when you prefer a warmer house . . . but we usually do not have time to pick through the pile, so we use the wood as it comes.

We began the fire with very dry wood, and once a solid bed of coals was established we used slower-burning green wood. The initial test proved successful. The unit heated the entire house and absolutely no oxygen was taken out of the living areas. The fire stayed in the firebox and the heat exchanger circulated heat into the house. There was no pollution in the house and we could put in logs up to 30" in length, which saved tremendously on wood-cutting energy. In fact we only put in one full wheelbarrow every evening and the fire kept slowly burning. Where it gets its oxygen is a bit of a mystery because we keep the damper shut most of the time. We only open it to get a sudden burst of heat after coming in from the cold.

2-40 *Outer plywood door with heat-reflecting foil.*

The stove's efficiency is amazing. When we put the logs in the burner in the evening they turn into charcoal during the night and that charcoal gives off heat practically throughout the entire next day without giving off much smoke. When the damper is opened, cold air gets in and takes all the heat up the chimney, so we made sure to keep it closed as much as possible to save fuel and increase efficiency.

Cleaning Out the Ashes

It takes approximately two months of constant everyday use before the firebox needs to be cleaned out. When the ashes reach the clean-out slot we move the hot embers to the rear and take out the cold ash. These ashes are then taken to the garden because they are an excellent source of lime and should never be wasted. Because the clean-out slot is located a bit lower than the manifold damper, the ashes never interfere with the damper. We also found that creosote collects in the heat exchanger and never interferes with the damper.

Another discovery we made was that even after we left the fire for a couple of days it did not go out. Very little heat rises because the damper is shut; thus the heater is constantly giving off combustion heat.

Sometimes we went off on short trips, came back after the weekend, stoked the fire with dry wood and waited . . . and it would eventually start smoking again. It never failed. We lit the first fire in September and it burned through to April, nonstop.

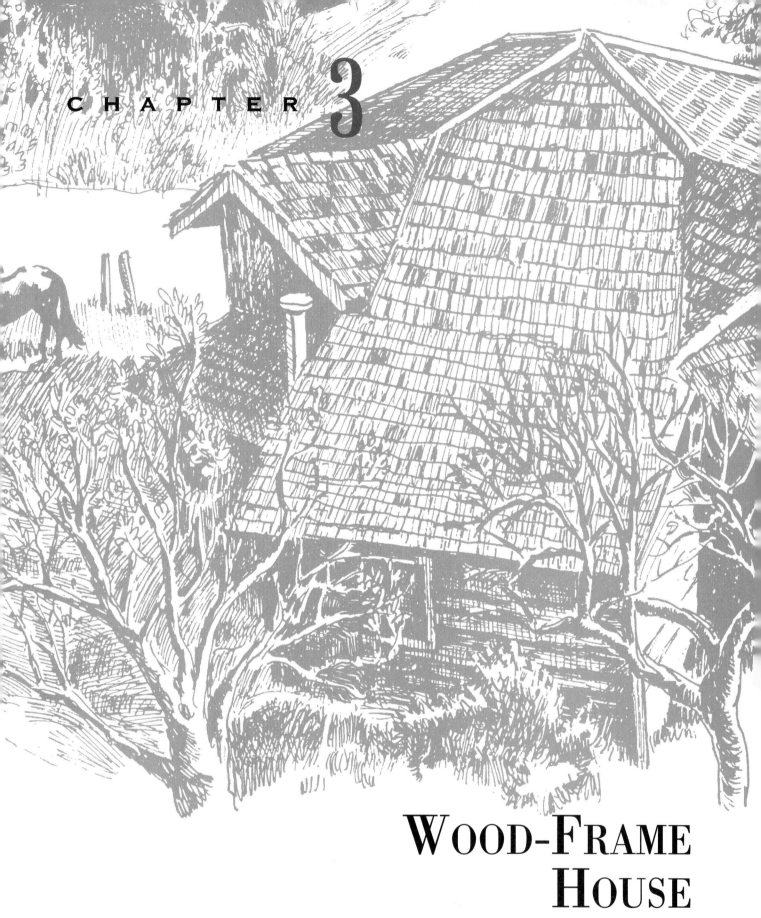

CHAPTER 3

WOOD-FRAME
HOUSE

Spaces
and
Relationships

Instead of constructing this house themselves, William and Rose hired an architect to design it and carpenters to build the structural portion of it. They were happy with the form of the traditional American wood-frame house, but yet they wanted their home to be special, something uniquely their own, as do most people. Being practicing artists, they desired their house to be aesthetically interesting in itself. To achieve that purpose, they themselves put in the finishing touches, using the mediums they knew best. They enhanced their home's structural beauty and made it a visible example of their own creative personalities.

Many architectural offices decline invitations to design small, individual houses because it is a tremendous amount of work for a modest fee. But there is usually a young architect around, a few years out of school, apprenticing in an office, who would love a chance to design a house (traditional moonlighting). The particular fellow they found was working as a night-shift janitor in a local pub when they hired him to design the house. In fact, he did most of the designing in between his janitorial duties. He had "dropped out," as they used to say, leaving a large architectural corporation because he decided "it wasn't good for his health."

Designing around a Budget

Rose and William wanted a two-bedroom house to fit their limited budget, so a design was developed that could be built in stages.

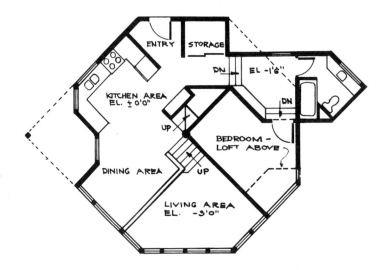

3-1 First-stage octagon idea for the house plan.

The first stage was an octagon, 12' on a side and about 30' across. It would contain a completed kitchen and dining area, bathroom, sleeping loft, and living area. The living area would be temporarily partitioned off to provide a closed-in bedroom under the loft. The octagonal core would have one high, open ceiling space, and the areas would be divided by changes in floor levels, each level spiraling around the center pole (3-1). The first stage would be well within their budget.

The second stage would add a mudroom and a pantry at the entry, another bedroom, and a small, partially covered terrace deck off the kitchen. The partition in the living area would then be removed, and that space would

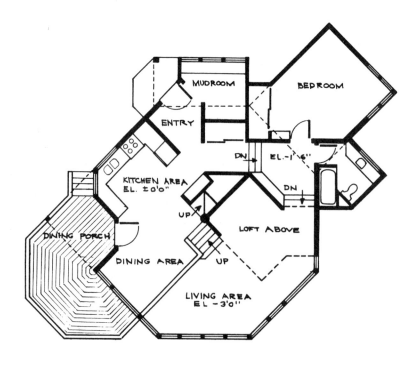

3-2 Second-stage evolution of the house floor plan.

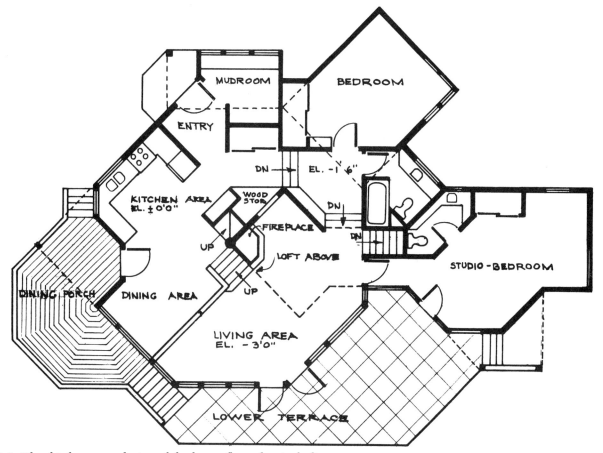

3-3 The third-stage evolution of the house floor plan including terraces.

double in size when the bedroom was added (3-2). They chose to go this far with the structure at the beginning.

The third stage allowed for a large terrace off the living area and another bedroom which would extend from the east side of the octagonal core. This section could be built onto, almost indefinitely, as funds allowed (3-3).

Site Selection

The owners chose a site on the slope which provides complete southern exposure (3-4). It includes a view of the surrounding mountains and overlooks the nearby river. The southern exposure also provides the greatest amount of year-round sun.

Though the slope has a 6' in 30' grade, it produced no problem. In fact, it inspired the multi-leveled floor layout which follows the slope and sets the house into the landscape.

3-4 Southern slope inspired the multi-level floor layout.

A single-level floor design would have forced the house to be lifted out on cantilevers and look like an object that did not belong. In order that the structure properly fit in with its surroundings, it had to be built as close to the ground as possible, making each level stay with the contour of the land.

Using a Model to Visualize

Since it was difficult for Rose and William, and everyone else without proper training, to visualize the architect's ideas from the drafting plans, the designer built a scale model of the house and explained its spaces and relationships. The house and its inner areas were positioned in relation to their exposure to the sun and the airflow (3-5). The southeast bed-

3-5 Site exposure to wind and sun.

room would get the cool, morning sun; the living area, because of its southeastern southern, and southwestern exposures, would get the sun at different angles throughout the day; the dining area and kitchen, to the west

and northwest, would get only the afternoon sun as it began setting behind the sparse forest in back of these areas.

Eaves, 3' long, were designed to extend over the southern and western sections to shade them from the direct sun but allow sufficient light to enter through the many windows. The low-opening windows at the south allow cool air to enter the house, while higher vents let the warmer air escape.

The design and the actual building practices were changed to suit the owners' style. Since William is 6'-4", the ceilings of each enclosed section were lifted 4". High shelf spaces were allowed above closets and partitions for open storage of his pottery. The loft was designed as a semiprivate place in which Rose could do her writing. Many shelves were built into the loft railing for her books.

The whole central core has a spiraling effect around its center pole axis. Each space moves into the next by natural progression, yet each is distinctly individual. The spaces are broken up for quietness and privacy by varying levels and short partitions. There are no dead ends within these areas.

William and Rose were pleased with the designer's concepts, except for the lack of basement space. The site was wet in the springtime with runoff which flowed down from the background mountains. This made such a space impractical.

Getting Construction Underway

Construction started just after summer solstice, on June 22nd, with a traditional batterboard-and-string layout, but, because of the many angles of the octagonal core, it proved to be more difficult and complex than the usual.

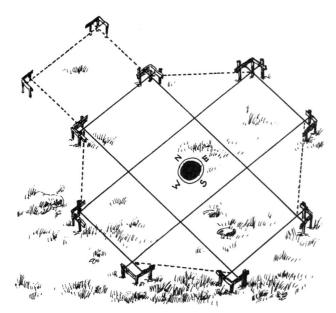

3-6 *Batterboard layout for octagon.*

The trio and a few of their friends shared quarters in the old house and tents on the property. Rose became head cook and vegetable gardener. Everyone was involved with the sense of building a truly creative structure.

The builders roughed out an area approximately 12' × 45' and set up the batterboards at the four corners. Another rectangle, about 12' × 30', crossed the first one 8' from the southern end, making the basic octagonal shape. These rectangles were then checked to make sure they were true (3-6).

The Fireplace Slab & Footings

After the area was laid out, an 18'-long trench, 3' deep, was dug for a concrete block, stabilizing wall. It ran southwest to northwest in the middle of the octagon, where the central level change occurred. The stabilizing wall proved to be structurally unnecessary. The fireplace slab, which was incorporated into it, could have been made separately as an additional footing (3-6, center dotted lines).

The crew consisted of three relatively inexperienced builders and a master carpenter who visited the site every two weeks to solve problems and give advice where needed. Joel headed the crew. Though he was not a journeyman carpenter himself, he had apprenticed under the master carpenter. The owners' son was the second crew member. The designer was hired as the third member, to assist the others in carrying out his design.

House-Building Shock

As the carpentry got more complex, Rose and William felt as if they were spectators to something that was running away from them, rather than controllers of what was happening. William was teaching pottery at a nearby college and Rose was working on her doctorate, growing vegetables, and cooking for the crew.

The house seemed to be the private adventure of those who were working on it; Rose and William did not feel it was theirs. In fact, they found their own living quarters and privacy overrun by the crew and their occasional visitors who freely used the old house's facilities whenever they felt the need. At times, William even found it necessary to lock himself in the bathroom to escape the omnipresent crowd. What was happening on their own land was indeed *house-building shock*—a kind of cultural shock—to them. They were not used to living as communally as they were forced to. But they could not complain; the work was going well. After all, how else would they get a custom job like this done for such a small monetary investment?

Footing holes were dug at each of the 12 intersecting points of the octagon and at each angling point in the remaining sections—22 in all (see below). Their holes were 3' deep to insure their being safely below the frost line.

Joist Hangers

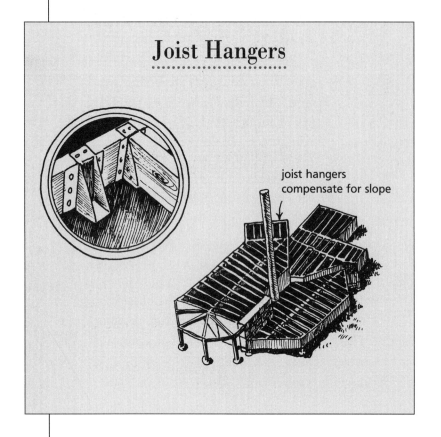

joist hangers compensate for slope

The forms only surrounded the 12" squares which protruded above the surface, because the sandy ground below acted as a natural form for the rest (3-7).

The cement for the footings was poured. As the concrete began hardening, spikes, which would later be driven into the 6 × 6 upright posts that supported the floor beams, were sunk into the tops of the slabs. The varying heights of the upright posts were determined by the surrounding terrain. If a footing was lower because the ground dipped, its post would be longer to compensate for it and to make it level. The posts have asphalt vapor-barriers below them to prevent the sweating concrete from prematurely rotting them.

Realizing the Design

The design of this house incorporated three separate levels to keep the structure as close to the sloping ground as possible and to act as a space divider for the various areas. The living area and fire-nook floor is the lowest. The hall, bathroom, and bedroom level are 18" above it. The kitchen, dining area, terrace, and mudroom are on the upper deck, which is 18" higher than the second one and 3' above the living area. To insure that each level would be as close to the contour of the slope as possible, joist hangers were used as needed. In areas such as the main bedroom, which is very near the ground on the north end, the hangers make it possible to keep the joists at the same height as the floor beams instead of lifting them 8" above these beams. Joist hangers are widely used and are known to be structurally sound.

The double 2 × 8 floor joists were spaced 16" on center (o.c.), and 4" of fiberglass insulation was tacked between them. A 1× subfloor was then nailed over them.

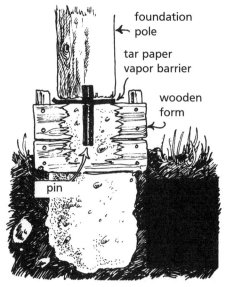

foundation pole

tar paper vapor barrier

wooden form

pin

3-7 *Concrete foundation poured into a freeform cavity.*

3-8 *Wall framing for the octagon.*

Framing the Walls

Next came the framing of the walls. The crew decided that the easiest and most accurate method of assembling each wall was to first lay out its pieces horizontally on the level deck, nail them together, then raise the finished frame and fix it into position. This method made tedious toenailing unnecessary, and provided the carpenters with a straight surface on which they could line up and measure the 2 × 4s.

The studs were placed at 16" centers and appropriate spaces were allowed for windows and doors (3-8). Where a window was to be put in, the cripples were cut to meet the horizontal sills. A cripple is any vertical stud which is interrupted by a horizontal piece before it spans the top and bottom plates. Single 2 × 4s were used to frame the windows and doorways. Any additional framing and spacers to absorb the settling of the completed structure were put in later.

The raised walls were plumbed with levels and the bottom plates were nailed through the subfloor to the floor beams. The wall sections were then joined together at the ends with flattened tin oil cans and they were capped with a second top-plate of doubled 2 × 8s on end. The 2 × 8s lapped the first plates on the wall ends to provide an additional tie to keep the walls in place.

Because most of the inside partitions were not bearing any structural load, they were framed with single studs, placed at 24" centers, and were topped with single plates. When the framing was finished and the walls and partitions were in place, the once simple, visually appealing, multi-level decks were transformed into a maze that looked like a forest with trees going every which way. There did not seem to be any continuity within the structure. But after the plywood sheathing was nailed onto the outside of the walls, the maze developed meaning. "Aha, there's the kitchen and the mudroom; this mess is really becoming a house."

Raising the Roof Pole

After the decks, walls, and partitions were in place, it was time to provide the growing organism with a center-pole axis to support its roof and convert it into a spatial masterpiece.

The raising of that 16' cedar pole brought a welcomed celebration. As it was put up, cheers filled the air. Rose prepared the festive table. By then she was ready for anything. There was plenty on hand to make the celebration last all night, and it did. The bunkhouse and old house were filled with merrymakers. Soon, exhausted by the event, Rose found her way to a quiet hillside and slept in the bracken.

The next morning the weary crew began assembling the loft area. They cut spaces for the huge, custom-made beam hangers into the center pole. These hangers hold up two of the double 2 × 10 beams which frame the loft. Four of these beams surround the loft and span from the center pole to the southern and southeastern walls. A ridge of 2 × 4s was nailed to the inside foot of the beams to support the heavy, 4 × 6, double tongue-and-groove deck.

A low railing was later placed around the loft area. The crew then set a bookcase into the front railing for Rose's books (3-9).

Building Trusses

During the design stage, Joel and the designer spent some time trying to figure out a suitable roof support. Joel thought of airplane hangars and how their roofs were held up. After studying that type of truss system, he and the master carpenter designed a similar system which would intersect the original octagon and not detract from its open, spatial beauty by cluttering it with a network of ceiling joists.

The four trusses were hung from a four-way iron hanger located at the top of the center pole. Each truss spans to opposite walls. Their main function is to hold up the collar beams which form a 12' square around the center

3-9 *Loft area.*

3-10 *Truss supports for the roof.*

3-11 *Center pole and trusses.*

pole to brace the roof. Two of the trusses also act as gigantic hip rafters which support the hip roofs. The other pair are hip rafters until they meet the collar beams, then they continue as ridge boards for the gables over the front door and loft areas. Each has two double 2 × 6 frames with webbing bolted between each side (3-10 and 3-11).

Creating the Ceiling

The roof in this dwelling is multi-layered. The interior roof is made up of 2 × 6 nailers which are spaced at 36" centers. These nailers are visible from the interior and span from the collar beams outward. Not only do they enhance the spiral effect of the ceiling, but they also act as nailing strips for the materials above (3-12). This gives the carpenters the advantage of not having to nail upward from below; instead they work comfortably from above. That feature alone justifies the extra use of materials. The nailing boards also provide a deceptive sense of structure which confuses even skilled carpenters. From the interior they look like rafters placed too far apart which hold up an uninsulated cedar ceiling.

After the interior nailing boards were in place, the 1 × 8 ceiling was put on. Economy-grade cedar was bought for this job. The usable, unrotten, and unsplit sections of each board were sawed out and nailed up. The rest was used above the outer rafters to nail the shakes onto. Nothing was wasted. The cedar

3-12 *View from the entryway.*

3-13 Roofing with shakes.

1×s were spaced ⅜" apart to allow for shrinkage. Since shrinkage is inevitable, the spacing was a method of developing uniformity in the size of spaces between the boards (3-13).

When the ceiling was finished, the designer laid on the loft floor and studied the fissures of light which shone in through the spaces between the boards. He watched as they seemed to spin around the center pole, giving the roof the desired spherical appearance. To finish the ceiling, the shining light had to be shut out. A layer of black building paper was stapled to the boards to cover them and to act as a temporary vapor seal until the finished roof was put on.

Placing Rafters & Ridgeboards

The outer 2 × 6 hip rafters and ridgeboards were cut and placed. The roof rafters were then spaced at 24" centers, nailed over the ceiling, and supported at the outer walls, collar beams, and hip rafters. The angle to which each rafter was cut depended on the pitch of the roof and the angles of intersection with the ridge rafters. The rafters and ridgeboards extended 3' beyond the walls as eaves to shade the interior and protect the exterior clapboarding from direct precipitation.

Blocking was put in between each rafter directly above the collar beams to keep the long, spanning rafters from spreading. Six inches of fiberglass insulation was then tacked between the rafters. Though some may think this thickness is unnecessary and prevents air circulation, the roof is excellently insulated and the snow does not melt on it, preventing damage from ice collection.

The 1× cedar scraps left over from the ceiling material were nailed across the rafters to support the finished roof of cedar shakes. The 24" shakes used on the roof were store-bought, but they could easily be made from cedar bolts. The shakes were lined up on the cedar nailing strips, which were spaced 6" apart (3-13 and 3-14).

3-14 Roof from the north.

Finishing the Interior

Normal preparation for plumbing and electricity was made before the interior 1 × 6 cedar ship-lap paneling was nailed on. It was then time to begin the interior finishing. The coming months of winter would make it impossible to work, and very little funds were left; so the crew decided it was time to depart. The following spring, Rose, William, and their daughter became more involved in the house and finally felt it was theirs. They learned to use hammers and saws. They put up most of the plywood and became skillful in paneling with cedar.

For a long while, they could not decide on the material they were going to use for the finished floors. William turned creatively to the art form he knew best. It took 500 pounds of clay to make the unglazed tiles which he used, but it could have taken more had he not left the plywood and subflooring under the carpets untiled.

He also made copper-red glazed-tile counters for the kitchen and bathroom. Rose finished off the bathroom shower area in a tile mosaic made mostly of unsatisfactory pots which, in the potter's tradition, had been hammered into pieces (3-15). Not everyone is a potter, but most people have some special skill. Many other materials could be used for the finishing touches.

The designer was pleased with the way the owners incorporated their own talents and

3-16 Kitchen area.

imagination into the house. It would never have occurred to him to use handmade tiles for the finished flooring or make cupboards out of the same paneling as that of the rest of the interior.

Living in Their New Space

This wood-frame house, built into the slope, succeeds in becoming a masterpiece of spaces and relationships and blends well with the background forest and mountains. Its gabled roof entranceway protects people from the weather even before they enter into the backlit mudroom area where they may remove their overcoats and kick off their shoes. The spaces beyond the entrance foyer are shielded by a partition. From above this shield, the center post, trusses, and living-room lights can be seen. People can be heard from those areas. One has time to become oriented and choose one's route. To the right, past the open cupboard featuring many of William's useful ceramics, is the kitchen. To the left, down to a lower level, are the bathroom and bedroom.

The kitchen is an open area with windows that frame the hillside apple orchard and expose a narrow corridor into the woods (3-16). From this area, you can see into the

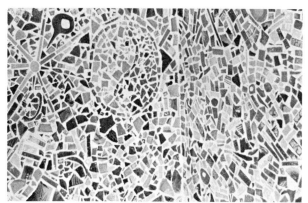

3-15 Tile shard mosaic in the bathroom.

dining area which is only divided from the kitchen by its own rectangular shape and its different floor. From the kitchen you can also look out the high windows of the lower living area.

Between the dining and kitchen spaces there is a Dutch door which leads out to the roofed section of the terrace, past the west wall. The terrace is partially covered by the end of a hip roof. Its open deck extends from the west wall out to a railing which will soon be sheathed in with cedar clapboarding to protect it from low breezes. The terrace overlooks the large mountain range and a nearby stand of aspens (see 3-17 and refer to 3-4).

The afternoon sunlight streams in through the many windows of the dining area and makes the huge, carved-wood table glow within this space. This table is where Rose chooses to do most of her writing. This space is divided by a short partition and a few steps that lead to the lower living area. One can stand at the partition and view the whole lower area or sit at the table and feel completely closed off

from it. From the living area the spiraling ceiling and the large, spanning trusses seem to be much higher up than they really are. This effect is created by the many windows which surround the area.

Beside the living area is another space about the same size. Yet, because of its low ceiling, it gives the feeling of being much smaller. This area is a fire nook which will soon be enhanced with a beautiful brick-and-clay fireplace. (Refer to Chapter 2 for more on creating a fireplace.)

The upper loft towers over the other levels and allows one to look down from its sides and see the spaces of the basic octagonal core. When standing, one can even gaze out of the high living-area windows. When sitting, one is in a private space created by the encompassing railings.

Two other separate areas with closing doors are additions to the original octagonal core. The bathroom is a tiny, five-cornered room fully equipped with bath, shower, sink, and toilet. The wall behind the bath and shower is decorated with a tile mosaic which Rose has pieced together. The sink has a copper glazed-tile counter. For the purpose of viewing the upper meadow, the toilet is located in the center of the room, facing the window.

The adjoining bedroom has a shed roof which slants down away from the octagonal core. Its gypsum wallboard walls break the cedar-paneling style and help to make this room different from the rest of the house.

3-17 *Schematic layout of floor levels.*

Site Visit Update

We visited Rose and William not long after their frame house was completed. They were delighted with the house, its views, and its spaces. They felt it was truly a house tailor-made for themselves. They were glad to have done as much as they did in the actual building of it, but in retrospect would have liked to participate even more. They found there was more satisfaction in making something your own, rather than having it made for you.

Before our return to this site several years later, we were aware that Rose and William had sold the property. The new owner, an experienced carpenter, enjoyed the design of the house, but was unhappy about some of the workmanship. He taught carpentry at a local college and periodically brought his students on a field trip to his home to show them some of the ways not to build a house.

His main concern was that he felt the foundation was inadequate. This was the first thing he corrected. He dug around the perimeter of the house and formed-up, then poured, a concrete retaining wall completely around the structure. He also set up a drainage system that controls the flow of the spring runoff, directing it away from the house.

His next concern was the roof. Though he liked the roof design, he thought it a poor

Dining area as seen from the loft.

idea to put cedar shakes on such a shallow-pitched roof— moisture remains on the porous wood surfaces and seeps into the dwelling below. A tin roof would be the solution.

The new owner and his wife liked the architect's concept of the third stage and planned to incorporate it into the house.

Fireplace nook in the living room.

Loft.

CHAPTER 4

LOG HOUSE, VERTICAL STYLE

INWOOD '74

From Many Creeks Flows a River

The simple log house that John and Janey built came only after a long search for a piece of land to their liking, and an even longer search within to discover the life they wanted to live. They had appeared on top of it all, sitting at their picture window, sipping cocktails in a luxury high-rise apartment in the heart of a large eastern city. As told from John's pont of view:

The 15,000 people residing on our block shared its conveniences, but very few of us even cared to pass the time of day with each other. We felt like bees in a filing cabinet, anonymously struggling for the betterment of the hive. We were servants to the protective security it offered us.

To maintain our personal sanity in that situation, we surrounded ourselves with hundreds of material conveniences. There always had to be an immediate reminder that what we were sacrificing, in terms of our health and emotions, was being compensated for by the pleasure we received from the manufactured world which surrounded us.

Our greatest enjoyment came when my wife and I were lucky enough to share the same day off together. Then we'd jump in our car and join the multitudes who also found it necessary to periodically escape from the noise and pollution of urban life. After several hours of driving, we found peace in secluded forested spots, beside small clear-water lakes. There we'd picnic and skinny-dip. We'd forget our cares and appreciate the natural beauty of the place. We'd lie in the tall grass and smell the pine-scented, refreshing air. We felt more comfortable and secure there than in the locked confines of our expensive apartment. But always too soon, the beehive summoned us to return.

We began craving those carefree excursions into the country. Thoughts of actually changing our life-style began to dominate our spare moments. We spent two years reading available information about living in the woods and preparing a plan for a homestead that would provide us with food and shelter. In that period we realized how important it was to find a place of our own (4-1), a place where the sounds we heard would be the flowing of creeks, the chirping of birds, and the whistling of the wind through the trees instead of the roaring of subways, honking of horns, and people always seeming to be arguing.

4-1 Searching for a place of our own.

Finding Our Piece of Land

It was a long search. Though the searching was very enjoyable, and put us in touch with many fine people who were living in the style we wanted to, it left us short of cash.

We had just enough money to buy the land and rent a small cabin until we could build our own house. I found a job at the local mill, in order to raise the money we needed for our supplies. For months, I sweated on the "green chain," lifting wet boards and transferring them from one place to another. For some strange reason, though, I rather enjoyed that job. It readied me for the hard work I had ahead of me on my own homestead. It also put me in touch with several of the local people who were later very instrumental in the construction of my house. In fact, a few of those fellow mill workers have become my closest friends and working companions.

We bought our place in February, but we didn't really get started with the building of the house until late spring. Those first few months were filled with planning of the layout of the homestead. Before we made any decisions of placement, we had to prune some of the wild growth so we'd know what the area looked like.

4-2 Limbed trees.

I took on the chore of limbing each tree in our thick, six-acre forest. I cut off every branch as high up as I could reach with an ax (4-2). This may sound like a lot of work, but it was very satisfying. By limbing the trees in that manner, I opened up the forest and turned it into a park with many paths and walkways. I also became sensitive to the land and looked forward to every task on it with a Zen-like enthusiasm. I knew I was where I wanted to be.

As far back as February when we had bought the piece of land, we watched the arc of the sun. We wanted the house positioned so that in the cold winter the kitchen and dining areas would receive the warm morning sun through the windows. While welcoming the winter sun, it was also important that the house be in such a position that the summer sun's light would be shaded by the roof eaves (4-3).

4-3 Keeping track of the path of the sun as the seasons progress.

Scouting for Logs

In the early spring, long before we began the foundation, I went out searching for logs for the vertical-log walls. A farmer up the road wanted some acreage cleared. He asked me to tell everyone who wanted firewood or logs that they were welcome to cut on his property. I told everyone, and before long all the timber was cleared away. My first plan was to cut down live trees and buck them to 7' lengths, then to peel off the barks and let them dry a season. But when I arrived at the site I came upon a pile of aged, fallen timbers. They were mostly pine, tamarack, and fir. By the end of the day we transported home enough logs to do all the walls. I was really pleased with my find.

Since the logs were already aged, I could use them immediately. They were light to handle and I wouldn't have to worry about any drastic shrinkage. One thing I didn't figure on, though, was the problem of peeling aged logs. After struggling with a drawknife for many hours and only completing a couple of logs, I decided there must be a better way. I rounded up several spuds and drawknives and invited all the local teenagers to my "peeling party." They accepted my invitation, ate my food, and listened to my music, but by the end of the day only a few of my logs had been peeled. In the days that followed, a couple of the more industrious youths peeled most of the remaining logs for a set fee per log.

A lot of the dark pitch from the bark did not come off the logs. At first I thought the discoloration was ugly, but once the walls were up I began liking the effect of the dry, peeled texture and the color patterns of the logs.

Siting the House

After much experimentation, we finally located a site for the house that would provide proper sunlight. We kept this site completely surrounded by trees to keep it cool in the summer and make it warmer in the winter. Trees are a natural windbreaker that shield an area from the icy winter winds. Before we staked off the exact house site, we made sure to cut down any snags or standing dead trees which might possibly fall on the structure we would build. Every cottonwood tree was also removed because this species has a weak root structure and cottonwoods have been known to fall for no apparent reason.

The area we chose was also well out of sight of the public road, but close enough to it to be practical in winter. We have no problem carrying our groceries and supplies down the short path to the house, yet we are not assaulted by car lights and constant road noises.

COTTONWOOD

Long before we actually started construction, we put stakes around the proposed perimeter of the house. And every morning we came to the site from our nearby cabin and inspected that area. Some mornings the area would seem very tiny, so we would enlarge the perimeter. Other mornings the area would seem huge. Those mornings we'd make it smaller. We soon began "playing house" in the area. We figured out where the various sections would be and how much space would be necessary for each. In the kitchen we measured areas for our refrigerator, stove, sink, cabinets, and cupboards.

Then one of us would pretend to make a meal and the other would go into the living room, stoke the fireplace, and sit down on the couch! We'd pretend to entertain friends. We'd pass each other in the hallway and sit down in the dining room to eat. Though we didn't stick to a plan for the finished product, we had a good idea of the space we needed. It turned out that 20' × 24' with an adequate loft area would be sufficient space for us—we had no immediate plans for enlarging our family.

We wanted a house where the rooms were defined by layout of furniture, not by walls and partitions. In conventional houses, the kitchen is separated from the living room and other areas. If a conversation is happening in the living room, the cook in the kitchen cannot participate in it because of the space barri-

ers. We are gregarious people, and we like being with others—so we eliminated partitions on the ground floor. The only separate space is the mudroom, sealed off to keep out drafts.

Laying Out the Foundation

After we set up the batterboards to make sure the 20' × 24' area was square, I dug 20 holes, four rows of five, for the cement piers which would hold up the sills. There wasn't any span greater than 6' in any direction between them. I felt it was necessary to have that many piers so as to prevent the floor from sagging and to make sure the foundation was good and solid. It's a real drag to have to reinforce a poorly planned foundation as an afterthought.

Gin Pole

Each of the holes for the piers was about 2½' deep and was wide enough for the forms which framed the 6" × 6" piers. The frostline was only 18" below the surface, but the soil was clay and was not as stable as rock or other porous soils. Because of this factor we had to dig an additional 1' to support the piers on a firmer, sand-type soil. The piers stuck out above the ground about 10" to prevent the sill logs from coming in contact with the clay soil.

We used a mixture of 5 parts clean sand and 1 part Portland cement for the piers. Many larger rocks and pieces of scrap metal were tapped into the concrete to save on cement and add to the strength of the mixture.

The area was relatively level, but there was a slight difference in height among the finished piers. We made up for these differences in height by setting various lengths of log-rounds above the piers. Then we placed small squares of black building paper between the log-rounds and the piers. The squares of paper acted as vapor barriers to protect the logs from the dampness of the concrete.

Placing the Sill

The four sill logs were notched in place (4-4). We dealt with the two outer sills first. They were raised to the height of two string levels, and both ends were notched onto the pier rounds. The depths of the notches were determined by the log's relationship to the other sills. The notches made them level with each other. If the log being worked was higher than the other sills already in place, its notch was made as deep as necessary until the sill was lowered to the height of the others. The space under the sills can be used for storage.

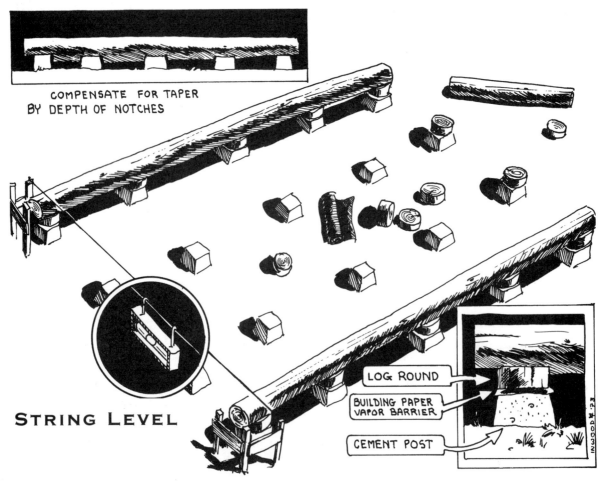

COMPENSATE FOR TAPER
BY DEPTH OF NOTCHES

STRING LEVEL

LOG ROUND

BUILDING PAPER
VAPOR BARRIER

CEMENT POST

4-4 Notching the sill logs in place.

Drainage System

Before we went any further on the construction of the house, we dug out the drainage system. Because the soil is clay and does not allow for proper drainage, we had to dig a deep dry well which is 8' wide, 10' long, and 12' deep (4-5). This hole is located about 5' east of the kitchen and shower areas. It is far enough from the house to prevent flooding the foundation piers, but close enough to save on expensive drainage pipe.

After the drainage system was dug out, we refilled 9' of it with many pickup-truck loads of large rocks. The bigger the rocks, the better the drainage. One end of the 2" plastic drainpipe was placed above the rocks, then the hole was covered with large cedar logs. A layer of 2" boards and a black building paper vapor barrier were placed above the logs, and a final covering of dirt was shoved over the other materials to protect this system. For additional foundation support, and to seal off the area under the sills from cold air, we built a rock retaining wall around the perimeter of the house. For this wall, I dug an 18"- wide and 2½'-deep hole between the outer piers. The bottom of the hole was filled with 4" of mortar, 3 parts sand, and 1 part masonry cement. The masonry cement, when dry, produces a white finish which is more appealing to me than the darker finish of regular cement. It also takes less time to dry. Large rocks were then fitted into the wet mixture, and other rocks were mortared over them until the wall sealed off the area between

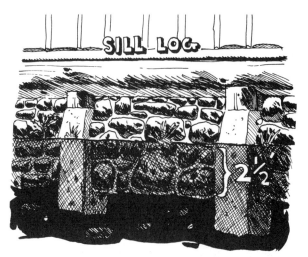

4-5 Deep dry well.

4-6 Sealing off the area between the ground and the sill logs.

the ground and the sill logs (4-6). The rocks touching the sills were then wedged in for a tight fit. We left a 5' space at the west wall for a store entrance.

Laying the Floor Joists

The 2 × 8 floor joists were then placed over the sills at 16" centers (4-7). Over the joists we nailed a subfloor of low grade, 2 × 8 tongue-and-groove cedar. Fiberglass insulation

4-7 Laying the floor joists.

in 4"-thick strips was stapled under the floor joists. We nailed a subfloor of low-grade, 2 × 8 insulation and the subfloor. You should take care when installing the insulation. If the fiberglass is not properly sealed, the 4" space between it and the subfloor will be a wind tunnel instead of a dead-air space.

To seal off this space properly, overlap the ends of the paper backing whenever possible and make sure the open joist ends are covered (4-8). Though there is zero heat loss through the floor, this area must be well protected to prevent cold air from entering.

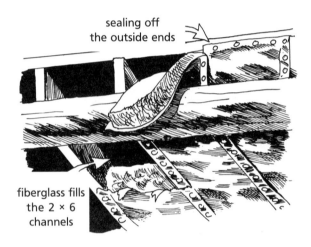

4-8 Insulating the floor.

4-9 Raised dining area.

One of the subtle room divisions that we designed is an 11"-high raised platform for the dining area. It is roughly a 9' × 12' area wedged against the south wall (4-9). The height of the raised area was determined by what we considered a comfortable setup.

One day after the subfloor was finished, we sat around drinking wine. We were celebrating our achievements to date and were so inspired by what we had already completed that we decided to begin on the walls soon.

Starting the Walls

We nailed the 2 × 6 bottom wall plates in place, then set up boards outside each of the four perimeters of the foundations. They were actually long batterboards which were nailed into the sills. Each of these eight 2 × 4s extended upright over 7', so a string could be attached near its top. The boards were positioned so the guide strings would be half a log's thickness, or 3", inside the perimeter of the building. This would make the strings intersect at half a log's diameter at every corner. These points of intersection would designate the exact center of the corner log (4-10 inset).

A black line was then drawn along the center of the 2 × 6 bottom wall plate. A log was centered over this plate. To make sure the upright wall log was exactly plumb, I attached a weighted string to one of the intersecting strings that crossed above the log. A fishing sinker was used to hold this vertical string plumb. The wall log was adjusted according to the plumbness of the string. It was then braced with a diagonal board, and the weighted string was transferred to the intersecting corner to check the other side of the wall log. The log was again braced, and was considered to be plumb (4-10).

Using a level is an inaccurate way to check how plumb an upright log is. No log is perfectly straight from end to end unless it has been hewn or milled that way. All logs have protrusions and low spots. What may be level in one

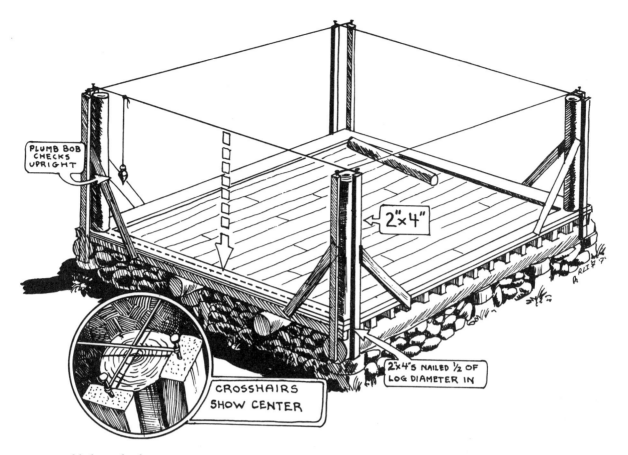

PLUMB BOB CHECKS UPRIGHT

2"×4"

2"×4's NAILED ½ OF LOG DIAMETER IN

CROSSHAIRS SHOW CENTER

4-10 *Establishing the four corner posts.*

3'-section does not necessarily give a true reading for the entire length of a log. I had doubts about my method of plumb-reading until I saw the electric company setting up our power pole. They put it upright with all their expensive equipment, but had to do a final check with a string and a bolt which they hung from a stick beside the pole.

By the end of the day, we had one log up. It protruded from the flat subfloor like the monolith from the film "2001." There was something spiritual about that log and what it represented to us. We didn't put up another wall log for days after. We did other chores instead, and just marveled at our "monolith" standing against the forest background.

The following wall logs went up quite fast. Each of the corner logs was put in place and checked for plumbness. Then each was nailed to the bottom wall plates with 7" Ardox nails, using one nail on the inside and one on the outside. Ardox nails were chosen for their

incredible holding ability. The only frustrating thing about them is having to pull them out if you make a mistake—forget it. We then braced each corner log with diagonal 2 × 4s.

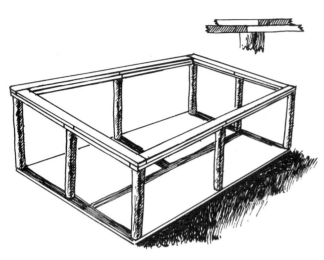

4-11 Pattern of lap joints over upright posts.

Installing the Top Plates

I laminated two 2 × 6 top plates together and nailed them over the corner posts (4-11 and 4-12). These double-laminated plates were nailed together every 16", and the nails were staggered to add strength to the plates. In putting up these plates, I overlapped an end of each so that the plates of one wall interlocked with the double-laminated plates of the intersecting wall.

After the top plates were in place, we filled in the full-length wall logs of the west wall, leaving adequate space for the windows. A 3" strip of fiberglass insulation was stapled to the bottom and top plates and along each log. The log to be placed was pushed in as close as possible at the bottom plate by one person, while a second person toenailed it in. We made sure the log was plumb before nailing through the top plate (4-13).

All the full-length wall logs were put in place and the window spaces were roughly outlined. To secure the corners and strengthen the walls, 2 × 6 diagonal bracing was used at each corner except for the dining area, or the southwest corner, where it would remain exposed if used. The bracing is hidden in the other corners by a brick wall, a shower stall, and a kitchen stove. These 2 × 6s start at the

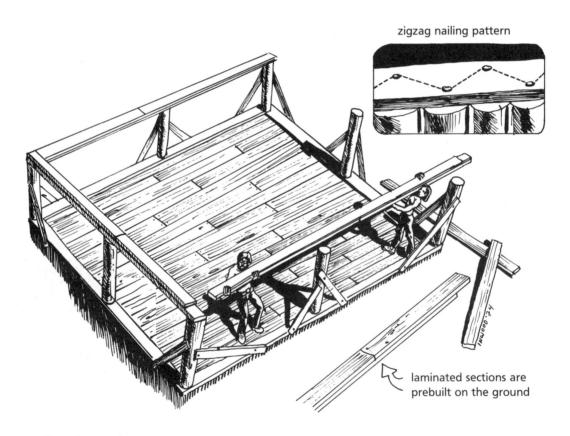

zigzag nailing pattern

laminated sections are prebuilt on the ground

4-12 Installing the top plates.

fiberglass
fills cracks

spiked at
top &
bottom

4-13 *Filling with full-length wall logs.*

bottom plates of each wall, a few feet out from the corners, and meet at the corners 5' above the floor. Each is notched into the wall logs (4-14). The other full-length logs went in by the same manner.

Most of the log structures I've seen in this area have small windows. Their interiors are dull and dingy because not enough light enters to brighten them up. I asked many of the builders of these houses why they wanted such small windows. They all gave me the same answer: they wanted the small windows to prevent heat loss and to conserve on wood and other heating materials.

We designed our windows big because we wanted light and we desired a view of our beautiful homestead. I would rather cut an extra cord of wood during the winter, when I'm in the house most of the time, than have small windows and be enclosed by four dingy walls. Anyway, large windows at the south wall bring in more of the sun's heat even during the coldest part of winter.

At the west wall we framed a 6' × 4' window space high enough to be able to see out of when we are eating. To frame a window when using vertical logs you simply cut your top window header two logs longer than the desired opening so the header log can rest on the vertical sleepers on either side of the window opening (4-15). Since there is no wall stress on the bottom windowsill, it is cut to the size of the window opening and toenailed to the sleepers on either side. This 2 × 8 sill is tilted downwards towards the outside so water slides off and does not collect and seep into the house. After the sill is nailed in place, cut short uprights and fit them into the space between the header and the bottom plate.

CORNER BRACING

4-14 *Each brace is notched into the wall logs.*

WINDOW FRAMING

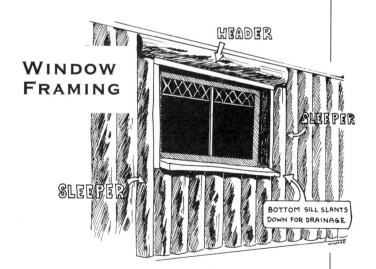

HEADER

SLEEPER

SLEEPER

BOTTOM SILL SLANTS DOWN FOR DRAINAGE

4-15 *Framing a window using vertical logs.*

4-16 Window construction showing insulation staples between the wall logs.

Then staple insulation between these short upright studs (4-16).

The second window at the west wall extends 11" lower than the dining-area window (4-17). It brings the afternoon light into the living room and gives us a view of the

4-17 West wall windows.

forest and the chicken coop. On a homestead, it is wise to position your windows so your livestock is in plain view, in case they get into danger.

The north wall has a large window in the center, above the woodbox. We close the window off in the winter with a heavy curtain because no sunlight comes in from that direction. Since no sunlight enters from the north, it is the coldest wall and should be the most protected. Our Franklin fireplace is located here. It has a brick wall in back of it to shield the log wall from its heat (4-18).

4-18 Franklin fireplace is positioned against the cold north wall.

Built into the north wall, beside the Franklin fireplace, is a firebox. It has a large outside entrance at which we load the box full of cordwood. This entrance is covered by a latched door to keep the cold from entering. The box has a lid enabling us to take the cordwood out of the box on the inside after we load it from the outside. This firebox helps prevent the heat loss which would occur if we were opening the house door to bring firewood in. It also keeps the floor clean from the wood chips and pieces of bark which plague many a wilderness floor (4-19).

There is a temporary door at this wall that we used until the main door and front porch had been constructed. This door is very light in weight, studded with 2 × 4s, and sheathed with cedar 1 × 12s. The main door is at the east

WOOD BOX

4-19 *The wood box allows wood to be replenished without repeatedly opening the front door.*

wall. This wall is double-logged between the shower room and the kitchen to frame in the mudroom and storage area. We used logs for this purpose because they were a cheap material and went well with the interior design.

The mudroom (4-20), which is 5' wide and 11' long, is a necessity for homestead living. It is a separate area where people can enter without disturbing the other occupants of the house with a cold draft and lots of noise. It is a

living room

mudroom entryway

front door

exterior front porch

4-20 *The mudroom helps keep the mud and the cold from geting into the house.*

4-21 The front porch and kitchen window.

place to hang overcoats and take off muddy boots. It is a reorientation corridor to prepare a chilled and road-weary traveler for the warm and cozy indoors.

To save on space, both the inner door to the living room and the outer door of the mudroom open towards the outside. The outer door opens to a large enclosed porch which is 6' wide and 20' long. This porch is framed with logs and has log rafters which extend 2' past the porch as eaves (4-21).

To make the stairs of the raised porch platform, I hewed flat the tops of two log pieces. The first was imbedded in the ground, and the other was perched 11" higher up on log uprights.

4-22 The kitchen.

The south wall has many large windows for heat and light. The huge 4' × 6' window in the kitchen brightens up that area so whoever is cooking does not feel trapped in a dingy little space. This window almost makes it seem like we are cooking in an outdoor kitchen. It makes us feel that we are part of the forest which surrounds us instead of closed off from it (4-22).

For the same light and heat purposes, we have two larger 4' × 4' windows in the dining area behind the table and two elevated windows in the dormer area above that space. These elevated windows bring in the higher-arched, summer sun to both the living room and dining areas (4-23).

4-23 Windows in the dining area, showing the two elevated windows in the dormer area.

Also bringing light into these areas are the windows of the west wall. They are very important because they allow the afternoon sunlight, which filters through the tall evergreens, to warm the house and prepare it for the cooler evening.

Though all the window spaces were framed and ready, we did not put in the glass the first year, mainly for two reasons. We wanted to give the walls time to settle and we were running out of money.

The last task, before the walls were completed, was covering the insulation strips and sealing in between the wall logs. At first I was thinking of cutting out quarter-rounds from larger poles for this purpose, but a nearby friend had a grove of young cedars. He let me thin out the grove and use as many of the narrow poles as I needed for the house. I brought home a truckload and proceeded to peel them. Even though they were green, they were as hard to peel as the dry logs because it was late in the season and the sap was low. But after a few days of constant scraping, they were ready. I beveled the ends of each pole and nailed them into the wall logs tightly over the insulation (4-24).

With the walls finished, it was time to get started on the loft and roof. I hashed over various roof designs with a few friends who had volunteered their labor and ideas. We decided to cover the kitchen and entryway areas with a bedroom loft, and leave the area above the living room and dining room open as a high, cathedral-style ceiling. A 45-degree pitch for the roof seemed to be the best because it made for a spacious ceiling, allowing a distance of 10' between the top wall plates and the ridge peak. The 45-degree angle, as we found out while working with it, was the easiest angle to use. Rafters could be simply measured and cut on that angle, and even insulation pieces and sheathing boards for the gable ends could be cut out with the minimal amount of waste and planning.

Constructing the Loft

It was time to begin the loft construction and we did not even have a center pole or a crossbeam for the joists. That problem was quickly taken care of, though. A hemlock tree was cut down and two logs were sawed from it. The logs were quickly peeled and brought to the house site. The 7' log was positioned upright near the center of the floor and the 14' one was notched in above it (4-25). It spanned between that upright and the inner east wall, where the other end was notched in place. As we pounded the spikes in, the logs spit back at us.

4-24 Covering the space between wall logs with sapling poles.

4-25 Joist placement beneath the left extension. To enter the left bedroom, you climb the ladder and step through the curtained entranceway.

The longer log extended well past the halfway point of the house which was designated as the end of the loft area. Since the pole was longer than necessary, we decided to modify our loft design and add a 36" extension to the north side of it. This space was used for a bookshelf and a reading area. The north end of that additional platform was later closed off for a small linen closet. The loft joists were spaced 16" on-center and spanned between the north and south walls. Every other 2 × 8 joist was doubled, to add support to the loft floor. These doubled joists also acted as braces to prevent the walls from spreading out under the weight of the loft. and roof.

A subfloor of 2 × 6 fir was nailed across the joists and a finish floor was laid diagonally above it. This diagonal finished floor is another precaution against the walls collapsing. It prevents the stockade walls from twisting by bracing them against leaning in any direction. Some people accused me of overbuilding, but I don't think I did. I just wanted to make sure our house stayed around for a long time.

Next came the rafters. The rafter sets were put together assembly-line style, using a simple matrix (jig) framework consisting of blocks nailed to the floor. First we laid out one set of rafters and cut their tops at 45-degree angles. The "A" brace was then cut and positioned and the rafter bottoms were notched to fit the top plates. Blocks were nailed around the rafter set in all the necessary places: two at the feet, a few along the sides, and two near the top of each. This method assured us that all the rafters were uniform and it gave us a guide for each of the necessary cuts (4-26).

After a few sets of rafters were finished, we laminated two of them together as a double set for the end rafters. One helper stood on the floor with a long board extended, raising the set by the "A" brace, while another helper and I spiked the rafter bottoms to the top wall plates.

4-26 Rafter layout jig and raising the roof rafters.

Rethinking the Design

At this point, Janey and I stood on the loft floor and tried to figure out how much space we would have for our bedroom under that simple gable roof. Neither of us was satisfied. We wanted a larger room. We recalled how some friends of ours had turned a small attic space into two good-sized bedrooms by incorporating a large shed dormer into the roof of that structure. We liked the idea and designed our roof to include three shed dormers, one on either side of the bedroom area and one at the south wall just above the dining area, to bring the morning sunlight into the lower spaces.

Adding Shed Dormers

We wanted the shed dormers in the bedroom to be 8' wide. Since we had to be able to stand in them, 5'-9" was a good height. This came to about a 22-degree pitch. I am glad we stopped long enough to decide on that extra roof space because at that point the dormers were easy to install. At a later time it would have involved tearing out rafters or maybe even replacing an already completed roof. We found over and over again that it pays to stop and live in the house at every stage of construction.

All the rafter sets were then spaced at 16" centers and nailed into place. Wherever the rafters braced the ends of the three dormers, they were doubled like the first two sets. The others were single sets. To frame the bedroom dormers, four jack rafters were cut at

4-27 Roof and dormer framing plan.

22-degree angles, and each was nailed to a peak of one of the four double-rafters. These extending jackrafters were then supported by several 2 × 4 upright studs spaced 16" apart (4-27). At the peak, the jack rafters were connected by an 8'-double 2 × 6 which spanned between them. Another 8'-double 2 × 6 was then placed between the bottom end of each of the jack rafters, and these headers were braced in the center, between the spaces for windows, by two 2 × 6 uprights (4-28).

4-28 Exterior view of north and west walls showing completed dormer and asphalt shingles.

The living room shed dormer was framed in the same manner. Being a smaller dormer, its jack rafters were cut at 35 degrees. This allowed for a space 8' long by 2½' wide in which two windows were put.

Finishing the Roof

After the roof structure and gable ends were framed, they were sheathed on the outside with low-grade 1 × 6 hemlock. To protect the roof sheathing, we covered it with a finish roof of asphalt shingles. Asphalt shingles were chosen because they are safer and last longer than cedar shakes and they are more aesthetic than aluminum. Cedar shakes are more natural and pleasing to the eye, but they are dangerous and are known to ignite with the least little wild spark. In fact, a friend of ours this winter lost his house because a spark set fire to his cedar-shake roof.

Finishing the Interior

With a protective roof over our heads shielding us from the autumn rain, we turned our energies to the loft interior. Again we stopped and figured out the spaces we needed. For comfortable, uncluttered living, plenty of closets and cupboards are essential. With our shed dormer design, there was adequate cupboard area under the dormer windows (4-29).

4-29 The loft interior.

For a closet, we set up a divider wall between the bedroom and what became the reading platform. This wall closes off the bedroom from the rest of the house, making it a separate area. The closet space is two rafters (32") wide and extends from the north wall to the center crossbeam. It was also partitioned off at the loft doorway entrance.

Because the house is specially designed for togetherness and has no totally separate spaces except for the mudroom, there is no door to the bedroom, just a heavy velvet drape hung from over the entrance to control heat. When the drape is open it allows the rising heat from downstairs to enter and warm the loft area. When it is closed, it prevents the heat from entering that space.

The inside ceiling of the bedroom and the open cathedral ceiling were sheathed with 1 × 8 boards, using the clapboarding method. This method was used to prevent having spaces between the boards and to seal off the insulation more efficiently.

Because more heat escapes through roofs than any other section of a structure, I took care to make sure ours was well insulated with 3½"-thick fiberglass. It is also important to block off the sections between the rafters where they meet the walls. I stuffed loose insulation in those ends and nailed on 15" board sections to protect the fiberglass.

Building the Stairs

To figure out a design for a set of stairs for the loft, I positioned the temporary ladder at various angles to find out which would be the most comfortable. An angle of about 45 degrees seemed to be about the best. I put up two 3"-diameter rails at that angle and made notches in them at about every 16" on-center for the 2½"-diameter pole steps. The rail on the right was longer and extended 3' above the loft floor to enable the climber to make a graceful entry onto the loft platform in whatever condition he or she might be (refer to 4-25).

Site Visit Update

When we revisited this site four years after John and his wife, Janey, had finished their house, we were already aware that they had split up some time before. John had stayed and Janey had gone on. What we were not prepared for was the dramatic change of life-style. This was reflected not only in the spaciously redesigned house, but also in the immediate surroundings. What was previously a quickly cleared, yet tidy niche in the woods, and a sufficient, but very small house, was now an estate which any successful couple would be proud to own.

John and his new companion, Sharon, had been housemates for some time. They both had good jobs and could afford to rethink the homestead's design. Sharon felt that the previous design had been too small and, with John's agreement, she had decided on some major modifications.

Included in her plan was a large extension off the west and north walls, and an addition to the east wall. These changes provided adequate space for several rooms, including a dining area off the front porch, a spacious bathroom, a large studio, shower and sauna facilities, a guest bedroom, and a music conservatory. The new dining area extends off the kitchen and front porch at the east wall. The exterior walls, as well as the dining areas, are built with horizontal and vertical logs and are skirted with cedar shingles.

On the upper level, beside the bathroom, is the studio area. The exterior of this area was framed with log posts and filled with short horizontal logs under the windows. The guest bedroom is located on the upper level at the northwest corner. To the south of it is a large enclosed porch.

The front porch and the east wall area were changed the least. The bathroom and its graveled, shed roof is the only extension to the north, and the dining area protrudes to the south. The outside surroundings have been carefully landscaped to enhance the beauty of the clearing.

John and Sharon are both enjoying their renovated home and the inspiration they receive from it. They both enjoy horses and have built a beautiful shelter for their animals in the spacious tradition of their own home.

The vertical-style log house (right) with the extension under construction to the left (west).

CHAPTER 5

LOG HOUSE,
SADDLE-NOTCH STYLE

Doing What Comes Naturally

Harry and June came to live on an old homestead which had some poorly maintained buildings on it. The old buildings were marginally usable until they could replace them with structures more suitable to their needs. The homestead has an abundance of water which rushes down from a large creek, irrigating the fields and providing enough electricity to power lights and a few smaller appliances. It has plenty of timbers for construction and heating purposes, and has excellent soil for their garden and hay crops. It is also isolated from neighbors and far enough away from town to be free of noise and pollution. The homestead was just what Harry and June had been looking for. They plan to stay on it for a long time. As Harry tells it, the urge to thoughtfully develop it into exactly what they want goes back a long way for him:

When I was a young boy my father once bought me a Lincoln Log™ kit. That set of miniature logs captured my interest for hours at a time. Between chores I would sit in the front yard and explore the many building possibilities the kit had to offer. One day when I was pulling firewood out of the bush with our old horse I got an idea to use real logs, modeled from the Lincoln Logs™, to make a larger fort—a fort which I could use as a hideout when I wanted to go off alone into the woods.

Appreciating the Woods

That fort had everything the smaller set had—only bigger. Even the window and door frames interlocked. But the only problem with my bigger fort was that it was too hard to disassemble and rebuild elsewhere when my hideout was discovered, so I had to construct another one every time this happened.

Designing log forts got to be my primary interest. Whenever I wasn't doing schoolwork or chores I was designing and constructing new forts and figuring out new methods of skidding logs to my sites. I even figured out new ways of bringing in the firewood because I was tired of harnessing the old horse and having to hook him up to logs so he could pull them to our woodshed. It wasn't his fault though—he was a nice old horse. I was just bored with doing that same chore every day. So I devised a pulley system, using an overshot waterwheel to skid the logs to the desired site (5-1).

I really consider myself fortunate to have grown up in a natural environment where I could learn how to take care of my own needs by utilizing readily available materials. I quick-

ly learned to appreciate the woods. I still use whole timbers in my construction, to make use of most of the tree and to escape from having to buy expensive lumber and insulation materials. Admittedly, building with timbers is a painstaking and sometimes tedious process, but it beats working long hours at a job to save enough money to purchase prefabricated materials. Also, I get a certain fulfilling pleasure from shaping each timber and making it fit snugly into place over the others. Each tree that was used was selectively thinned out from my own land and very little was wasted.

Starting Slowly with a Root Cellar

Once June and I were settled on our site, we thought carefully about how to develop the homestead into what we wanted. Our first building project was to replace an old root cellar which had rotted with age. We find it very important to have adequate food storage sepa-

5-1 The pulley system to skid logs. "Doing what comes naturally."

rate from the house because of the possibility of fire. A root cellar also provides a constant cool temperature which keeps fresh fruits and vegetables very well.

The cellar was replaced with tamarack logs (Western larch). The inner and outer walls were 4' apart and filled with planer shavings for added insulation. Its roof was constructed gambrel-style to allow for storage of empty jars, boxes, and other odds and ends (5-2). This smaller structure got us back in the practice of building and readied us for the next project, the house.

Selecting a House Site

We chose for the site of the house a slope which overlooks many mountains in the area. This slope is part of a plateau in the center of our land. On one side of it were the hay fields, to the rear was the new barn site, the old barn, and the garden area. In front of the site was a terraced area which we later developed into a tree reserve. Here we've been pruning evergreens so they grow as full as possible.

We began cutting the tamarack logs for the house in late winter. Most of them came from the mountainside across the field. After they were cut, we left them in place and peeled them with a square-nose shovel before all the

5-2 The root cellar.

sap was up. Peeling them before much of the spring sap flows helps keep them from mildewing and discoloring so readily. The logs remained on the hillside until the snow thawed enough for the horses to skid them to the building site (5-3). The logs were placed there on pole skids and were left to dry for a couple more months.

5-3 Skidding Western larch (tamarack) poles with a horse.

We mainly used tamarack logs because they have little taper and are usually very straight. These timbers have few limb knots and are quite durable.

5-4 *The wall on the left shows how the stone foundation steps gradually up the slope.*

Designing the Foundation

While the logs dried, we measured off a 28' × 30' area and outlined our foundation. The logs were 32' × 34' in length to allow for at least a 1' overhang on each side. We did not make any attempt to level the slope. Instead, we built our foundation with steps gradually going down the slope (5-4). The steps of this stabilizing wall went down at almost two-log intervals, allowing the adjoining logs to interlock with the flat rock and cement foundation for added structural support. Each of these adjoining logs was grooved at the bottom so it fit snugly to the log beneath. They were trimmed on the underside instead of the overside to prevent moisture from collecting in the grooves.

One of the reasons for the combination of rock mortar and log in the foundation was that the rock mortar had to be used where there

was contact with the ground. The logs would rot quickly if they were touching dampness. Logs, which we didn't have to buy and which were more pleasing to look at, were used where they were not on or below ground level.

The slant of the slope provides the house with a 14' × 30' basement with full headroom. Here, firewood can be stored and a Pelton waterwheel can be kept and protected from freezing. This area also houses an old wood furnace which heats the upper sections as well as the basement. A cement floor was poured for this area and was slanted slightly downhill for drainage. The surrounding logs are interlocked with round notches as are the wall logs above. A long car axle was driven into these logs at each side to reinforce them where they join the rock-and-mortar (5-4 inset).

The stabilizing walls on the 28' sides were 5" higher than those on the 30' sides to compensate for the stagger of the wall logs. They were constructed 5" higher because 5" is half the diameter of the 10" logs that were used as the end logs.

Placing the Sills & Joists

The longer sill logs rested on the lower wall sections. The end logs, which would be notched into these sills, were raised by the higher wall so they could properly interlock with the sills and begin the necessary stagger (5-5). Anchor bolts, 12' apart, were sunk into the concrete for added support of the bottom logs.

We spaced the joists 2' on-center and notched them into the sills with a lap joint. The joists were left round on the sides and bottom. Their tops were sized and hewed with a foot adz and a broadax to provide a level surface for the rough-cut 1" subflooring. Before I adzed the joists, I made vertical cuts into them every few inches with a very sharp ax (5-6). It is important to keep your ax very sharp at all times. Then I chopped out the pieces with a 9-pound-head broadax and went

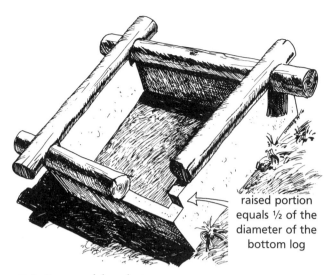

raised portion equals ½ of the diameter of the bottom log

5-5 *Staggered foundation.*

over the cuts with a foot adz to finish them off smoothly. If used correctly, a sharp foot adz will make a hewn surface look as if it had been planed by a mill (5-7).

We set up stringers or uprights every 6' as supports under the joists where needed. Their lengths depended on the sloping of the hill. Their tops were notched and spiked into the spanning joists and their bottoms rested on large rock pillars.

We chose to notch all our corners with round notches because we've found from past experience that this notch looks best and lasts the longest. It allows the wall log to extend

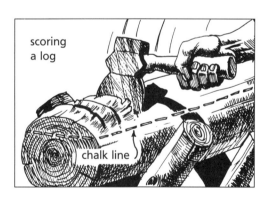

scoring a log

chalk line

hewing with a broad hatchet

5-6 *Using a very sharp ax to hew a log.*

5-7 *Lap joint notching floor joists into the sill log.*

beyond the corners, making the notches both beautiful and strong. Our log ends are staggered, one long, one short, so the long one completely covers the shorter one, preventing moisture from collecting on it (5-8).

I've torn many an old log building apart, and, in most cases where dovetail notching was used, the corners were the first place to rot because they were not protected by any overhang. in my opinion, the round notch is also the easiest of the notches to make.

5-8 Saddle-notched round-log ends.

Starting the Walls

We started the walls by placing the first end log across the two sills, making sure there was an equal distance of overhang on either side. It was secured in place with log dogs. I then took a plumb bob and centered it on the highest point of the log end to line up the new log over the ones below. If you do not have a plumb, any pointed weight—a fishing sinker for instance—would do just as well. I used this method to keep my walls straight.

To keep the wall logs uniform, I placed any log that was oval or unround so that its widest part was going up and down. Then I hewed it, to prevent obvious gain. First I used a pair of calipers or dividers to measure the gap between the stabilizing wall log below and the log which was to be notched (5-9). This gap would be equal to the depth of the notch prior to hewing.

The dividers were opened to this size and were held vertical at all times as they were run along the contour of the crossing sill log's end. The upper point duplicated the sill log's contour onto the log above, a gap's width higher than the lower span. The outline of the notch was then marked on both sides of the upper log with a thick lumber crayon (5-10).

The log was turned over with a peevee and again dogged into place. Then, with a very sharp double-bitted ax, we scooped the notches out to just beyond the crayon's outline to allow for hewing. The double-bitted ax I had been using was modified for this process. I heated the blades in a vise and slowly bent them into a curve. I then ground off the ends of the blades to round them, so they wouldn't gouge into the sides of the notches while I was cutting them out (5-11).

Lifting Logs into Place

We learned many times over that it never pays to lift heavy logs into place without the aid of some animal or some simple machine. Too many people cause their bodies needless strain by trying to lift objects that are too heavy for them. Why chance wrecking your back when, with just a little thought and research, you can invent a tool to do your lifting? To lift heavy logs we devised a swinging boom setup that is based on the principle of the log derrick which at one time was used by professional loggers.

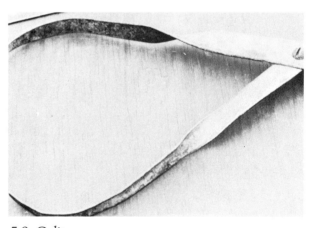

5-9 Calipers.

POSITIONING & HOLDING A LOG IN PLACE FOR MARKING

log dog

divider

determining area
to be cut out,
using a divider

5-10 Preparing to cut the saddle notches.

To make this swinging boom, we first set up a long vertical pole. This is called a stiff leg because it remains stationary. It can be supported by either a tripod brace or a stiff guy fastened to either a floor joist or a nearby solid structure. At the top of this pole, a block-and-tackle is connected to control a suspended, double-poled, swinging boom. At the bottom end, these boom poles straddle the stiff leg and are held in place by a block of wood and a

cable. This boom is free to swing around from the bottom and is able to lower logs onto any of the walls. A hand winch is bolted to the bottom of this boom and a pulley is attached to the top of it. The winch's cable goes over the pulley and is attached to a pair of log tongs

5-11 Axing out a saddle notch.

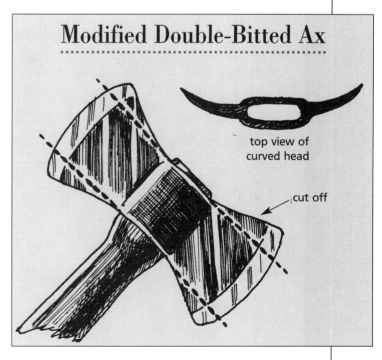

Modified Double-Bitted Ax

top view of
curved head

cut off

which grasp the center of the log, raising it and lowering it to the desired position. I found this device invaluable in my work (5-12).

The walls of the house went up relatively quickly, mainly because many of the logs we used were straight and had little taper. Many of them needed little more hewing than the 3" flat surf ace on top and bottom. These logs could be hewn easily enough by marking them with a scribe and scoring them with an ax or a chain saw, then chopping out the scored section with a foot adz. I made the scribe out of old scrap metal which I found in the dump, and I ground the marking tips out of old cobalt steel files. The tips were then welded onto the metal. One set of these tips is held shut with a piece of wire and the other can be adjusted to various gaps by a block of wood (5-13 and 5-14).

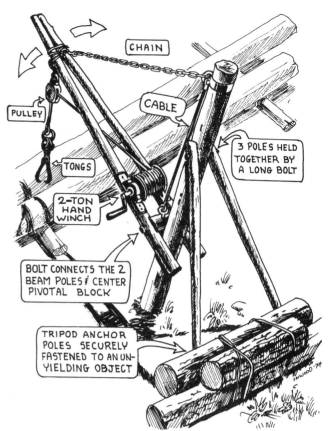

5-12 *The basic swinging boom.*

The principles of the Chinese windlass.

Hewing the Logs to Fit

Some of the logs were very difficult to fit in places and had to be turned several times before they were straight enough to lay flat over the logs beneath them. These logs either had large tapers or serious bends in them. You'd be surprised how much a log can be corrected by hewing. There are many purposes for hewing the tops and bottoms of the wall logs, including placing insulation, guarding against checking, and aesthetics.

Anyone who considers her or his log building a work of art and who wants to appreciate it for many years to come will come to know that every log, no matter how uniform it may appear, has some taper and some bend to it. Unfortunately, most logs have a noticeable taper and some high spots which prevent them from seating snugly on the log underneath. To compensate for taper you must hew the gain accordingly. It is also important to

5-13 *Homemade scribe.*

5-14 *Hewing with a foot adz.*

stagger your logs—butt, tip, butt, tip—to prevent having to hew off larger portions to compensate for gain. This method makes the most use of each log.

Insulating a Log Wall

We used a mixture of cotton and jute between the wall logs of the house. These materials were the stuffings of a couple of old mattresses we had laying around and a davenport I found at the dump. When I ripped open the old davenport with my knife, people at the dump gave me strange looks. I wonder what they thought I was looking for!

Since building the house, we've been using fiberglass insulation. I take a few rolls of the fiberglass and cut through each of them with a saw to get 3" strips. It is much easier to cut these strips while the wrapper is still on the roll, rather than stretching it out and cutting from long lengths of it. To use it, I just lay out a 3" strip and staple it to the top of a log which has been placed and hewn. It compacts very nicely between the logs and insulates extremely well.

create long strips by sawing through the coiled roll

fiberglass fills the channel

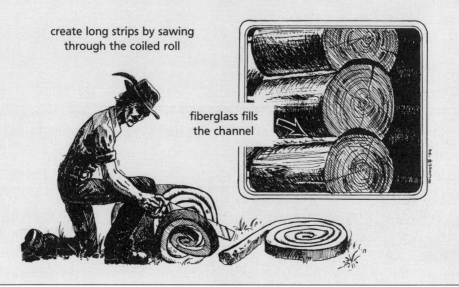

Each wall was made up of full logs, 32' or 34' in length; I used no pieces. After each log was notched and fitted in place, a 1" auger hole was drilled halfway through it on either side of the proposed door- and window-openings. A smaller-diameter hole was then drilled below the 2" auger hole to start the 12" spiral spikes.

These spikes were countersunk with a drift punch and mallet to secure the logs together. It is important to spike any future opening from log to log, to prevent the loose wall ends from collapsing when you are ready to chain saw the doorways and windows. The countersinking requires two steps to prepare the logs for the spike (5-15).

Purposes of Hewing

To provide a shelf that insulation could be compressed into so it won't be exposed to the weather.

To guard against random checking or cracking. Logs have a tendency to split where the sapwood dries out the quickest or where the sapwood is worked off. Some species, such as young 12"-wide cedar, have as much as 2" of sapwood all around them. If the log is left round or is hewn evenly on all sides, it will check the heaviest on the side exposed to either heat from indoor sources or heat from the sun, whichever is greater. If the sapwood is cut away from one or two sides, the larger checks will develop in those areas. If the logs were hewn on the tops and bottoms, the checking would be bidden between the logs.

To compensate for taper. Unfortunately, most logs have a noticeable taper and some high spots which prevent them from seating snugly on the log underneath. To compensate for taper you must hew the gain accordingly. If a wall log has a 9" tip and an 11" butt, you should hew both top and bottom in such a manner that you gradually cut off an inch more on each side at the butt than you do at the tip. When dealing with a crooked or bowed log, you put the crook or bow up and down and hew the high points until the log is snugly seated. This sometimes takes many turns and much handling before the log cooperates.

To avoid or correct "mouse holes" that tend to collect moisture, which promotes rot. A common mistake in building log walls, which can be corrected by hewing, is the forming of mouse holes. These are spaces caused by notching too deeply.

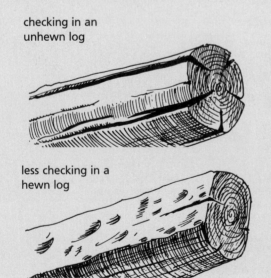

checking in an unhewn log

less checking in a hewn log

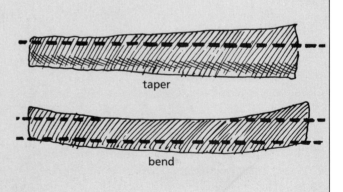

hewing to compensate for . . .

taper

bend

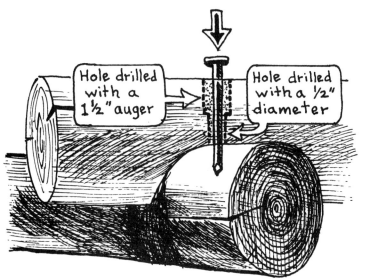

Hole drilled with a 1½" auger

Hole drilled with a ½" diameter

5-15 *Countersinking a spike.*

5-16 *Living-room corner.*

Making the First Doorway

The only disadvantage to using full logs seems to have been my wife's objection to working so long without knowing what the inside of our house looked like. Upon completion of the walls, I immediately chain-sawed a doorway so she could inspect the interior. She was very pleased with the effect of being surrounded by golden tamarack logs, and insisted that we find some way to protect them from rot and prevent them from losing their color. We did, in fact, coat them with a plastic preservative called Kemwood™, which is a brand of ure-

thane. The house has been standing for more than eight years and the interior looks just as new as it did the day we finished it (5-16).

After cutting out the first doorway, we tenoned the newly exposed wall ends with an ax and a homemade chisel. The end of the chisel was made from an old car-bumper support which I ground sharp on my grinder. The blade part fits into a cut piece of 1" galvanized pipe. I carved a piece of hardwood and wedged it into the pipe. This is the part hit with a mallet (5-17). I've used this tool for months at a time without having to sharpen it, the blade is so hard.

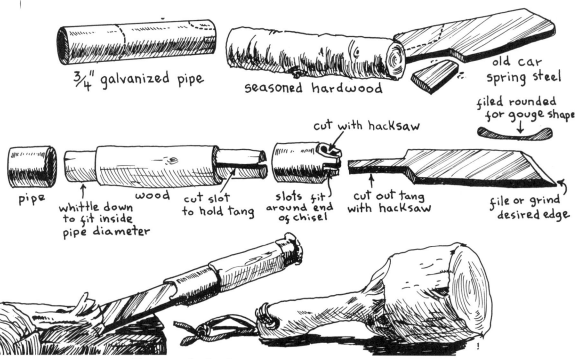

¾" galvanized pipe

seasoned hardwood

old car spring steel

filed rounded for gouge shape

cut with hacksaw

pipe

whittle down to fit inside pipe diameter

wood

cut slot to hold tang

slots fit around end of chisel

cut out tang with hacksaw

file or grind desired edge

5-17 *Constructing a good homemade chisel.*

The ends of the logs at the door and window openings were tenoned so they could be sandwiched by the double 4 × 4 door frames. Two 2" holes were then augered into both tenon ends so the log walls could settle independent of the door frame. The double 4 × 4s which I hewed out of logs were placed on either side of the tenoned ends and two smaller holes, large enough for ⅜" bolts, were drilled into each of them at the bottoms of the 2" auger holes. The bolts fit through the entire frame, and the larger holes allowed the walls to settle without damaging the frames. Pieces of doweling were fitted over the bolts to conceal them (5-18).

Framing the Windows

Window spaces were then cut and framed. Hand-hewn 4 × 12s were placed vertically against the wall ends and 3 slots, each 2" long, were drilled into each of them. Spikes were then hammered in at the bottoms of these narrow slots. A 2" space above the frame was left open to allow for settling. This space was filled with cotton and jute (mattress- and davenport-stuffing). When the walls settled, they compressed the insulation, preventing damage to the windows and window frames. The windows were put in loosely and were held in place with ¾" lumber strips (5-19).

Before the top-plate logs were placed above the 30' walls, several 4"-square laps were notched every 2' on-center into the highest logs of these walls. Ceiling joists, which I hewed to a flat 4" top and bottom, were then spanned across from wall to wall and their ends were fitted into the 4"-square laps (5-20). The ceiling joists were supported in the center by a similarly band-hewn crossbeam which spanned across the building to support these beams. The top-plate logs were then notched into place.

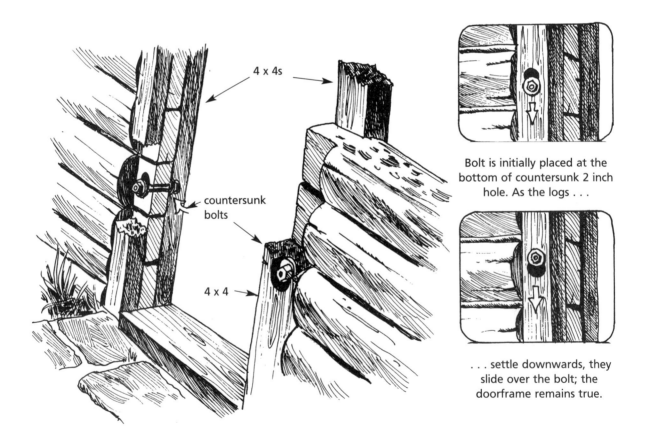

4 x 4s

countersunk bolts

4 x 4

Bolt is initially placed at the bottom of countersunk 2 inch hole. As the logs . . .

. . . settle downwards, they slide over the bolt; the doorframe remains true.

5-18 Framing a doorway.

marginal space filled with spongy insulative material

as logs settle down-wards, nail slots pre-vent frame warpage

5-19 *Framing the windows.*

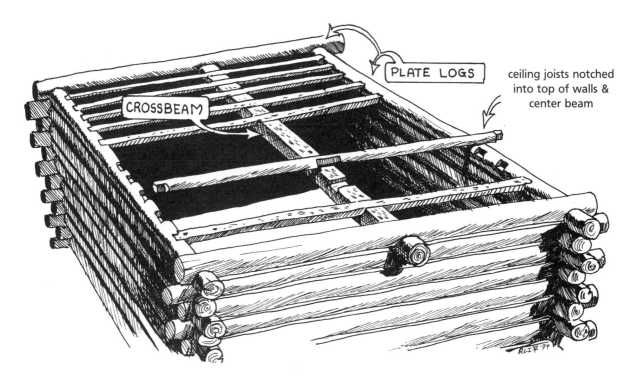

CROSSBEAM

PLATE LOGS

ceiling joists notched into top of walls & center beam

5-20 *Laying second-floor joists.*

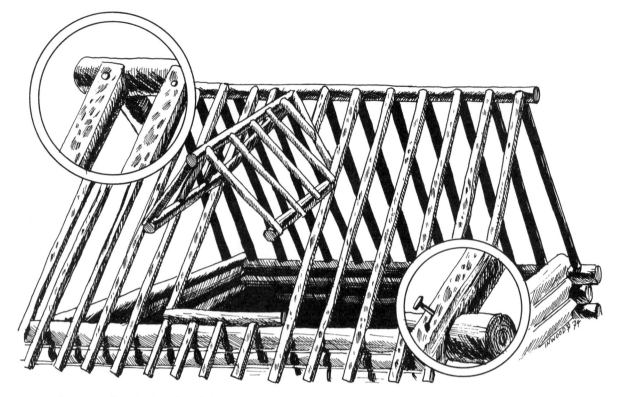

5-21 *Pole framing of pitched roof and dormer.*

Except where the dormer was to be fitted in, 7" cedar rafters were round-notched over the top-plate logs every 24" on-center above the ceiling joists. Then the shorter rafter pieces were toenailed to a header above the dormer. I used dividers to measure the width of the top plates, then cut my notches accordingly. The tops of the rafters were joined together at a final ridgepole which spanned the building at the roof's pitch (5-21).

Pole-Framed Dormer

We had decided that we wanted extra living space in the roof area, so we designed an 8' × 10' log dormer that has 7' of headroom in the center. This area was supposed to be a sewing room for my wife, but it turned out to be a guest room for occasional visitors. To frame the log dormer, 2 × 8 boards were first placed on the already hewn dormer-support rafters and were nailed into them. These boards extended from the roof's eaves to where the dormer-roof supports would intersect these support rafters.

5-22 *Cutaway view of log dormer construction.*

5-23 *Log dormer.*

5-24 *End wall with stone chimney.*

They provided a flat surface for the beveled ends of the cedar side logs. The cedar side logs were round-notched to the front dormer logs in the same manner as were the wall logs, and their beveled ends were spiked into the 2 × 8s (5-21). Where the top side logs intersected the support rafters, the bottoms of the valley rafters were nailed in. Their tops met at the ridgepole peak and marked the top-center point of the dormer. At this point the dormer's ridge log was connected to the ridgepole and the valley rafters. It extended horizontally out to the front of the dormer. Dormer rafters were then round-notched to the top cedar side logs and their tops were connected at the dormer ridge. Jack rafters were nailed between the valley rafters and the roof ridge-beam for additional support. The front window space was later cut out and framed in the same manner as the wall windows (5-22 and 5-23).

Closing In the Gables

After the dormer was finished, the gable ends were closed off with 1" lumber and later paneled over with cedar shakes. Each gable end has a 16"-square ventilator near the top for air circulation (5-24). 1 made nailers for the cedar roof shakes out of smaller poles which I hand-hewed, with a sharp ax, on two sides to a thickness of 2". Very few of these nailers were straight poles; in fact, a lot of them were quite snakey. But even with their bends, hewing them flat on two sides made them ideal nailers for shake roofing.

The Shake Roof

We split all the roofing shakes from cedar bolts with a shake froe. The job did not take long and was very satisfying. After we split these shakes, I took a drawknife and went over them to smooth their surfaces. This, I later found, was a mistake. Shakes should have a rough surface for proper drainage. The rainwater goes into each of the rough crevices and rolls down off the roof. When the shake is smooth, the water tends to penetrate through instead of rolling off, causing leaks in the roof. So much for perfectionism.

The roof eaves are protected from ice buildup by an 18"-wide sheet of aluminum which I nailed to them. The top of the aluminum is covered by the bottom shakes to prevent leaks.

5-25 *The living room showing the antique Franklin stove used for heating.*

Building the Chimney

With the main structural chores out of the way, it was time to add the finishing touches. We had been collecting rocks for quite a while. In fact, whenever we took a vacation we brought back several beauties (see Chapter 2 for more on chimneys). Our collection consisted of various different types of rocks from Idaho, Washington, Montana, and all parts of western Canada. In my spare time I used to practice splitting the rocks with a rock-splitting hammer. I tried to get them as flat as possible for a rock chimney. This chimney is now located at the northern wall, outside the living room (refer to 5-24).

A 2'-square hole was cut out of that wall to allow for the chimney pipe of the antique Franklin stove with which we heat our living room (5-25).

Constructing the chimney was very interesting. I first gathered several possible rocks for it and hit them each with a blow of the hammer to check if they cracked easily. The ones that did were discarded because they were too brittle to work with and too dangerous to use. Such rocks have a tendency to explode when heated. We bought a commercial flue which

has an 8" × 16" draft opening, and began fitting rocks around it. Because it is very difficult to locate the grain in most rocks, I found I had to use the trial-and-error method of facing them. I had good luck with many of them and was able to split them in half and get two flat faces from one rock. After facing them, I trimmed them so that when in position they would want to tip backward, towards the flue. This way they stayed in place while the mortar was drying. I made other cuts on the end stones to square them off (5-26).

The mortar I used was a mixture of half dolomite grit sifted through a screen that had 200 sections per inch and half Portland masonry cement. I mixed small amounts, only as much as could be used in half an hour. Before I mortared the rocks in place, I checked them once more to make sure they would tip inward instead of outward. When I was satisfied with the fit, I added the cement. Where there were small openings around the flue after the facing was in place, unshaped rocks were added to fill the gaps. An opening for cleaning out the creosote was allowed at the bottom of the chimney (5-27). For safety, the chimney extends 5' above the roof.

I built forms around the chimney as I mortared the rocks, to help it maintain its tapered shape. Each form was a small section, no more than 24" high, to cover the portion which was being worked on. Each was propped up and held in place with poles that spanned from the top of the frame to the ground. The ends of the forms were also nailed to the walls for added support. Later, when the mortar began setting, but before it dried, I removed the forms and swept the excess mortar from the rocks and joints (5-26).

Finishing the Interior

After completing the chimney, I worked on the interior again. I framed in the room dividers with lumber, built a simple stairway to the basement, and constructed a spiral-type staircase to the upstairs bedrooms. (We needed a spiral staircase because of our lack of space.) My wife and I agreed that we wanted a large living room, dining room, and kitchen, which would not be separated by closing doors. In the space left over, we wanted a good-size bedroom, an ample bathroom, and a staircase. With our design, the staircase had to suffer. its width could only be about 36", which is convenient for everyday travel but impossible for transporting furniture up and down. All the larger bedroom supplies had to be brought in through the dormer window.

For finishing touches in the house, I also built outdoor planters out of logs. They attach to the front of the house above smaller supports. These logs were dug out with a chain saw and final cuts were made with an ax to clean them out (5-27).

TYPE OF HAMMER USED FOR BREAKING AND FACING ROCK

WIRE TWISTED AROUND FENCE STAPLES DRIVEN INTO LOGS BOND THE MORTAR TO WOOD SURFACE

FLUE

MORTAR

PLACE ROCKS WITH AN INWARD LEAN

TEMPORARY FORM MADE FROM SALVAGE 1"x MATERIAL

2"x4" BOARD NAILED TO LOGS

CLEANING HOLE

INWOOD ▢ 74

5-26 *Constructing the chimney.*

5-27 *Outdoor log planter.*

Site Visit Update

Soon after the house was finished, we visited June and Harry. We all stood back and admired the completed house. They were both extremely satisfied with it. The one aspect of the site we all agreed we didn't like, though, was the rocky mound in front of the house. Harry and June said that they wanted a proper lawn to accentuate their house's rustic beauty. They had found it impossible to grow anything on that rock mound.

The next year we went back to visit them and instead of the rock pile there was a big lawn in front of their beautiful home. Harry explained that they had been frustrated with that area until they began plowing the hay field. At that time, he said, he had an idea. By carefully lifting large sections of turned sod and placing them in his pickup truck, he was able to haul the grassy turf sections to the front of their house. There he neatly fitted them together like a patchwork quilt covering the rocky mound. Before long the grass grew out and the sections grew together to make one big lawn for the front of their house.

That summer Harry and June were still in the process of building their barn (which is fully described in Chapter 12).

On returning to this homestead eight years after it was built we found very little had changed. Harry and June were still just as friendly and cordial as they had been before and their place looked just as manicured and cared for as it had always been.

Four years later their home and their relationship with each other was as solid as the log house they built twelve years before-and it would probably last just as long.

The only change in the main house after twelve years was a new roof. The original shake roof was not leaking, and would have been fine for probably another twenty years, but it was an unnecessary fire hazard. Harry

Saddle notches, still tight.

A log planter, still blooming.

chose a painted, galvanized roof. Instead of taking the previous roof off, he simply placed 2" x 2" spacers 16" apart along the roof, one at the center of the metal sheets, and one at either end as nailers, and fastened the roofing onto these strips. The strips at each gable end sealed off the gables. The eaves were not sealed, but left open to have ventilation between the two roofs.

Instead of buying the expensive peak-capping material which one usually has to purchase to seal off this joint, Harry simply extended one side of the roofing a few inches beyond the peak to cover the joining side.

Visiting the the site at the end of the millennium, we took all of the photos that appear on these two pages. A gate had been added to the main driveway, and a waterwheel built. The details of the house remained intact including a remarkable durability of the basic saddle-notch log con-

struction. The house had undergone further evolution with the addition of a new room. The house is as strong and beautiful as when it was first built nearly thirty years before.

The saddle-notch-style log house visited in the summer of 1999.

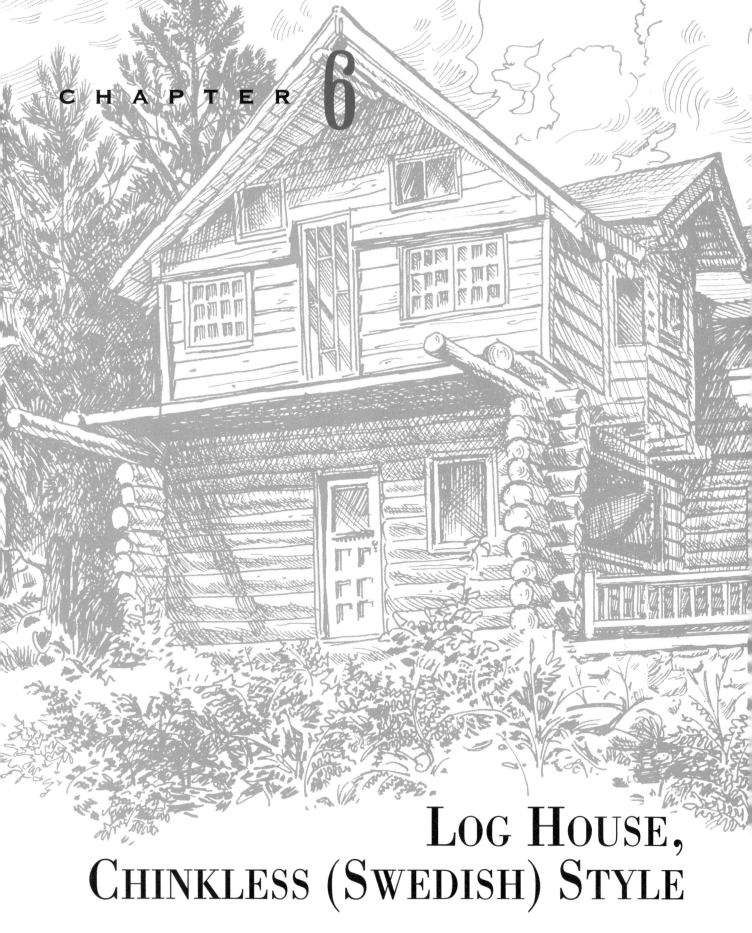

CHAPTER 6

LOG HOUSE, CHINKLESS (SWEDISH) STYLE

An Author Builds — Christian Bruyère

W e, the authors, Christian Bruyère and Robert Inwood, originally researched the material presented in these chapters in order to design and construct our own homes. This house was designed by Chris and his wife Margee for them and their son. They feel that it will provide them with inspiration and space to grow in during the coming years. Chris tells the story of their house:

What we wanted was a good-size log house that could be built by two people. Margee and I figured out various designs, but each was either too small or too impractical. The logs we would be using were from trees that a friend asked us to clear for him. They would have to be trucked in our 3-ton, staked-bed truck. The longest logs we could carry on its 12'-long bed would be 20', with butts towards the cab and a heavy-duty chain binder around them. Even that was kind of pushing it. In fact one day I almost flipped the truck, driving a load up the hill to the building site. The front tires came off the ground and the front end hung in midair until I got some of the load off the truck.

Elements of the Design

Keeping in mind this limitation on the length of the log, we figured out a design which would give us ample room, but be a bugger to build. The design called for 11 logs per tier in a modified, double interlocking-square floor plan, with a basement under the 20' × 20' southeast square. Sound complicated? You're lucky you didn't have to build this monster!

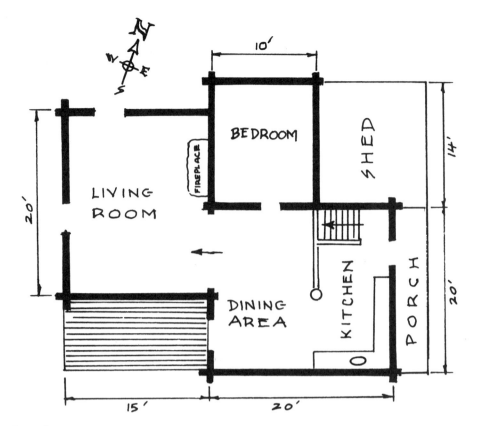

6-1 *Main floor plan.*

Constructing the Basement

Being in a northern climate, with long, cold winters, we wanted a basement for the appliances and the wood furnace. A lot of builders prefer to pass on this convenience because of the cost and difficulty, but we felt we needed this subterranean space and are glad we expended the energy. Being underground, it is one place that won't freeze if we leave during the winter. The basic layout looked simple enough but perhaps it was the scale that seemed intimidating (6-1).

Actually, the basement was not that hard to construct. A friend of mine with masonry experience was between jobs and agreed to trade his labor for a few days in return for our two billy goats and my help on his barn. The deal was made. I hired a Caterpillar™ (a "Cat") to come in and dig out an ample hole, and we immediately began forming a 12"-wide × 8"-high perimeter footing around the 20' × 20' floor space. We poured the footing, reinforcing it well with continuous horizontal lengths of rebar tied in at each corner.

Pouring the Slab

Then we poured the 4"-thick slab, setting in four 2 × 4s lengthwise as nailers, in case we wanted a wooden floor later. These on-edge 2 × 4s also acted as guides for tamping the concrete (6-2).

6-2 *Constructing the basement.*

To smooth the floor, use a straight board and straddle it between two nailers, sliding it back and forth over the concrete to work it in. Be sure not to forget to form a drain hole at this point because it's a hell of a job to do as an afterthought.

Using this method, the floor was poured in three stages. Each pouring filled an area between two sunken 2 × 4s.

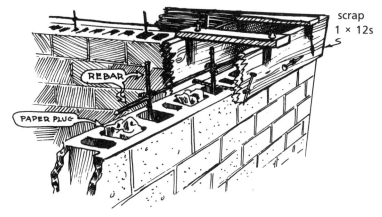

6-3 *Foundation walls using a block cap form.*

Building the Foundation Walls

As I was tamping the floor, my friend began laying the concrete blocks. He suggested I use this material instead of forming up walls and pouring cement, because the blocks were cheaper (at that time) and easier (for him, anyway).

I wanted to learn his trade for future reference, but as we went along I personally could only lay a few inside blocks. Most of my time was being spent mixing his "mud" and keeping him supplied with blocks.

The basement walls went up extremely fast. In less than a week we were 12 tiers up, or 8' high. I highly recommend at least this height for proper headroom.

Capping the Walls

After the block laying was completed, my friend told me how to form up the cap and instructed me on the filling procedure of the blocks. Since I was forming up a cap for horizontal logs, I had to modify the method he explained to compensate for the stagger, making a 4"-high cap on the cast and west walls and an 8" cap on the north. The south wall is 28" lower to allow for windows.

As a makeshift form for these caps, I used scrap cedar 1 × 12s straddling either side of the top rows of blocks with these boards (6-3). To hold them in position above the blocks, holes were drilled at the designated points, 8" down from the top of the boards

for the north and south side and 4" down at the east and west sides. A doubled-up piece of wire was placed through one hole, with a nail in the loop, braced against the inside board. The loose ends of this wire were put through the outside board and held by another nail, which was twisted until the boards squeezed tightly into the straddled blocks. The tops of the forms were held apart the width of the blocks by scrap nailers, nailed into the upper ends of the form.

After the forms were in position, I crumpled some heavy paper into the tops of every other hole to keep the concrete out, then placed a length of rebar down each of the uncovered holes. This rebar should be long enough to go to the bottom of the hole, with its top sticking out far enough to be wired onto a crossing round of horizontal rebar which circles around the perimeter (6-3 and 6-4).

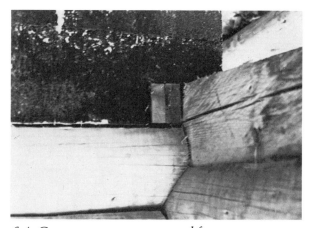

6-4 *Concrete cap corner prepared for stagger.*

6-5 Setting the floor joists.

6-6 Floor joist placement over a basement floor beam post.

After the cap was poured, I formed up the piers for the other section of the house. Since the ground was sloped, I set up these pillars at undetermined heights, letting upright posts of various lengths provide the level needed for the floor beams and floor joists.

Setting the Floor Joists

The floor joists were set over the beam at approximately 6' intervals, going east and west. Because I wanted the floor to be as low as I could get away with, I used 2 × 4 materials for the joists, spacing them across the beams at 12" intervals. This is sufficient when using a 2× fir subfloor—the floor is quite solid (6-5).

We wanted our son's bedroom, the dining area, and the kitchen to be a step up from the living room for a multi-level effect. We also didn't want to clutter the basement with upright braces for the floor above. With these purposes in mind, we used 1 × 12 floor joists for this area. These joists span over 9' before crossing the floor beam above the basement. The floor is solid and the joists are well within the "1" thickness to 1' of span" formula.

The floor beams under our son's room go north and south, and the 2 × 4 joists span across them to the top of the basement wall on the south and to a beam on the north (6-6).

Building the Log Walls

Now the log work began. The sill logs were either butted or notched together, depending on how the intersecting walls met. We used round or saddle notches for the outside corners and hidden-shoulder dovetails for the inside corners or junctions (south living-room wall to west dining-room, east and west bedroom to south bedroom, and north living-room to west bedroom).

We did not want to deal with chinking; therefore we decided to take the extra time to lay the logs in the Swedish, chinkless method, but little did we know what we were getting ourselves into. Using this method I could lay two full logs a day; some of the professionals can lay three or four. Because we had 11 full sides per tier, we did not see much progress for some time.

Cutting a Saddle Notch

To begin the "simple" outside-to-outside cornered logs, those with one saddle notch on either end, you begin by setting your log across the logs you will be joining it to. For interior finishing and aesthetic appeal, we, as most builders do, plumbed the inside wall, and let the outside taper in or out, depending on the log. To plumb the log, take your level and hold it upright against the log, parallel to the log you are notching. Shift the log until it comes up against the plumb level and dog it in place with a log dog (6-7).

Next, take your scribe, making certain that its handle remains at all times exactly horizontal, and scribe the shape of the intersecting ends of the log lying beneath onto the ends of the log you are notching. To figure out how wide the tips should be spread for the preliminary notch, find the narrowest distance between your log and the log below. Spread the tips and block them at a width ¼" shallower than this space. Be sure to start your scribe mark at the apex of each log end and go down from that point, making the lines on the sides meet under the log. If the scribe is not held perfectly horizontal, the ends of the notch will either be too tight or too loose (6-8 and 6-9).

6-7 *Initial plumbing of log.*

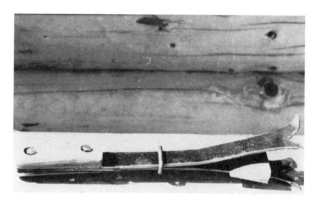

6-8 *Homemade scribe gauge with block.*

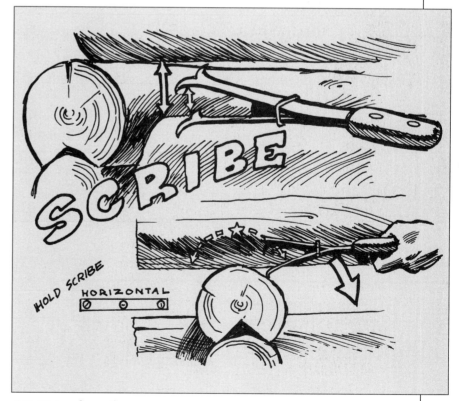

6-9 *Using the scribe gauge.*

6-10 *Christian Bruyère lining a notch using his homemade gouge, seen in 6-11.*

6-11 *Homemade gouge.*

After making the scribe mark, turn your log over, marked side up, and again dog it in place. Now outline the scribe mark with a shallow gouge, making sure to cut in deep enough to prevent splitting when chain sawing. A friend of mine made me an invaluable tool for this purpose from an old leaf spring (6-10 and 6-11).

How Long Will It Take?

Our house had 11 logs per tier and 13 tiers (143 logs). Using the described method, we were able to lay two logs a day. That works out to about 75 days' labor, not counting the felling, peeling, and hauling. We had a particularly rainy year and could only work, on the average, three days a week. You don't want to work on a log building in the rain; I tried it once and fell off the slippery logs. Because of such potential difficulties, we decided to hire a couple of friends, professional log-builders, to assist on the house. I went out on a lucrative tree-planting contract and made enough per day to pay both of their wages. Though I felt this might be seen as a cop-out, now I know it was the best move I could have made under the circumstances. I had to give up quite a few "pioneer points" for this compromise, but it probably kept me appreciating the house.

After the contract, I returned and joined in, then finished the last few tiers alone, or with Margee, or with the help of occasional visitors. One such visitor, an old friend from the city, came by and was immediately indoctrinated into the lifestyle. We purlined up a few top logs and I cut in the notches to seat them in place.

After the roof was completed, we escaped south for the winter and returned in the spring for tree planting. After tree planting, I went to work on the stone fireplace, again trading labor with my mason friend who helped with the foundation.

To cut out the notch, first chain-saw several vertical kerfs into it, then knock out the cut pieces and clean the seat in swift, steady motions with the tip of the chain saw (6-12, 6-13, and 6-14).

6-12 Notch with kerfs.

Christian Bruyère prepares to build his log mansion for himself, his wife, and their son.

6-13 Knocking out the kerfs.

6-14 Using the tip of the chain saw to clean out the notch seat.

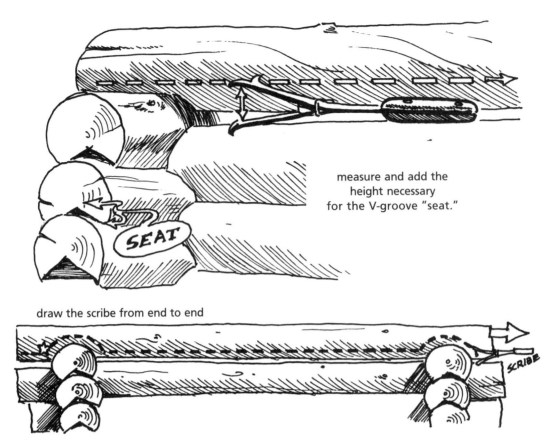

measure and add the
height necessary
for the V-groove "seat."

SEAT

draw the scribe from end to end

SCRIBE

6-15 Using the scribe.

Seating the Log

After this primary notch is cleaned out, roll the log over and place it in the previous position, plumb to the inside wall. If the log does not seat on the notch, turn it over and try again. If it does, notch it in place. Now take the scribe, again being careful to hold the handle horizontal, and trace along the length of the bottom log, carefully scribing its contour on the log to be notched. To figure out the depth necessary for this scribe, examine the bows and dips in the upper and lower logs, and adjust the tips so they will cut into the top log enough to provide at least a 3" seat along its course (6-15). With bumpy logs this seat could vary from 3" to more than 5".

This final scribe line should begin at one end of the top log, go around the saddle notch, go the length between that and the saddle on the other end, over this notch, and then run back to the original end (6-16-A).

Cutting the Groove

Once the scribing is carefully completed, roll the log over again and begin the cutting. Your success with these cuts depends on how well you scribed and how well you follow your lines. It might help to darken the line with a pencil.

We usually begin with a long, lengthwise cut from notch to notch. The area beyond the notches should be trimmed with a hand tool because this area won't be filled with insulation. To make the first cut, turn the log about 22 degrees to the left or right and rip vertically along that line just deep enough so your cut can be joined by the next cut, which will be at right angles to this first one. You need to cut at this acute angle to prevent the log from riding on the inside shoulders rather than on the scribed line (6-16-B). You should by no means make the cuts deeper than half the log's diameter because this would weaken its strength.

This rip should be made at high revs, with your saw held at approximately a 45-degree angle. Never attempt to saw exactly on your line; most of the time it deviates too much from the log's contour. Trim the line later with a chisel or sharp hatchet. When you finish with the first length cut, turn your log about 45 degrees and cut vertically down the opposite side, meeting the cuts in the middle (illus. 6-16-C).

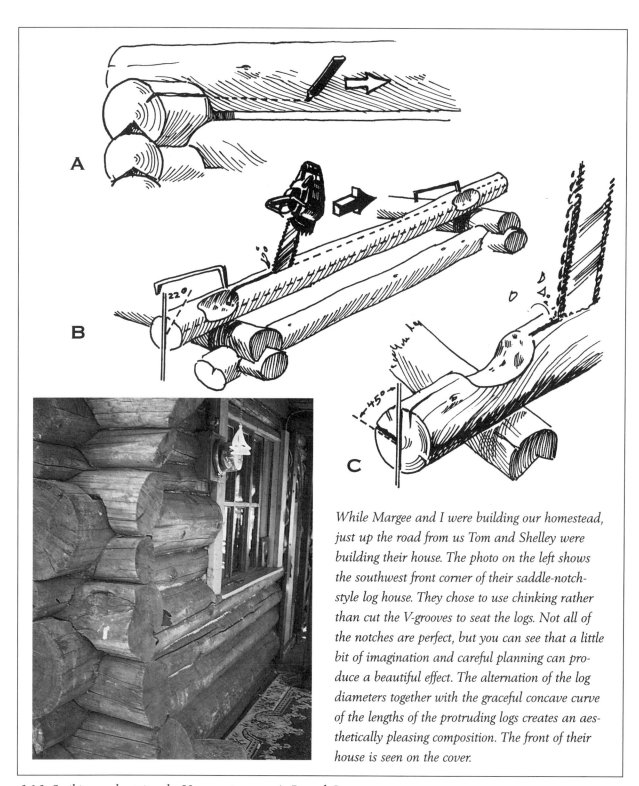

While Margee and I were building our homestead, just up the road from us Tom and Shelley were building their house. The photo on the left shows the southwest front corner of their saddle-notch-style log house. They chose to use chinking rather than cut the V-grooves to seat the logs. Not all of the notches are perfect, but you can see that a little bit of imagination and careful planning can produce a beautiful effect. The alternation of the log diameters together with the graceful concave curve of the lengths of the protruding logs creates an aesthetically pleasing composition. The front of their house is seen on the cover.

6-16 *Scribing and cutting the V-groove in steps A, B, and C.*

Details of actually making the V cut, trimming the scribe line and the finished V cut are seen in 6-17, 6-18, and 6-19.

6-17 *Making the length cut.*

6-18 *Trimming the scribe line.*

6-19 *Length cuts and trimming completed.*

Adjusting the Notch

Next, make the final notch cuts. The notch is again outlined with the gouge in the same manner as before, but this time going as deep as possible to save on "chain saw jitters"; the chain saw is used enough as it is (6-20). Then I cut some small kerfs, going deeper in the center than at the edges, giving the notch a concave seat for the fiberglass insulation which will fill it. These seats are also cleaned out in the same manner (6-21).

6-20 *Outlining final sadle-notch cut.*

6-21 *Final saddle kerfing and cleaning.*

Trial Fit

After this and the end trimming are completed, your log is ready to be rolled over to see if it fits snugly in place. This trial fit should be done before tacking on the fiberglass-and-oakum sealer, because getting a perfect fit the first time is rarer than getting a hole-in-one on a tough golf course. Not even a pro can boast of more than a perfect fit once a week. Often I have to turn the log as many as five or six times before the fit is exact. The major problem is usually that the log is riding on the notches or on an inner ledge. To find the problem points (riding points), hit the log in several places along its length and over the notched areas, then turn the log over. Wherever there is a crushed point or new discoloration is usually the place where your log is contacting the lower log. Either chain-saw or hew these spots down with an ax. If the log is riding on the notch, carefully mark the spots and trim them with the gouge (6-22).

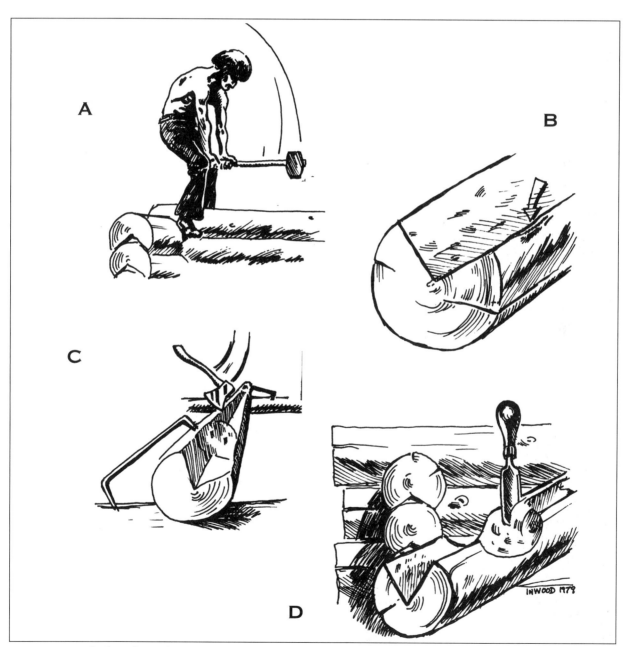

6-22 Seating the logs through steps A to D.

Then try to seat the log again and again, until you achieve the perfect fit (6-23 and 6-24).

6-23 Well-fitted wall logs.

6-24 Well-fitted notches.

Cutting Hidden-Shoulder Notches

The round saddle notches were a breeze compared to scribing and seating the inside, hidden-shoulder dovetails. These are tricky notches to execute, but they are quite beautiful. Try not to get frustrated if it takes you half a day to complete a log with one of these notches on it. That's how long it took me—there may be easier ways, but none as aesthetically pleasing.

To prepare for making these notches, cut the log to be joined to the proper length. This length should be long enough to notch one end and to bring the other end half into the width of the joining log. Scribe your primary notch on the other end. Measure the diameter of this end, find the center point, and with a level mark a plumb line from top to bottom. Measure 2½" in either direction from this line and mark two other plumb lines, 5" apart, centered on this end (6-25). Now measure a line 3" in from the end, at the top of the log, eyeball straight behind the center end line, meas-

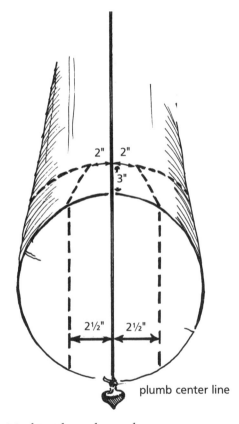

6-25 Marking the male member.

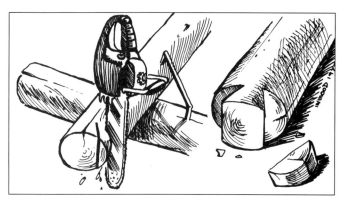

6-26 *Cutting a male dovetail.*

6-27 *Hidden shoulder dovetail joint.*

ure 2" in either direction at this point, then draw another line. This line should be 4" long and centered. Make a straight diagonal line on either side, joining the 5" lines with the 4" lines (6-25).

Now adjust your log so the end is hanging free of any obstacles and make your primary cuts. Being careful that your chain saw is held in exact plumb and you are cutting straight up and down, guide the saw across the log on either side of the intersection of the diagonal and crossing lines (the 4" lines), then rip down the diagonals until you meet these cuts. The end piece which is left should be a vertical, dovetail shape (6-26).

Make your round notch on the other end. This will allow the log a seat and eliminate the need for the dogs. Where the dovetail end intersects the crossing log, draw a line on the lower log, then trace the body of the dovetail. Note: with the exception of the bottom wall logs, this primary dovetail cut is already in the lower log.

After an inset is made into the lower log to receive the male dovetail end, place it into the slot. If it is not a snug fit, don't worry about it. It will not be seen. If the male end does not fit into the receiving, female end, trim it down (6-27).

Now, as before, adjust your scribe to the desired width for the length of the log and the saddle-notched end. Make

your scribe lines, then carefully scribe the contour of the upper log's shoulder on the facing sides of the lower crossing log, making certain that the scribe handle remains exactly horizontal at all times.

Now remove the top log and gouge out the meat along the scribed line to the depth of the male end. When the log is ready to be set into place, it should fit snugly into this notch, with its shoulders hidden within it (6-28).

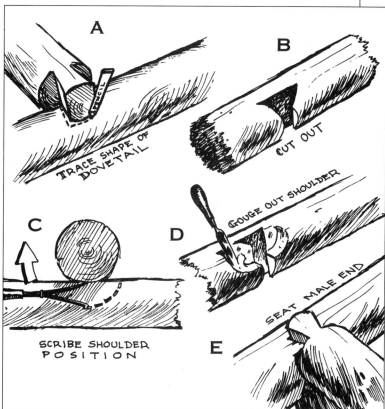

6-28 *Scribing and seating dovetails.*

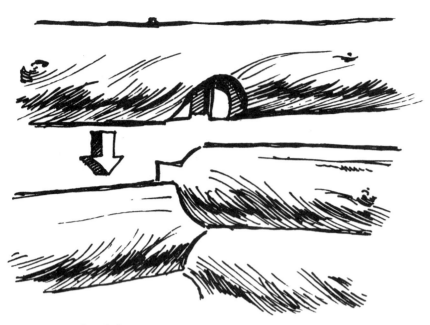

6-29 *Top female log seating.*

Now, scribe the remainder of the log. Using the same adjustment on the scribe, trace the intersecting shoulder of the dovetailed end on either side of the facing, female slot. Gouge along these lines and trim out the notches.

After a log is ready for fitting, tack shipbuilder's oakum along the inside edge, completely around the grooved inside, including the end notches. This substance waterproofs and seals the joint. Inside the grooves and notches, a sufficient strip of fiberglass is set for insulative purposes (6-30 and 6-31).

Once this log is in place, it is ready to receive the lower half of the next crossing log. First plumb and position this log over the male dovetail end and trace that piece on the underside of the log to be notched. Turn this log over, making certain it is exactly upside down. Check the plumb line on the end with your level, then carefully cut out the female (6-29, same cut as in 6-27)

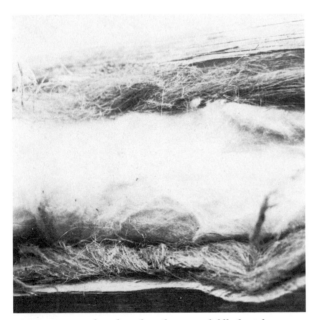

6-30 *Groove lined with oakum and filled with fiberglass insulation.*

6-31 *Finished hidden-shoulder notches.*

Building the Roof

Then the top logs are purlined up and notches are cut to seat them in place. Here is one such top log which fits over the ceiling joists of the living-room north wall (6-32 and 6-33).

Installing Ceiling Joists

The ceiling joists were round-notched over the walls and their tops were hewn for the 2 × 6 tongue-and-groove cedar subfloor and ceiling. This material was used because it provides a visually appealing ceiling for the lower areas (6-34).

The tops of the top-plate logs were then hewn to provide a flat surface for the 2 × 6 framed pony walls of the second story. We decided to use frames to save time and energy. We had to have a roof on by winter and we were becoming exhausted. These walls were sheathed on the inside with spruce tongue-and-groove because this is a light wood and would contrast with the exposed log rafters.

6-32 Log-ascending purlins.

6-33 Log after being notched.

6-34 Ceiling and joists over the living room.

6-35 *Bathroom ceiling and finished walls.*

The bathroom was sheathed in cedar and then gypsum wallboard (drywall) was installed to give a finished wall 6-35).

On the outside, the walls were braced with plywood. The plywood was given a vapor barrier of black paper and was exterior-sheathed with 1× cedar in a clapboard style. We didn't buy actual clapboarding because the cost was prohibitive. We chose this style because we thought that the clapboarding would blend well with the logs (6-36).

6-37 *Log framework of the bedroom dormer.*

We wanted the exposed, log-rafter ceiling over the bedroom, studio, and bathroom (6-37), and were willing to do the extra building to have it. A sheathing of 1× hemlock, another light wood, was nailed over the rafters

6-36 *Southwestern view showing log constuction on the ground floor and clapboarding on the second floor.*

6-38 *Rafter layout.*

shingles

plywood

insulation and 2 × 6

1 × 6

rafter

ROOF SHEATHING

and a network of 2 × 6 boxes for the insulation was built above it, crossing the rafters. The box section was covered with a layer of ⅝" plywood and the roof was finished with two-tone green asphalt shingles (6-38).

We deviated from the normal wall construction to put in a dormer and a bay window in the bedroom and studio (6-39) because we wanted to bring in more light, much as our neighbors, Tom and Shelley, up the road from us have done with their playful gable. (Tom and Shelley's house can be seen on the cover and in 6-16.) This also changed the basic rafter design in the interior. The inside framing of these openings was constructed out of log so it would blend with the rafters (see 6-37).

6-39 *Our studio bay window and bedroom dormer on the left. Tom and Shelley's gable on the right.*

6-40 *Unfinished fireplace.*

Building the Fireplace

My mason friend who helped with the foundation and I built the slab. Then we set the metal heatform in place and built the necessary blockwork around the flues.

With this core completed, I went north to a section of blasted granite and brought back a few truckloads of angular stone. Since what is beautiful in stonework is a matter of personal taste, I built most of the fireplace alone (6-40). The stones go beyond the ceiling, into Margee's studio. (See Chapter 2 for more on fireplace building.)

Cutting Openings

After the fireplace was completed, I began cutting out the door and window openings. Before making these cuts, I measured the openings and framed them with plumbed and leveled 1×s. Then I carefully chain-sawed the vertical cuts, cutting flush against the guide boards. The most accurate way to cut is to start near the top and cut with the tip up, higher than the body, at about a 45-degree angle. This way

the blade is cutting down into a few logs at a time, guiding itself down a straight line. Always use a safety chain and cut at a fast speed to help prevent the saw from jumping back at you. Always saw downwards, trying not to bind the tip more than necessary.

After the vertical cuts, I set up a horizontal guide on the outside of the bottom jam, or sill log, under the opening. This guide was level with the inside board. I made several kerf cuts down to the guides and broke off the excess pieces with a mallet, then hewed the sill flat with an ax (6-41). When cutting this sill you should not go any deeper than a third of the way into the log because of the previous V-groove along its length. Then measure the height of your opening and follow this same procedure at the top.

Splines for Window & Door Frames

After the openings were cut, we splined them with 2 × 2 splines to hold the log ends in place during the settling process. When making these cuts for the spline, you should gouge a bit deeper so you can back the boards with insulation to fill the uneven spaces. The length of these splines should be 2" shorter than the opening to allow for settling. Do not nail these splines in place.

6-41 *Making horizontal cuts.*

Site Visit Update

Chris and Margee were dedicated to building the ultimate country house—and they succeeded! What's more, they lived in their finished house for more than a decade.

The design proved very practical. Bob Inwood revisited the site and took these photos in the summer of 1999. The house is still a home to subsequent owners. They have added a balcony off the second floor bedroom, a bay window and an an exterior chimney for the kitchen, and a large deck area off the kitchen porch.

For Chris and Margee the process of forging their own special abode had challenged their problem-solving abilities and given them enormous personal satisfaction. After they completed the roof they went south for the winter, returning in the spring for the tree planting. After all of this work, they were looking forward to living in their homestead. All the details were finished by the next winter. Chris said, "We're happy we built our house the way we did, and appreciate the rustic beauty that only natural building materials and an unspoiled countryside can provide."

The chinkless-style log house built by Chris and Margee Bruyère, visited in the summer of 1999.

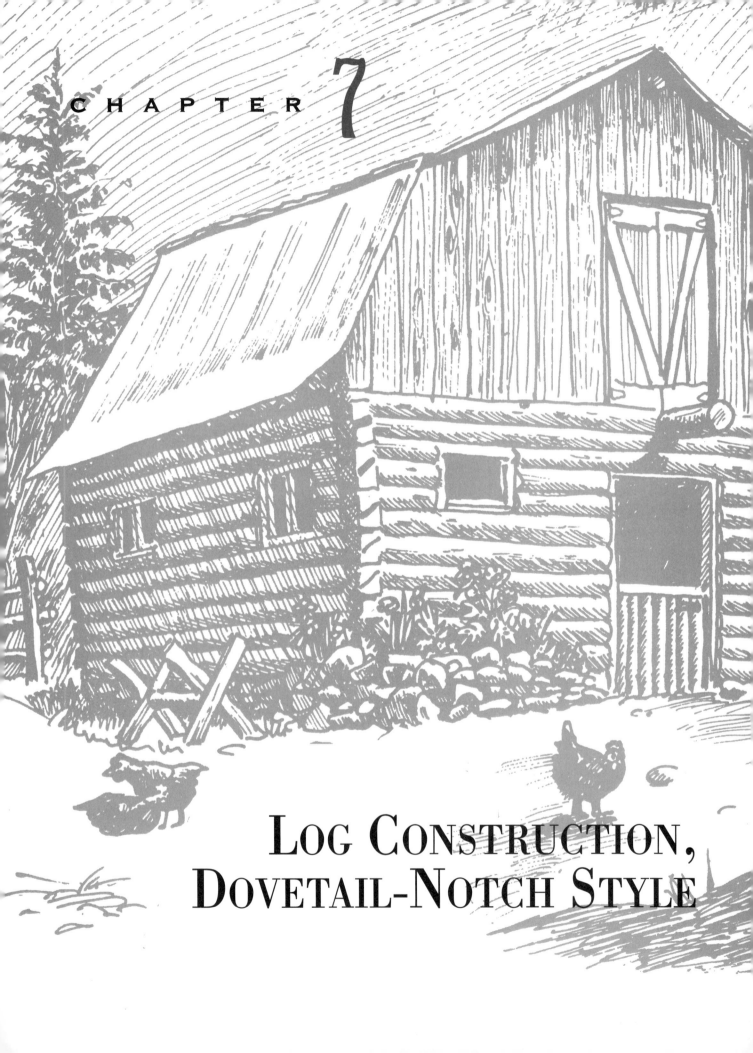

CHAPTER 7

LOG CONSTRUCTION, DOVETAIL-NOTCH STYLE

Overcoming Difficulty through the Help of Others

Before they had felt ready to build their main house, Christian Bruyère and his wife, Margee, learned by building a barn on the homestead property they had found. As Chris tells it, the process began with the urge to move on and the desire to visist some friends who had recently escaped the city and suburban sprawl to the North Country:

When we got to their homestead we expected them to relate their hardships in trade for ours. But, though they were living out of a temporary one-week wonder which they built out of scrap lumber, and though the temperature was just above freezing, they had nothing but good to say about their new home. All was going well for them. They were working together for something they believed in. They loved the peacefulness of their riverfront forest and would not trade it for anything.

Instead of sinking under the weight of our negativity, they began teaching us new things. They showed us edible mushrooms and plants that grew wild which were there for the taking. They showed us the forest and told us their plans for a new log house. Before long we helped them cut and peel logs and prepare the firewood.

From Dream to Reality

Our friends, being city dwellers like us, did not have any knowledge of building with logs or any other material. But they were determined to build their log house. Within hours after their project had started, many neighbors, both old-timers and new "textbook pioneers," offered their assistance. Some of them helped physically and some expounded theories over homemade elderberry wine. We were impressed with the cooperation and helpfulness of these people. They were truly neighbors.

After working with our friends for a while and learning from some of their mistakes and experiences, we decided that this area would be a fine place in which to settle. The folks were really friendly and the valley, surrounded by large mountains, was very beautiful and protective.

Finding a Site

We searched for a short while and soon located an old homestead complete with house, barn, root cellar, and outbuildings.

Soon after we moved in, the roofs of the old barn and storehouse collapsed. We examined the remains of the barn and found that most of the massive 12"- to 16"-diameter cedar logs which comprised its walls had decayed into rotted pulp, good only for composting. We invited a few neighbors to help demolish the structure and shared whatever firewood we could salvage.

The root cellar was the next to go. The only thing usable from that mess was the concrete front. The rest went to the dump.

At least we could live in the house for a while. It had no actual foundation, just a few rock piles it rested on. Its walls and floors slanted in various directions, but it was warm and cozy—and the price was right.

Acquiring a Menagerie

We really got into the rural frame of mind fast. We wanted to immediately become self-sufficient and raise many useful animals. We bought a horse for riding and farm work (so we thought). We purchased a Black Angus heifer for milking and breeding, and goats for immediate milk.

7-1 *Making a peeling spud out of an old shovel.*

Planning for a Barn

Since the winters are cold in this area the first construction project was to build a log barn to house this menagerie. I wanted to try building with log, first because of its rustic beauty, and second, because it is plentiful in our area and there are many sections of land that could use a little selective thinning out.

We have an adequate wood lot on our land, yet we wanted to get the logs for the structure elsewhere for the time being. A neighbor from across the river needed some land cleared. He made me a proposition I couldn't refuse. If we would clear the land for him and raise his pig along with ours (yes, pigs too) until it was ready to be slaughtered, he would let us keep all the tamarack we needed for the barn. He suggested we use tamarack because of its durability and straightness. We found that it was also a very easy wood to work with because it had few limbs or knots except near the top.

We trucked the logs to the barn site and immediately began peeling off the bark. We did not have a peeling spud, so we improvised with an old shovel that a neighbor lent us. Its round tip was cut off an inch from the end and the new edge was filed sharp to cut more easily. This proved to be an excellent tool for the purpose (7-1).

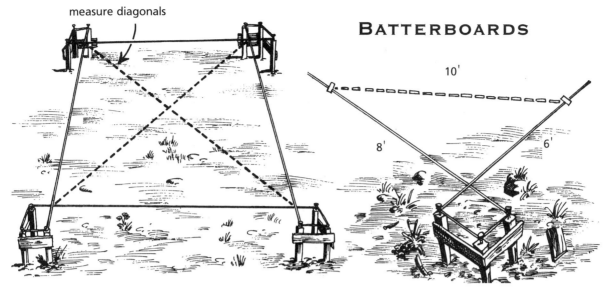

measure diagonals

10'

8'

6'

7-2 *Setting of batterboards.*

The bark stripped off easily because the logs were cut in the early spring when the sap began running. But as the weather became warmer, we found it increasingly harder to peel the logs, not only because the sap was drying and we had no shelter from the hot sun, but also because we made the mistake of having our work area downwind from the pigpen.

As we cut and peeled the logs, many neighbors came to give us a helping hand and offer us advice. Some of the advice, I must admit, was rather unsound, but most of it was necessary and useful. I started trading labor with some of the locals. One neighbor helped me set up batterboards and showed me how to rough out a square 22' × 22'. He checked the square by measuring a line 6' on one side and 8' on its perpendicular. In order for the corner to be an accurate 90-degree angle, the diagonal of the lines had to be 10' long. We measured each corner, then double-checked the crossing diagonals. They had less than 1" difference in length (7-2).

In return for this help I worked on his place with him. Though I didn't know much

about construction or farming, I was eager to learn and he was happy to have my help. It was all a valuable experience for which I was grateful.

Laying Out the Footings

We decided to use ten 24" footings as the primary foundation for the barn. We dug the holes: one at each corner, one at the center of the sides without doorways, and one on each side of the two doorways. Each hole was 12" deep and more than 24" wide. The footings were 24"-high pyramids, 12" square on top graduating to 24"-square bottoms for maximum support (7-3). We made rough 1 × 6 forms and braced them with thin strips of 1× on the outer

foundation posts

WHEN WATER IS SAME HEIGHT AT BOTH HOSE ENDS, IT IS LEVEL

7-3 *Laying out the footings.*

7-4 *Mixing the cement. "Overcoming difficulty through the help of others."*

and poured into the forms. We used a mixture of 1 part Portland normal cement, 2 parts gravel, and 3 parts fine sand. We also added quite a few large rocks for volume. This saved on cement and didn't seem to take away from the strength of the footings (7-4).

Luckily the area for the barn was relatively level so each footing stood between 8" to 12" above-

side. Each one was set in a hole. I checked the levelness of the forms by filling a hose with water and stretching it from corner to corner on one side (7-3, inset). The ends of the hose were bent up to just above the tops of the forms. If the forms were level, the water levels within each hose would be horizontal with the tops of the forms. If that wasn't the case we would adjust the depths of the forms. If the water level was too high, the hole was filled until the form was the height of the others.

The cement, gravel, and sand were then measured on a platform, mixed with water,

ground. The sill logs would rest on top of these footings.

The Earth as Floor

We figured that the best floor for a barn was a natural one of porous soil. Urine seeps through it and after a season or two the decayed bedding and uncollected manure break down on it and produce an excellent humus topsoil which can later be put into the garden.

There is a problem that arises, however, when building a log structure without a floor. All four of the bottom logs will be sill logs of

CENTER POST SLIGHTLY HIGHER TO COMPENSATE FOR START OF STAGGER

7-5 *Adding stonework to fill between footings.*

the same level. When using any notching method to join logs, the logs must be staggered. Two parallel logs should be set on the pillars and two crossing logs should be notched a half log above them. The space between the crossing logs and the center pillars can be filled by making these pillars half a log higher than the others. The higher center pillars will then support the raised end logs. The space that is left between those logs and the ground can later be filled with stonework or other foundation material (7-5).

Another way to rectify this problem is to make notches in the underside of the two lower logs. These notches should be at least ⅓ of the logs' diameter in depth, and should be long enough to cover the top of the pillars they will be resting on. Notch the crossing logs to these with dovetail notches or any other notch you prefer (7-6).

Dovetail Notches

Dovetail notches are widely used when working with milled or hand-hewn logs because of their ability to interlock. Their design prevents them from coming apart no matter in what direction stress is applied. They pull each wall log towards the center of the building, making it impossible for the logs to fall outward (7-7). The same principle holds true when using round logs. Because of this interlocking ability, we found it safe to use this notch without having to spike the corners. We saved ourselves money on materials and prevented premature decay in the notches. Nails and spikes contract and expand at different rates than wood. After a period of time, the moisture and oxidation which collects between the two surfaces will rot the wood and weaken the corners.

We cut dovetaill notches in each successive log until the walls were finished (7-7).

Since we were lucky enough to have plenty of good logs to choose from, we built the barn walls out of solid logs wherever possible. But

END LOG

7-6 *End logs start the stagger.*

we miscounted the number we needed, and we ended up not having enough long logs for the whole structure. Consequently, the back wall was constructed of 8½'-long pieces. An 8½' piece on either side left room for a 5' doorway in the center.

7-7 *Interlocking dovetail notches.*

7-8 *Establishing a vertical line for flat sides.*

MAKE VERTICAL CUT
TO SAME DEPTH AS
MARKED ON LOG END

7-9

7-10 *Removing the side slab.*

Cutting Dovetail Notches

Dovetail notches are simple to make. First you use a level to find two parallel lines (north to south) at each end of the log. In our case, the lines were about 1" to 1½" in from the outer circumference of the log end (7-8). Then measure the diameters of the crossing logs which are to be notched above. Mark these measurements on the side of the prospective ends of the lower sill logs.

A sharp pruning saw is used to cut in against the grain to meet the depth of the parallel lines (7-9). We knocked each of the pieces out with an old ax and a hammer (7-10). Then place the log in position.

Rest a square on the end of this log and slanted it at a slight (30 degree) angle, then mark a line across the log end. Make a saw cut at the rear of the notch to the same depth as the slanted line (7-11). This piece is then knocked out and a wedge-shaped log end is formed to interlock with a coupling notch (7-12).

A crossing log is put in position above the first logs. The level is again used to find two parallel lines, and the appropriate pieces are sawed and knocked out. As the top log is held in position, rest a square on the slant of the bottom-log notch and measure the distance between the high and low points.

The distance and slant are dupli-cated on the side of the upper-log notch with the high point being at about half of the log's diameter. Draw a line, saw a cut against the grain, and chop the piece out with a hatchet (7-13 and 7-14).

The log is then fitted into place, which usually means hewing its bottom until it fits snugly (see 7-15 on the following page). The amount of hewing needed with a relatively straight log depends on how care-fully the slants and distances of the log below were measured. If care was taken, it would fit tightly with-out any hewing. That was seldom the case. If the notch was cut too deeply, the log bottoms and tops would have to be hewed according-ly until the notch interlocked prop-erly. If the notch was not cut deep enough and the gap between the logs was too wide, then the bottom notch would have to be hatcheted or axed out until it was wide enough for a proper fit.

7-11

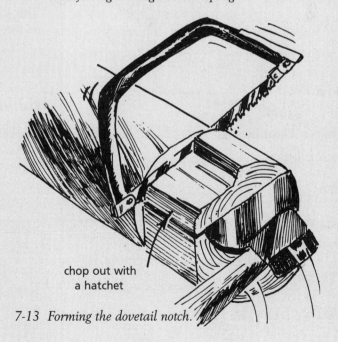

7-12 *Transferring the angle to the top log.*

7-14 *Dovetail-notch detail.*

chop out with a hatchet

7-13 *Forming the dovetail notch.*

Lifting the Logs

Though the logs were heavy—tamarack which had dried for less than two months—they were not very difficult to lift. Using a simple parbuckle, my wife and I managed to hoist most of them in place, and waited for visitors to assist us with the others.

Getting a Perfect Fit

If the notch is cut too deep, the log will keep the joint from fitting.

Correct the error by hewing along the length of the log . . .

. . . the joint drops into a snug fit.

7-15 Hewing until the notch fits snugly.

This parbuckle consisted of a long section of rope with both ends tied around the sill or a low log. The center of the rope was brought to the inside of the building, thrown over the wall, and looped around a log that was placed at the foot of the two skids. As the rope was again pulled to the inside, it raised the log on the skids and hoisted it to the top.

Making the Doorways

We spiked the fitted logs on either side of the proposed doorways to keep them in place after the openings were sawed through.

Some builders spike either side of the window areas, but we felt that would limit us in window design.

Placing Joists

We notched in a crossbeam above the walls before we placed the top wall logs in. The crossbeam is important structurally because it supports the ceiling joists. These joists have the dual purpose of holding up the loft floor and making an additional tie-in for the walls (7-16).

Each joist was placed at 19" center except for the one at the rear. There we allowed a 30" space between that joist and the rear wall for a trap-door. This trap-door is an inside entrance to the hayloft. It is large enough to easily allow hay bales to be thrown through it for the hungry occupants waiting below.

Building the Retaining Wall

At this point we finally located a portable cement mixer. A fellow up the road, who eventually became a good friend, needed to use my truck, so in trade he loaned me his mixer for a day. That entire day, and into the late evening, my wife and I mixed many loads of cement and gathered many large rocks for the stone retaining wall. By lamplight, before the night ended, a very solid and beautiful secondary foundation was completed. This retaining wall prevented logs from sagging and sealed in the sections between the footings (7-17).

7-16 Cutaway of interior stall layout.

7-17 Completed retaining wall.

detail of
lookout
construction

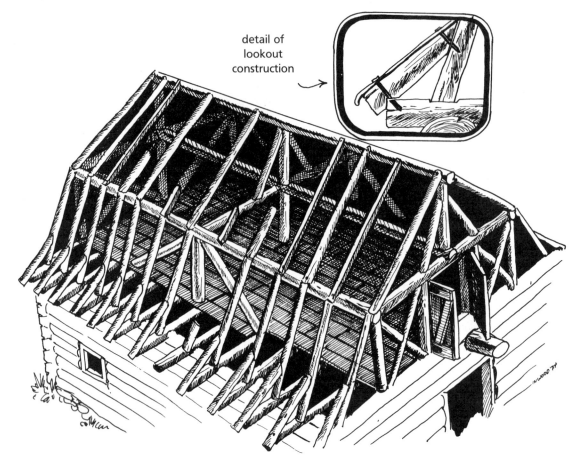

7-18 *Pole roof framing.*

Framing the Roof

Next came the roof. We chose to use a typical gambrel roof, because this style provides the most usable storage space for hay and grain. The first frame was constructed 14' wide, 7' high, and 22' long from front to rear. This space

7-19 *Lower roof rafters and support.*

proved to be more than adequate for at least four tons of hay and many sacks of grain. We used 5"- to 6"-diameter poles for the frame, and reinforced it with center posts, side braces, and double crisscrossed poles at front and rear. I found from seeing many old barns with collapsed roofs and still strong walls, that you cannot overbuild the roof section. It needs all the support you can give it (7-18 and 7-19).

After the frame was secured, a ridgepole complete with notches for a second set of braces was placed above it. The braces and a top ridgepole were then spiked in.

We cut 24 poles which were 4" to 5" in diameter to a length of 8' for the lower set of rafters. The bottoms of these poles were notched and spiked into either end of the 12 crossbeams. The tops were attached to the top of the frame. After these rafters were in place, 24 more were cut. Three vertical sections, each 4' in height, were set in the notches at the front, center, and rear of the ridgepole. After we braced them, we wondered how to hoist the final ridgepole. My wife was pregnant, and we thought it unwise for her to chance the chore. Before long, though, her cousin and his massive friend came for a visit. Without even being asked, the friend carried the ridgepole to the roof and hoisted it up. He then slammed the spikes in place and helped us connect the other rafters.

I examined the framework and decided that the pitch of the top rafters looked too awkward because of their height. We removed the few connecting rafters, chain-sawed 1' from each of the three extensions, and sledge-hammered the excess pieces from the ridgepole. We later replaced them and followed the friend's suggestion of enjoying a few beers for the remainder of the afternoon. A few inches were later cut off the upper rafters to compensate for the shortened extensions, and they were again spiked into place (7-20).

Thus far, building expenses had been nominal. We spent under 100 dollars, including the cost of feed for the neighbor's pig. But at that point, milled lumber was needed.

Shopping for usable but inexpensive lumber can be a big chore. We went from mill to mill to find enough economy-grade material to floor the hayloft and use as nailers over the rafters. Lumber prices are constantly on the increase. Even the lowest grade 1×s we found were over our budget. We finally located a private party who was selling his boards. He included enough 1 × 8 and 1 × 10 cedar, at a good price, to do our flooring and enough other 1× to use for nailers and gable ends.

The Loft Floor

The tops of the ceiling joists had to be hewn before the loft floor could be laid. After the hewing, cedar boards were quickly nailed

7-20 *Ridgepole, brace, and upper rafters.*

across the joists and a space was left for the trap-door. The nailers were then attached to the lower rafters. After they were attached, we found out it was not necessary to construct a solid covering. We then spaced the upper nailers 6" apart to save labor and materials.

The Roof Covering

We considered many different roof coverings. Although it was decided that a cedar-shake roof would have been the most aesthetic and least expensive, we chose to use an aluminum roof. The shake roof would have been impractical because of snow buildup on the upper sections and the difficulty of climbing on it in the middle of the winter to clean it off.

A freak mid-September snowfall reinforced our decision. The barn needed a roof immedi-

7-21 The completed barn in use.

doors and windows. I measured where I wanted to have the front door and nailed up 2 × 4s as vertical guides for my chain-saw cuts. Then I cut through the logs to make the opening. That opening was framed with a double thickness of 2 × 6 which acted as hinge supports and door frame.

Making the Barn Doors

It took me a while to figure out what design of door I wanted. I needed a solid door for weather, but I did not want a massive door that would be too heavy for the hinges. I looked through the scrap pile of log pieces that I had left over and found some short sections of 4"- to 5"-diameter cedar and tamarack. I set up a guide, using a 2 × 8 platform with two nails sticking out of it about 3" apart (7-22).

The log pieces were each cut to 38" because I wanted to have Dutch doors for ventilation and light. I hammered a log section down onto the nails of the platform and made it stand up-

ately. The aluminum roofing seemed expensive, but it was worth it. Though it lacks natural beauty, it is the most durable and maintenance-free of possible materials. It also sheds snow and is easy to install. Two of us put most of it up in a day. It was late November before it snowed again (7-21).

Now it was time for the interior work to begin and it was time for the barn to have

half-round slabs of alternating cedar (C) and larch (L) wood

7-22 Cutting half-rounds for making the doors.

7-23 *Dutch-style front door.*

7-24 *Applewood door latch.*

right as I ripped it down the middle with the chain saw. This process was quick and easy.

After the half-rounds were cut they were laid out in a line. I alternated the tamarack and cedar for appearance and structural reasons; nails hold better in tamarack. The cedar backing was then nailed on and one door was ready for hanging (7-22).

The second door was done in the same manner and applewood handles were added as

a finishing touch. We are very satisfied with the way the doors came out (7-23 and 7-24).

We framed the rear doorway and the hayloft doorway and decided to make those doors differently. They were made of three layers of 1 × 6 hemlock with one layer of black building paper sandwiched in as a protective vapor barrier (7-25). The first layer of hemlock was of short horizontal boards which were laid out on a flat surface. These

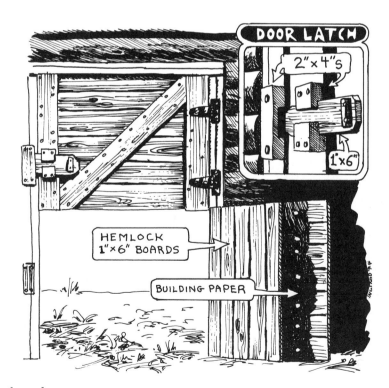

7-25 *Design of the front door.*

7-26 *Rear door of the barn.*

7-27 *Rear door latch.*

7-28 *Windows glazed with recycled automobile glass.*

boards were covered with the building paper. A layer of vertical 1 × 6s was placed over the paper and nailed to the bottom layer. A final diagonal piece and borders were added for support (7-26 and 7-27).

Glazing the Windows

The window spaces were next. I wanted to make sure the occupants of this building had plenty of light, but I knew I had to safeguard against window breakage, especially with our obstreperous animals. After searching through many of the junked cars in the area I found some nearly rectangular glass in a few early-model Dodges and DeSotos. This safety glass was easy to install and is very difficult to shatter (7-28).

We paneled the hayloft gables with the cedar 1× and wanted to start on the interior. We were none too soon: the weather was getting colder and the animals were still without shelter. But instead of starting on the barn's interior, we were forced to construct a root cellar because the frost was already destroying our pumpkins and winter squash. The root cellar did not take long to build.

Building the Stalls

On completion of that project a friend of ours saw the barn and, after praising it, asked us if we wanted to take care of his milking cow while he and his family went away for the winter. Fresh milk and butter, homemade cheeses, ice cream, and yogurt—what homesteader could refuse such treats? He and his family planned to leave in two weeks. Though our Black Angus was not giving milk yet, she would eventually, so one of the stalls was designed to house his cow now, ours later.

After figuring out the various stall sizes, we dug holes in the ground a foot deep to bury the bottoms of the upright supports. Their tops were notched and spiked into the ceiling joists above. The size of the stall depended on the animal it housed. The two identical stalls at the right front were built to house the heifers or meat steers of the year. Those stalls are about 5' wide and 8' long. Each contains a feeding manger and an area for a water bucket. They have crisscrossed log gates which hinge and latch to the upright supports (7-29).

Behind them we constructed an 8' × 10' goat stall to house two or three goats (7-30). It contains a feeding manger, and a bucket area in one section and milking platform with a feeder in the other. The horizontal dividers as well as the gate's crosspieces are spaced less than 4" apart and are over 6' high. They will be higher yet because goats are clever little devils, especially the ones we have. The goat pen also has a door which opens to a ramp that serves as a walkway to the corral outside. The ramp, when in raised position, is also the gate to the corral

7-29 Goat stalls.

(note, however, that over time these stalls proved inadequate; you should modify their design for ample space).

On the other side of the barn we built two more stalls. The 5' × 9' front one is for the horse. It does not have a gate. As long as there is an adequate place in the manger to tie a horse, there is little chance the animal will leave. Cows, on the other hand, should

7-30 Goat area.

be hooked to a ring and, if possible, have gates on their stalls. Our Black Angus heifer, Beulah, once unhooked herself and got out of her stall, ripped open milk cow's dairy mash, and ate what she wanted. When I came in, she ran to the Dutch door as the bottom partition closed. She took a leap, came down on that section and flattened it.

The 6' × 12' area to the rear is the milking stall. Behind the milk cow's stall is a space about 3½' × 8' for storing a couple of bales of hay and a few sacks of grain. A ladder goes up to a trapdoor which serves as the inside entrance to the hayloft. A simple rope-and-pulley system was designed to lift and lower the trap-door (7-31).

Chinking the Logs

Next came chinking. It has been proven that the easiest method of chinking a structure is to have a chinking party. Invite all your friends to help you and you will be done in one day. We set up a cement mixer and used a mixture of 1 part lime, 1 part masonry cement, and 5 parts clean, fine sand. When I rechink the walls after they have a chance to settle, I will just use masonry cement and

7-32 *Chinking the log wall.*

sand (1 part to 3 parts) because too much lime causes the mixture to be less durable and masonry cement already has lime in it.

We made palettes from plywood and supplied each helper with one, an inexpensive pair of rubber gloves (to prevent lime burns), and all the food he or she could eat and drink. First we hammered in many nails along the top of the logs, spacing them about 2" apart. They were bent in towards the building to hold in the chinking (7-32).

I controlled the mixer, but could never keep up with the enthusiastic workers. The work went well, but I noticed that as the huge punch bowl emptied, the chinking got sloppier. The following day, my wife, a friend, and I went over the walls with a wire brush and a whisk broom to level the sections which protruded. We then smoothed out the rough surfaces. Chinking should be concave and should blend into the wood. This prevents water from collecting on it and working its way between it and the log, causing premature decay of the walls.

After completing the chinking, the barn was almost finished. All that was left was repairing Beulah's damage.

7-31 *Trapdoor to the hayloft.*

Site Visit Update

Chris and Margee were determined to build their barn, to learn the techniques and skills needed so they could go on to build the ultimate country house. How they succeeded in creating their homestead is presented in Chapter 7 (see also the "Site Visit Update" on page 139). They lived in their special abode and worked in their barn for more than a decade.

Over a year after the barn was completed Chris said that he sometimes would think back to the pleasure they had building it. Each problem and each hassle that was overcome gave them a little more confidence and reinforced their belief in this type of life. In Chris's words, "We are very happy with it and we are proud of our achievement. And now, every time a neighbor or a friend wanders up to offer her or his help,

Cow-milking stall.

and every time someone makes a useful suggestion to us, my faith in my fellow human grows stronger and becomes more a part of me. More and more I've realized that the only way to be 'self-sufficient,' without the need of an established order, is to cooperate and communicate with those who also want to live in harmony with nature. It's surprising how many of us there are."

The completed barn in its first year of use.

CHAPTER 8

POST & BEAM, WITH STUCCO & "MASONRY" INFILL

INWOOD

Wood-Fired Sauna — Robert Inwood

Bob Inwood has gone through some quite significant changes since this project first began. He has switched from free-style cartoonist and illustrator to building designer and consultant. He has now built his own house.

This wood-fired sauna was his practice building, through which he experimented with many different techniques. The walls were framed with the post-and-beam method, and were filled with dimension lumber, cement, and stucco. The idea was to become familiar with these techniques through practice, and then he would be able to choose which mediums he preferred working with and incorporate them into his house. As Bob tells it, he carefully chose the site for the sauna in relation to the future house:

I built my sauna into a hillside, close to where I planned to build Lynelle's and my house. It was set into the hill to make full use of the insulative property of the earth. My design called for many pecautions to make sure that it would be well protected from runoff. I dug a hole, 9½' wide, 11' long, and 5' deep, for the structure—all by hand. This took several weeks to complete. But I did not want heavy machinery scarring my land. I needed a hole this size because I wanted to make sure the sauna would be large enough to accommodate six to eight people, but small enough to retain heat well. Many of the people we knew had saunas which were 8 × 8. That space seemed too small to us because it allows only a few bathers to be far enough away from the source of heat not to be scorched by it.

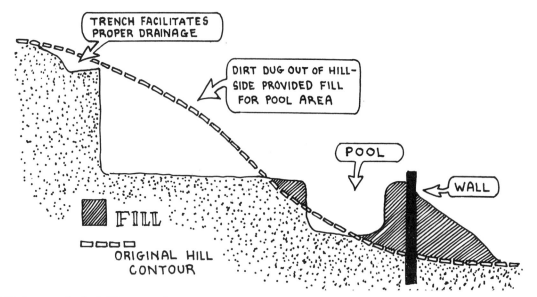

8-1 Working with the hill's natural contour.

Basic Construction

We used the dirt we shoveled out of the hole to create the walls of the pool, located on the downhill side of the sauna. Four upright posts with crossing boards prevented the earth from sliding any farther down the hillside. The ends of the posts were buried into the ground and the boards nailed across them to hold the dirt. On the uphill side the ground was leveled so the runoff would have a tendency to flow down the sides of the hill instead of draining in back of the sauna (8-1).

The walls were framed with the post-and-beam method and were filled with dimension lumber, cement, and a stucco mixture. To start them, I dug four corner holes in the 9½' × 11' excavation. Each was 3' deep and wide enough to accommodate an end of a creosoted railroad tie. These 8'-long railroad ties were discards that I bought very cheaply. They are excellent to use when in contact with the earth, because they were thoroughly soaked in creosote and will not rot out for at least as long as we'll be around to use the sauna.

After burying the bottom ends of the upright ties 3' into the ground so their top ends would be flush with the uphill side of the hole, I ran 2 × 4s above each of them and made sure, with a carpenter's level, they were all the same height. I then packed sand and gravel around them and plumbed them on two sides with the level (8-2).

8-2 Excavation for hillside sauna.

Why a Sauna?

We needed a place where we could cleanse and rejuvenate ourselves as we planned and developed our new homestead. The first and most important building which we constructed was the sauna. A sauna cleanses your skin of its surface dirt as well as ridding your body of its inner impurities. It also helps you unwind after a hard day of working and provides you with a warm, peaceful chamber in which to meditate.

A sauna cleanses you from the inside out by flushing your blood with its heat. This stimulates your sweat glands, and your sweat washes through your pores as it flows outward to cool your skin. Then, after your body is saturated with sweat and you cannot stand any more heat, you scrub down with soap and plunge into a pool of cold water or stand under a cold shower and rinse off. The cooling effect of the water momentarily stimulates you and closes your pores. Afterward, when you reenter the sauna or go to another place to relax, you will find that the previous combination of stifling heat and cold shock induces restfulness and loosens muscular and nervous tension.

Saunas have other healthful advantages which are beneficial to country living. They help heal surface wounds by bringing blood to afflicted areas. They act as vaporizers to clear out stuffy sinuses for sufferers of head colds—however, if you have a cold, icy plunges or showers are not recommended after this treatment. A nice hot sauna can relieve party hangovers because they work out the alcoholic toxins from you body by stimulating circulation. Saunas are also perfect for massages and are great places to get to know people.

WIRE SUPPORTS PREVENT BOWING

STAKES HOLD BOTTOM FORM BOARD STRAIGHT

8-3 Foundation forms.

The front uprights were temporarily held together with 2 × 4s so they would stay in place while I dug an 18'-deep trench between them. This trench was for a short retaining wall. The wall would extend from the bottom of the trench to 12" aboveground. I drove spikes into the sides of the uprights, and then nailed 1× forms between the ties. They were braced every 3' with narrow slats. I drilled holes into these slats and ran lengths of baling wire between them on either side. The wire ends were then wrapped around nails to hold them in place. These braces effectively prevented the forms from bulging as we poured in the cement. The mixture we used was 5 parts sand, 1 part Portland cement, and as many flat rocks as we could put into the mortar without weakening it (8-3).

Foundation Walls

The two side foundation walls were dealt with next. We built these retaining walls to a height of 2½' using square rocks which we trucked in from wherever they were available. The walls were mortared in without forms. Whenever you build such a wall it is important that you use flat, wide rocks which stack up well. We dug 10" channels between the side uprights, and nailed spikes along them to tie the walls together. A 4" layer of mortar, 3 parts sand, and 1 part masonry cement was poured into the channels dor the bottom rock to set into. The remaining wall rocks were mortared in above them until the walls were built to height, then they were checked for levelness with crossing 2 × 4s (8-4).

Framing the Roof

Above the upright posts, I put in a double-layer top plate of interlocking horizontal logs (8-5). These logs were 10" cedars that were peeled and ready. They braced the long, overhanging roof and raised the walls another 18". The first layer of side logs was notched over the uprights. The crossing logs were then round-notched onto the side logs (8-5, inset). To make mine notched, I eyeballed the contour of the lower logs, figured the approximate depth and width of the notch, and marked that on the log to be notched. Then, with a Swedish saw, I cut deep scores into the notch area to the drawn outline and knocked

8-4 *Front and side foundation walls in place with upright posts.*

the pieces out with a chisel. The upper layer was notched over the first in the same manner. The top side logs are 17' long, extending 2' beyond the rear wall and 4' beyond the front wall to support the roof's overhangs.

At this point, because the weather was getting cold and rainy, we decided to put on the sheltering roof instead of filling in the walls. I figured out a comfortable pitch for the roof and spiked in two 18" upright ridgepole supports

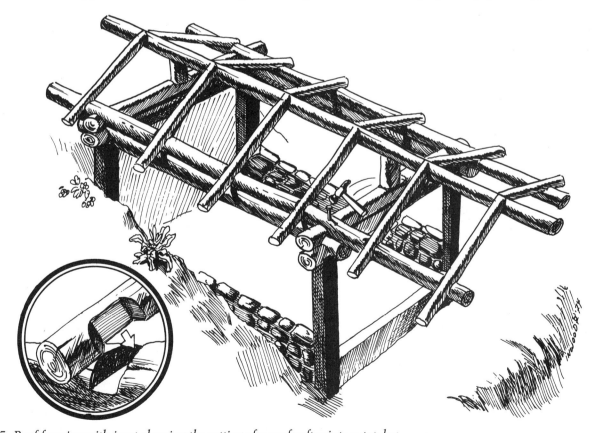

8-5 *Roof framing with inset showing the setting of a roof rafter into a top log.*

above the front and rear top wall plates. These uprights allowed the roof a slight pitch of less than 15 degrees. I didn't want the pitch any steeper because the heat would be more apt to escape through the higher roof. I also planned to finish the roof with sod. If it were any steeper than 15 degrees, the loose sod would have more of a tendency to erode off it.

A 17'-long ridgepole was notched over the short uprights, and the rafters were seated deep into the top side plates and the ridgepole. These six rafter sets were each spaced 36" on center. I lap-notched them deeplyto make them level with the tops of the side logs and the ridgepole. This eliminated having to use spacers between each rafter to fill in the usual gap between the subroof and top wall plates.

The lap joints were easy to make. I simply sawed and chiseled out the square laps at 36" intervals on the side plates and ridgepole. I then figured the angle for the rafter top by resting the rafter bottom above the side plate so the top met with the ridgepole. I eyeballed the angle and sawed into the rafter top (8-6). After spiking into the side of the ridgepole, I eyeballed the angles and depths of the bottom cuts in the same manner. If I were to seat the rafters again, I would hew the sides of the ridgepole just slightly instead of notching them. The deep notches weakened their structural soundness.

Adding the Subroofing

Because of the heavy sod roof that would be above it, I made sure to construct a strong, vapor-proof subroof. The first layer was of 2 × 8 cedar boards which were nailed lengthwise across the rafters. Over those boards was a layer of heavy building paper and another layer of 2 × 8s which crossed the first. I stuffed thin strips of fiberglass insulation between both sides of the peak and over the side-wall plates to seal off these areas. Then a ridgecap of aluminum flashing was put over the boards to prevent the rain from entering through the peak gap (8-7).

To seal this subroof, I spread melted tar over the top boards using an old broom. The tar came in 100-pound lugs which I melted down in an old bucket. I needed 200 pounds to initially cover my roof. Another thin coating will go on it when I spread the coarse gravel. This gravel will embed into the soft tar to keep the sod on the roof. Also to hold the sod, 4" poles were nailed around the outside edge of the roof eaves. They cross at and extend over the peak for an ornamental effect.

Support for the Front Overhang

Even then, without the final sod covering, the sauna roof did not leak at all. When the weather is hot, the uncovered tar has a tendency to

8-6 Bob Inwood eyeballing the rafter angle.

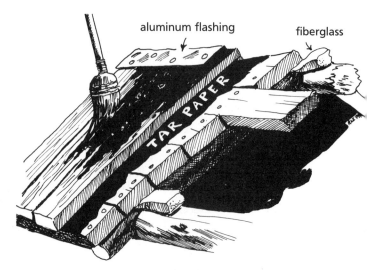
8-7 The built-up roof.

get soft and sticky, but it doesn't drip or run. The only problem which did occur with the roof was that the 4' front overhang, which shields the dressing area, sagged under the heavy winter snow load. I corrected that structural problem by notching in two diagonal braces to support the overhang (8-8). These braces span from the side-plate extensions to the center of the corner upright posts. They have successfully corrected the sag and add a nice aesthetic appeal to the front section.

I planned to put 2" to 3" of good soil on the roof for the sod covering. It will be seeded with white clover so the roots will help hold the sod together. The flowering clover will make the roof flow into the landscape of the hillside.

Finishing the Walls

When the roof was on and the sauna was protected, we returned to the walls, handling each in a different manner. Above the short rock walls on either side, we laid an 8" strip of fiberglass. A horizontal log was placed over each strip and was toenailed to the center of the top-plate logs above. Two 8 × 8 upright posts were then spiked into these notches. This created four smaller rectangular spaces—two at each side wall (8-9). I wanted these smaller spaces because the wood being used to fill the walls was short scrap stuff that was lying around. None of it would go the entire distance between the corner posts.

The outside edge of each of these rectangular area was framed with 2 × 2 nailing strips and three of the four sections were filled in with horizontal 4× planks. The fourth rectangular section was divided again with two 4 × 4 uprights. These upright posts support the small hewn poles which framed an 8" × 10" window (8-9).

8-8 *Bob and Lynelle's son in front of the sauna, showing the front entry and the knee braces added to support the roof overhang.*

Adding Stucco

To brighten the outer rectangular sections of the side walls and give them a rammed-earth effect, the spaces created by the 2 × 2 nailing strips were filled with a stucco-like mixture. To prepare the sections, I stapled a double thickness of chicken wire into each of the areas framed by the 2 × 2 nailers. The thickness closest to the inner wall was ¼" away from the

8-9 *Filling in the walls.*

8-10 *Adding stucco.*

paneling; the outer one was about 1" away from it. The strips were also lined with several bent rusty nails to hold the stucco mortar in place (8-10). The mixture I used was the basic 3-part sand, 1-part masonry cement mixture. The sand was a fine, river-bottom type. It was mixed dry so there would be less chance of shrinkage. I added water until the mortar was a paste-like and malleable consistency. I worked it into the chicken wire until the mortar covered it and came out to the edge of the uprights. Using this method I was able to build up the thickness over only one day. Applying the mixture in several coats, as is usually done with stucco, takes much longer.

Burlap was hung over the stuccoed wall and the drying mortar was sprayed with water for several days to cure it and prevent it from setting up too early. It set up well, without obvious shrinking or cracking, and the wall spaces were sealed in efficiently (8-10).

The Front Wall Area

To fill in the front section, I first laid burlap on top of the short retaining wall. The burlap acts as a gasket to prevent air from whizzing between the retaining wall and the 6 × 8 horizontal beam that was toenailed in over it. This beam provided a bottom wood surface for the

8 × 8s which were to frame the doorway. The uprights broke the front wall area into three rectangles, the middle one being the entrance to the sauna. The other two areas were framed with 2 × 4s that were nailed to the centers of the surrounding burlap-lined beams. Rough-cut 1× sheathing was then nailed to the outsides of the 2 × 4s, closing off these two rectangular sections.

A layer of building paper was tacked onto the inside of the 2 × 4s and an inner sheathing of 2 × 6s was nailed over it. I left a small area open near the top of the inside wall, to allow sawdust insulation to be shoved in between the walls. This sawdust was packed down as tight as possible so that it wouldn't have the tendency to settle. After the sawdust was packed in, the top sheathing boards were nailed in place (8-11).

The center 32" × 48" entranceway was then framed in and a door of 2 × 6 tongue-and-groove cedar was hinged in place. These cedar boards were held together with 2 × 4s which were doweled into them at top and bottom.

The Back Wall & Drainage

The back wall had to be structurally sound and able to repel any drainage that would come in from the hillside behind it. To create an ade-

2"×4" FRAMES INTERIOR

2"×6" BOARDS

BUILDING PAPER

DRY SAWDUST

1"×8" BOARDS

8-11 Insulating and sheathing the front wall.

quate vapor barrier, I nailed a big sheet of 6-mil plastic between the corner uprights. This vapor shield covered the entire wall section and acted as an outside form to protect the cement wall from the earthen hillside in back of it. The cement and rock portion of the wall was built high enough to shield the blazing heat stove which would be directly in front of it. An 8 × 8 beam was set above the retaining wall, and the remaining upper section was framed and filled with dimension lumber.

The Gables

The front and rear gable section that were created by the roof's pitch were the last areas to be filled in. It took me a while to figure out how I was going to deal with them. I had many ideas but few materials. My decision came at a friend's summer solstice party. There before me, in front of the musicians' platform, collected in boxes, was the material I needed. I took several cases of the empty beer bottles home for the sauna gables. The gabled areas were prepared with chicken-wire strips which I stapled from the top-plate log to the underside of the subroof boards in a zigzag pattern. Bent nails were also then added to grip the mortar (8-12).

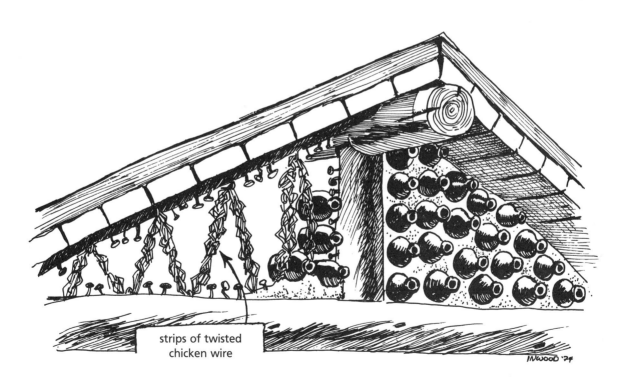

strips of twisted chicken wire

8-12 View of the inside wall as we are building the "masonry" infill using empty bottles.

The chicken wire not only held the concrete, but it also stabilized the large number of bottles as they were being cemented in. The job was simple and went very well. The setting mortar was sprayed with water for about a week to prevent it from drying too fast or cracking. The result was, and still is, a beautiful amber light shining in through the many tightly cemented bottle bottoms.

Finishing the Interior

The shale pieces that made up the floor were 1' to 2' slabs, ½" to 1½" thick, which were outcropping from a hillside in an area where this kind of rock occurs. Before we laid the shale mosaic pattern, we prepared the floor area with a 3" thickness of sand into which the slabs would set. The spaces between them were then mortared so sand wouldn't get on our feet.

How Do You Heat It?

This sauna is heated by a super-duper, homemade, 15-gallon-barrel wood heater, designed and built especially for the structure by a close friend. It sits on top of a cradle of 4" poles which is surrounded and covered with rocks to help it reflect heat out into the sauna.

The stove's chimney goes straight up through the roof, rather than making a bend into the wall. I think this is a safer method because there is no chance of creosote collecting in the bent areas and creating chimney fire. When creosote builds up in a straight pipe, this pipe can be cleaned out from above without having to be taken apart. The sooty deposits will fall back into the stove and burn again. To keep creosote buildup down, burn dry wood and let a lot of air circulate through the firebox.

Where the chimney goes through the ceiling, it is reinforced with a 36" length of Yukon-type, double-walled, galvanized pipe. This pipe has a 4" dead-air space between the walls for protection. We filled that dead-air space with clay to give it more of an insulatory value and packed additional clay around the stack where it comes out of the roof, to seek that opening.

Shale floor inside the sauna.

We throw water on the rocks to create steam for a hotter, wet-vapor bath. I personally like to start off dry and, after a while, throw a lot of water on the stove to fill the room with steam. This raises the temperature level and induces me to sweat until all my pores are saturated. Soon my body can't stand any more of the stifling heat. Then I run outside, jump in, staying in the cold water until I'm ready to repeat the process. I wind up feeling totally clean and relaxed.

The Problem of Heat Loss

One problem I've noticed about other saunas that annoyed me was that when people ran in and out, to plunge and return, they let so much heat out that it would lower the temperature of the room uncomfortably, and even cause drafts. I prevented this problem in my sauna by building a framed-in entry chamber to absorb the temperature change. This area is only 2' long and the width of the doorway, but it works well. To frame this area I set up two upright poles for the inside corners. I figured that as long as interior uprights were being set up, they might as well have some structural significance. I ran a horizontal rafter brace between two rafters on either side of the area and notched the uprights under them to hold them in place. This produced an extra support for a large section of the heavy sod roof (8-13). Horizontal poles were then nailed across the uprights, just above the top of the doorway. These poles created a ledge above the entrance chamber. A horizontal pole, spanning the side walls, was put in to continue the ledge to these walls. Slats 1¾" thick were notched into this horizontal pole on either side of the chamber ceiling. This raised platform is for people who like super-hot saunas (8-14).

The outer chamber itself was then walled and roofed with 1× boards which spanned from the inside posts to the narrow nailing strips that framed the doorway. A floor was put in this area so there would be two gradual 6" steps into the sauna instead of one giant step.

Building the Benches

Two vertical bench ledges were nailed to the back wall just above its 2½' high cement section. An end of each of the inside horizontal bench supports was nailed above them. These bench supports span from the rear wall to the front wall and were notched into the entrance chamber uprights so they wouldn't have to span that entire distance unbraced. A 2 × 4

8-13 Door open, showing the benches inside the sauna.

8-14 Details of the upper and lower benches.

was then run along each side wall just above the cement retaining walls. They were approximately level with the inside bench poles and provideda shelf for the outside end of the 1¾" bench slats. The inside ends were notched into the horizontal support and their tops were trimmed with a saw so there were no rough edges sticking out (8-15).

These slats were spaced 1" apart to allow heat to come up from underneath and circulate around the whole body of the bather. These spaces also provide an area where the excess moisture can drip off a person's sweat-soaked body so he or she doesn't have to sit or lie in the wetness. I might change the slat design of the upper platform because bathers on the lower benches sometimes complain about such drippings. Diagonal boards can be fitted between the slats so the bathers can lean against them at a comfortable angle.

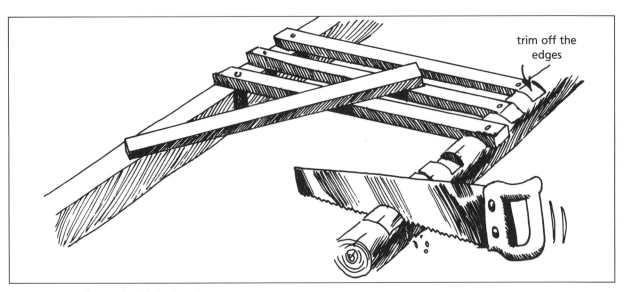

trim off the edges

8-15 Using slats to build the benches.

Site Visit Update

Author/illustrator Robert Inwood still uses his sauna and still lives in the homestead that he designed and constructed after finishing the sauna. "We enjoy our sauna and have had many compliments on its design."

It is comfortable, spacious, and heat seems to distribute very well throughout it. Even with six or eight bathers, it is not too crowded and the sauna room is easy to keep hot.

When the sauna was first completed Bob and his wife, Lynelle, used to bathe in it as many as three or more times a week. They used a temporary cooling device until the plunge was completed. It was a showerhead connected to an upright pole. It was fed by a plastic water pipe that ran down from a nearby mountain creek.

After taking such frequent saunas, they soon noticed they were gettting dehydrated and seemed always to be thirsty. By taking so many saunas in such a short time, the heat was pulling out too much moisture

Wide-angle view of the sauna interior.

from their bodies. They eventually found that a sauna once a week was a good balance and was best for their health.

Bob is a dedicated believer in the benefits of taking a sauna. "We are very pleased with the sauna and have been regularly enjoying its health-giving benefits. We consider it a necessary and important structure which should be an integral part of every homestead."

Looking at the interior view of the bottle "masonry" infill and showing the rafter supports.

POST & BEAM, WITH LOG
& CORDWOOD INFILL

INWOOD

Gathering Together

When the urge comes to establish your homestead, the enthusiasm you bring to it may have to take you through a few steps to get there. And the process may be one of self-realization. That is what happened to Glenn and Kathrina. They had been living in a small flat in a large West Coast city. A day came when Kathrina announced that she was pregnant. Glenn responded with the recognition that what he wanted was the security of a house—a home—for his new family. As he tells it, they both wanted to settle somewhere and have a home they could call their own. Their first impulse was to buy a house:

We decided to buy an old house just outside the city limits and fix it up as an investment. As we started fixing up the house, we began realizing the sad shape it was in. The plumbing was rusted out and leaking, the wiring was dangerous, the whole thing needed a lot more renovation than we were prepared for. What really got us, though, was the compound interest on our loan to buy the place. We'd need more than thirty years to pay off the mortgage. We still thought it a good investment and we knew we wouldn't have any trouble getting a good price for it when we decided to sell. But even from the very beginning, for some reason, this house never really seemed like home.

The property was surrounded by a beautiful wooded area that provided us with nearby peace and serenity—two luxuries rarely found so close to a city. As we considered these assets, so did someone else. Soon a logging company came in and logged out our little neighboring forest. What used to be a wooded playground was transformed into a graveyard of slash and stumps. We luckily unloaded the property for a little above what we paid for it and decided to look elsewhere for a home.

A Second Try

Some friends of ours were thinking about settling on some undeveloped rural land. They had heard about a place near a large lake, surrounded by picturesque mountains. Since we were into taking a vacation in that direction, we offered to go see the place for them. We went to the area but it was still early spring, and because of the muddy runoffs we could not get up the road which led to that parcel of land. However, the valley we were in was so incredibly beautiful that we decided to inquire around to find out what else was available.

We soon found just the place we wanted. It was bordered on one side by a large river and on another side by a rapidly flowing creek. It was deep within a thick forest of second growth. This land and the immediate area that surrounded it had been logged out many years ago and had been left forgotten. We camped near the river and stayed until the mosquitoes finally drove us out. But they didn't stop us from returning.

We came back with our friends and found that they shared our enthusiasm. Within a few weeks we made a deal for the land and bought it. Throughout the next few months I spent as much time as I could in the library learning about architectural design. I had visions of the home I wanted to build. It was an arch-shaped house with a courtyard in front. I was preoccupied with this vision because I had never really had a home before, not even as a child.

Finding a Site for a House

On returning to our land when we felt prepared enough to do so, we set up a tent and waited for the rains to stop. It rained for several weeks. We put up a quick "A"-frame to shelter us from the miserable weather. As we finished the "A"-frame the sun came out and shone for seven weeks straight. Kathrina and I spent many days walking around our section of the property, trying to decide where we were going to build our home. We wanted to be near the river and we wanted to have a southwest exposure so we would get as much sunlight as possible.

Noting Where the Sun Rises

Kathrina put markers up in a line, designating where the sun rose over the mountains on a certain date (May 1). She put another set showing where the sun set on that date. From these markers we calculated how much sunlight we would have at a given spot in the different seasons of the year. In May, the sun's arc was still pretty low, so if a site received plenty of sunlight at that time of year, it would receive even more when the sun's arc was at its peak in the summer. After several trials, we finally located the ideal building site.

Planning Ahead

While I was working on the plans for the house, I also figured out the quantities of lumber we would need. I checked the local mills and priced the boards. Prices always seem to be on the rise and materials are not always available. I knew that in order to get the best deal, I had to act immediately.

At that time I did not know anyone in the valley except for our partners in the land. I went out looking for a Caterpillar™ to make a road into our property. As I was searching, I met many fine people, especially a man with a "Cat." I asked him to do the work for me and I would pay him what he asked, but he said he had hurt his back and could not do it. I knew how to operate his machine, so asked if I could borrow it. It never hurts to ask; and a person doesn't get what he needs unless he makes his needs known. To my surprise, he let me use his machine. I made the road and

Problems Working Alone

Since I was working alone most of the time, I had an incredible amount of difficulty moving the first few beams. Such physical punishment just didn't seem necessary. I thought about various simple machines that could help me in my work.

Finding Solutions

I remembered a device I had come upon while traveling. I had seen it being used beside a mountain stream that was being mined by hand, gold-rush style. Pyramids of rocks were piled on the banks; some of those rocks were huge boulders. They had been taken out of the stream bed and piled on the banks in order to get to the stream's gravel bed. I asked an old prospector how they lifted those stones up and stacked them in such high piles. He told me about the gin-pole device they used. It consists of a stationary support pole and a swinging pole that is notched into its butt. The swinging "Gin Pole's" tip is suspended out in a 45-degree angle by a guy wire which is secured near the top of the stationary pole (refer to Chapter 4, page 85, the "Gin Pole"). A come-along, or a block-and-tackle, is attached to the tip of the pole to lift the huge rocks. The swinging pole is then guided to the bank by ropes. For the support pole, a substantial tree is used.

Making Your Own Lifting Device

If a strong tree is not around, you can use a scissor (a two-member tripod). It is made out of two logs latched together at the top. Hold the scissor almost upright, leaning it a bit towards the stream, by a guy wire which is attached to a solid stump or tree in the background. Then suspend a block-and-tackle down from the peak of the scissor into the water. Guide the block-and-tackle line to the bank by hand and lift the boulder, swing it around, and lower it onto the pile. This second method is less efficient than the first, but it prevents many an aching back.

For my stationary pole, I used a 50' cottonwood which was beside the building site. The tree was going to be felled anyway, so I cut a deep wedge-shaped notch into its butt for the seat of the swinging pole. The butt of the 35' tamarack swinging pole was trimmed and put into the notch. It was suspended at a 45-degree angle towards the house site with a guy wire secured to the stationary pole about 10' above the notch. This tree for the gin pole was later used for the roof's ridgepole.

How It Works

A chain block was hung from the swinging pole's tip, and a pair of log tongs was attached to the end of the tackle to grip the log or beam. I soon found the tongs to be a dangerous and inefficient method of gripping the logs because they only secured them at one center-balance point. I ended up using a chain that circled the log at two points and was lifted in the middle by the traveling block's hook.

What It Could Do

This pole could swing in a 150-degree radius and could reach any part of the building site. When this device was in action I could pick up the biggest log or beam, crank it up, swing it into position with guide ropes, and lower it down to where I wanted it. This was a slow process because of the time it took to raise and lower the beams with the chain block, but there was nothing difficult about it and I didn't break my back with the lifting that had to be done.

returned the "Cat" to him. I told him that I used it for 15 hours. He saw the road and said that it couldn't have taken that long. He asked me for 20 dollars for the use of the "Cat." I couldn't believe his generosity. Here was a man who was unspoiled by greed, a man who genuinely liked people and wasn't out to get all he could from them.

As I searched for a truck to haul the lumber, I met a family of people who were just as helpful as that man. Instead of making an impersonal bargain of renting a truck for cash, Kathrina and I traded our labor for the use of the vehicle. We worked in their nursery, and we learned much useful information from these experienced homesteaders who unselfishly traded their knowledge and good "vibes" for our respect and friendship. That was one of the best deals I've ever made. We are still reaping the benefits.

Whenever I had time to spare, I went around and searched out more of the local inhabitants. Never have I met so many compassionate people who were willing to share themselves so freely. Most of the folks here have two things in common: the willingness to communicate their needs and knowledge and the awareness that such sharing is a vital element of their lives.

Finding Unexpected Opportunities

In these local travels I also met a fellow who was building his house out of scrap lumber. I asked him where he was getting the material. He showed me an old lumber mill that was being torn down. The owners were going to set fire to it soon, but they allowed anyone who wanted to salvage what he or she needed. By the time I got there, all the usable 2" material had been stripped off. I walked around, feeling disappointed—I had missed the boat. Then I realized that there beside me was a huge 23'-long, 8 × 12 truss beam. Near it were several other large timber pieces that had been left to be burned. There were 8 × 8s, 10 × 12s, 4 × 4s, and 6 × 6s. Altogether, we got six pickup-truck loads from there.

9-1 Unloading the found railroad trestle timbers.

Shortly after that, we found an old planer mill that had caved in and been discarded. The owners let us dismantle it and take what we needed. Then, a few days later, the railroad was rebuilding an old trestle and was going to burn the old timbers. We loaded the timbers up and took them home (9-1).

A Plan to Match Our Resources

Before long, we had a mountain of such timbers. We measured everything and made a list of what we had. I then tried to figure out how we could best utilize the material in our carefully thought-out plan. The timbers could not be efficiently figured into the plan. Many of the pieces were too short, and the nice, long ones would have to be cut. So the original plan was thrown out and a new one was drawn up on the basis of the lengths we had. The dimensions of the house were changed in order to prevent wasting any of the long beams. The west wall, originally 20' long, was changed to 23', the length of the longest timber I found. The north wall stayed 20', the east wall became 16', and the south wall became 21'. So the house took on a trapezoidal shape (9-2).

Because of the massiveness and structural soundness of the timbers, I discarded the frame construction techniques that I studied for so long and decided to use the post-and-beam method. The post-and-beam method would give the walls more structural strength and would prevent having to clutter the house with all the interior upright supports our original plan called for.

Putting in the Foundation

It was already late in June before we started our foundation. Since the property is all level river-front land, we didn't have to deal with a slope. We were free to pick the best site on the basis of sun exposure and view of the river. Instead of having a foundation wall around the perimeter of the building, I chose to use a network of sill logs which would be supported on nine cement piers. The cedar logs were mill runaways given to me by a neighbor who had snagged them out of the river as they flowed downstream from the local mill.

I laid out the position of the foundation with traditional batterboards and checked the trueness of the two square corners. If those corners were true, the others would be also. At this point I checked the levelness of the ground with a surveyor's level that I borrowed. Then I dug the holes for the foundation piers. A hole 2' wide and 2' deep was dug at each corner, in the center of each side, and in the center of the building. These holes were well below the 18" frost line.

9-2 Layout for the foundation piers.

POST & BEAM, WITH LOG & CORDWOOD INFILL   177

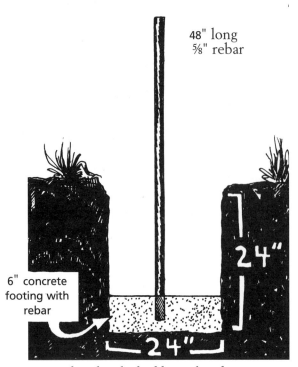

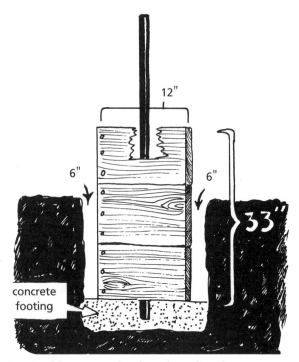

9-3 *Footing the rebar for building a foundation pier.*

9-4 *Building a wooden form for a foundation pier.*

The bottom slab of each pier is 24" square and 6" high. These slabs were poured first, without forms. A 48"-long rebar rod was then stuck into the slabs (9-3). When the slabs were nearly dry, 1× cedar boxes that were 12" square and 33" in length were centered over the slabs. Concrete was then shoveled into the boxes until each was filled. When the concrete set, the boxes were removed. Each pier stuck up 15" above the ground, to lift the sill logs well above the carpenter ants. It is said that these little devils won't climb over 18" of concrete to make their nests. The rebar pin extended far enough above the pier to go through the cedar sill beams and about 4" into the upright posts which rested on them (9-4).

Placing the Sills

The sill logs ranged between 9" and 14" in diameter. They were each notched so there was 8" of beam above the piers to make them level. I placed the larger-diameter butt ends directly on the piers and then notched them on both top and bottom to prevent too much from being taken out for one notch. You can

cut up to a quarter of a given log's thickness for each notch without weakening that beam and losing the structural value of the material. If more than a quarter of its diameter is cut out there is a tendency for the log to split lengthwise under pressure (9-5). I tenon-notched the thickest beams over the piers and lapped the perpendicular sills so they would fit over them. A hole was then drilled in each end to accommodate the rebar pins which would secure them together (9-6).

Setting the Floor Joists

After the sill logs were in place, the 2 × 8 floor joists were put in across them, running east and west. Though they were about 20' in length, they never spanned more than 8' between supporting points. A good rule to follow when putting in floor joists is to make sure the joists are at least 1" thick per foot of span. If the joists span 8', you need to use 2 × 8s. Actually this makes them more substantial than houses in the city, but most city houses nowadays are not worth the paper that the mortgage is written on.

9-5 *A ceiling beam showing severe checking.*

9-6 *Securing the lapped sill beams.*

To allow for a split-level main floor which would be a subtle divider between the living area and the dining and kitchen areas, I hewed the inside of the west wall sill and the side of the center sill that faced it (9-7). These surfaces were made flat to accommodate the double

2 × 4 lips which were spiked to the bottom of these sides. The lower joists of the dining and kitchen areas were notched over these lips to split the level of the floor. We then nailed in joists for the upper level over the crossing sills, making that floor 8" higher than the lower one.

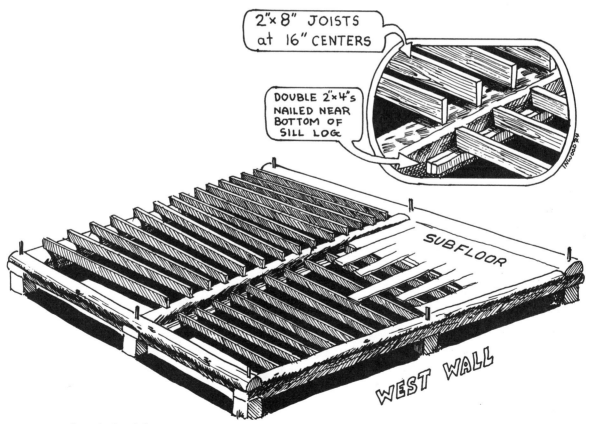

9-7 *Laying out the split-level floor joists.*

The 1 × 12 cedar subfloor was then put down so we would have a nice surface to work on. We nailed on all the flooring with Ardox, spiral-type nails. This type of nail prevents floor squeaking because it holds better and does not have a tendency to pull away from the joists as the floor is walked on.

Erecting the Posts

The eight upright support-posts were put in above the sills, over the outlining piers (9-8). A hole was first drilled in each of their bottom ends for the 4"-long rebar which stuck out above the sills. The four corner posts were 10 × 10s that were salvaged from the planer mill and the four inside posts were 8 × 8s that were runners for the carriage in the old sawmill. They were sawed on two sides. The sawed sides were used as flat surfaces for the wall logs or lumber frames to rest against. The round sides could be seen from the inside and outside of the building. These fir posts carry all the structural weight. The wall logs, or studs, do not carry any of it. Each of these posts could support as much as 100 pounds per square inch, so an 8 × 8 has the structural strength to support 6400 pounds above it.

The posts were checked for straightness with a level and were braced with diagonal 2 × 4s. The perimeter beams were then raised with the gin pole and lowered into position above the posts. The gin pole worked well, but it was a slow operation. When the huge, 1500-pound beams with poles and ropes were rigged, we stood clear and were careful not to get underneath them. We guided the suspended beams with the poles and ropes and stood clear until they were in position (9-8).

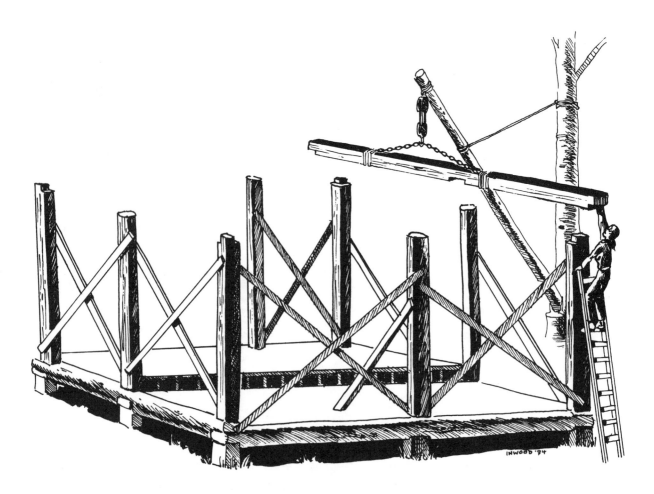

9-8 Lowering beams onto the braced posts using the "Gin Pole." (Refer to page 85.)

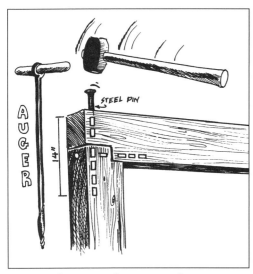

9-9 *Steel pins are driven into the corners.*

9-10 *Starting the hewing process.*

9-11 *Making a series of scoring cuts to the chalk line.*

9-12 *Using a shipbuilder's adz to form the center post.*

Puting the Beams in Place

We notched the ends of the beams and tops of the posts and augered a deep hole into each of the ends. Steel pins were then driven into each of these joining corners to secure them (9-9). The steel pins are lengths of ½" and ⅝" bar stock that I found in a local junkyard. Most of this material I made from tie bolts which I got out of an old boiler and which I hack-sawed to length. These super-hard steel rods were only 5 cents per pound and were a lot stronger, and much cheaper, than the softer rebar stock.

Next came the cedar-log center post to brace the ceiling beams. This was my first attempt at hewing a log on four sides. Eventually I wanted to carve the pole and make it an ornamental finishing touch to the house. To start the hewing process, I centered a 10" square on one end of the log and an 8" square on the opposite end, letting all the crossing lines go out to the edge of the ends (9-10). A chalk line was snapped down the length of the log from one line to its corresponding line on the opposite end. With a chain saw, I then made a series of scoring cuts into the side of the log to the depth of the lines (9-11).

After one side was scored, the log was dogged in place and the sections between the cuts were knocked out. This technique was repeated on each side, and the whole log was trimmed with a shipbuilder's adz (9-12).

Instead of raising the log so the 10"-square end was down, I put that larger end up to give the center post a tapering effect, making the building seem lighter. This effect would be even more pronounced if the center post were longer (9-13).

The four center 8 × 8 ceiling-beams were put in and joined over the center post. Each beam spanned only from the center of the wall to the top of the center post. I found out later that this was a structural error. Because the separate pieces joined in the

Notes on the Column

The unusual inverted taper is thought to originate with ancient Minoan tree cults. These cults believed that if a log was placed root end down, the tree could return to life, destroying the building it supported. Therefore the pillars were placed with the smaller top end down. The larger root end of the log eventually became the elaborate capital.

9-13 *Center post.*

greatest amount of sheer strength when tying a wall together, the sheathing boards should be put on diagonally. The diagonals create several triangles; this is the strongest form of sheer bond. If the ceiling beams were two continuous pieces notched over the center post, instead of four separate sections, their sheer strength would be considerably greater because they would, in fact, tie the walls together. After putting in the center beams, other ceiling beams were put in as braces for the 2 × 4 joists which span the three loft sections of the roof area.

The 2 × 4 loft-floor joists were nailed in at 16" centers above the ceiling beams and a floor of 1 × 6 tongue-and-groove was fitted together over the joists (9-14, inset). I used tongue-and-groove stock because a subfloor is not necessary with this interlocking material. No dust comes through between the boards, falling instead to the lower sections of the house. And with the joists at 16" centers, this 1× flooring is sturdy enough not to bounce or sag with weight (9-14).

center instead of making a continuous tie across the house, the design lacked sheer strength. Sheer strength is the tying together of the separate parts of a whole section to reinforce it. For example, in order to gain the

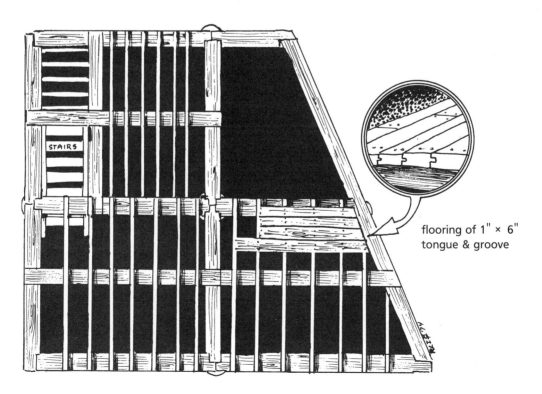

flooring of 1" × 6"
tongue & groove

9-14 *The floor plan for the loft.*

9-15 *A look at the outside of the loft area. On the right is a view of the northeast corner.*

Creating a Loft Space

We did not want a full second story, but we did want a loft space built into the sloping roof. The only way to have a full, open space between the ceiling and roof, without cluttering that space with a network of roof trusses, was to support the rafters at the peak with a ridgepole.

The ridgepole ties the rafter tops together and braces them. This prevents the rafters from sagging under a heavy snow load and spreading the walls with an outward force of pressure.

Because of the structural importance the ridgepole has in this type of design, it has to be a good-size log at least 8" to 12" in diameter. Our ridgepole is the 35' tamarack which had served us well as the gin pole. We just lowered it onto the loft floor and disconnected it from the stationary cottonwood tree. Five feet was then sawn off its tip to make it 30' long. This provided 5' overhangs on either side to keep the walls dry and to shelter the porch area below. This ridgepole runs east and west and is held 9' above the loft floor by posts (9-15).

Putting such a beam in place is always a struggle. Four of us broke our backs trying to lift that huge pole above the 9' uprights, but even with all that force it refused to cooperate.

After several clumsy attempts, we gave up this method of placing it. As I cursed and tried to catch my breath, a welcome solution came to mind. I put two 2 × 6 rafters in place, overlapped their top ends, and joined them together as a scissor brace. I secured them with diagonal supports and attached a block-and-tackle to their crossing peak. Then, with the aid of my helpers, one end of the beam was hoisted up. I was able to hold what they gained by lifting while they set up another pair of rafters and raised the other end of the ridgepole in place at the peak (9-16). Both ends were then spiked to the crossing rafters, and the three supporting uprights were notched into the underside of the ridgepole. The overhanging sections that protruded past the walls were braced by diagonal poles which were notched into the ridgepole ends and the uprights.

After that mighty beam was put in place, I framed in a 5'-high pony wall on the north side of the roof directly over that wall. On half of the south side, above the floored loft area, another 5' pony wall was framed in (9-17). The other half of that side was left open and the rafters for that section were notched in place over the south wall beam. They spanned from 2" beyond that top beam to over the ridgepole and were spaced at 16" on center.

9-16 *Hoisting the ridgepole into place requires some able helpers.*

PONY WALL

9-17 *Pony wall and rafter layout for the loft.*

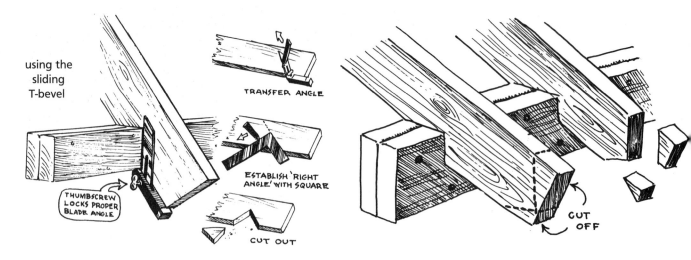

using the sliding T-bevel

THUMBSCREW LOCKS PROPER BLADE ANGLE

TRANSFER ANGLE

ESTABLISH 'RIGHT ANGLE' WITH SQUARE

CUT OUT

CUT OFF

9-18 Seating the rafters and trimming the rafter bottoms.

Framing the Rafters

The rafters were spaced at 16" on center to efficiently carry the heavy, 4' snow load that sometimes collects on the roofs in this area throughout the long winter. This design enables these 2 × 6 rafters to support between 150 and 175 pounds per square foot, which I hope is more than they will ever have to carry.

The rafter bottoms were notched over the pony walls and the top wall beams in the conventional manner. A wedge-shaped, double-mitered piece was sawn out of each rafter bottom, and the rafter was then spiked onto the top plate. To figure out the various angle cuts, since I was doing all the cutting with a handsaw (we did not have electricity), I used a sliding T-bevel. This is a square that can be adjusted to any angle. I figured out the angles on the first set of rafters by trial and error and put those rafters in place. I loosened the thumbscrew which holds the adjustable bevel blade and pushed the tool into the intersecting corner of the top plate and rafter, with the body on the top plate and the blade snug against the angling rafter. I then locked the blade in place by tightening the thumbscrew, and transferred this angle pattern to the next rafter (9-18).

I cut each rafter bottom end so it was vertical. This was partially a decorative effect, but also a way of prolonging the life of the rafters. This prolonging cut gives the rafter end more exposed surface, so it remains drier and the rotting process is slower. To lengthen the life of the rafter ends even more, I also cut off the bottom point, which would collect moisture (9-18).

Roofing

By the time it came to sheathing the roof, I was exhausted from the past months of steady sunup to sundown physical labor. Some old friends from the city dropped by, saw my condition, and volunteered to relieve me of the chore. Within a few hours, all the 1 × 12 boards were up and the house was ready for the finished roofing of 90-weight asphalt building paper. For the next few days I expressed my gratitude the best I could, by showing my friends around the beautiful valley.

The rolled asphalt went on very fast. As soon as the roof was finished and the house was protected from the fall rains, we brought the tent and cookstove inside and moved into our new home.

Log & Framed Walls

Next came the walls. We wanted to design each a different way. I cut down some standing dead tamaracks which were bone-dry from age

9-19 *Window placement in the northwest corner.*

9-20 *Dining area windows on the northeast wall.*

and filled in the west wall with log pieces while Kathrina framed in the north and east walls. Since whatever materials we filled the walls with did not have to support any structural weight, I used pieces rather than full logs so I could position and frame the windows as I built the walls. I took time to carefully plan the window placement. I set each window up on sawhorses and stood back to see the effects of every placement. Then, when I was finally satisfied, I framed it in and went on to the next. We wanted a lot of window space on the west wall because it faces the nearby river. The windows would give us a fantastic view of its relaxing waters while we were at the dining table or in the kitchen (9-19 and 9-20).

Since it was canning season already, Kathrina worked several hours a day both canning and framing. She framed in the north wall with 2 × 4s at 16" centers. She built the frames on the floor, then put them in place between the posts and spiked them in. The outside 1 × 12 cedar sheathing was nailed on with galvanized nails to prevent board rot around the nail holes. (Galvanized nails do not oxidize as regular nails do.) We put 3½" insulation in between the studs, and covered it with a layer of black paper as a vapor barrier. The inside cedar sheathing was nailed on later. This wall does not have any doors or windows because it is the coldest wall and does not get any winter sun. The fireplace and staircase are located along it on the inside and a woodshed protects it on the outside (9-21).

9-21 *Fireplace and stairs are set along the coldest wall.*

9-22 *Living room area.*

Kathrina built the east wall in the same manner. Here she framed a large 5 × 5 window which gives us a view of the small, open area that we landscaped and of the forest surrounding it. It brings in the morning sunlight to brighten up the long living-room area (9-22).

The southern wall has two parts. The section west of the middle post is a log wall made of aged white pine and tamarack. The logs were extremely hard to peel, even with a drawknife. These short logs span between the middle post and the long, 18" × 72" window to the far west. This long window helps to distribute heat. The cold air comes off the bottom and rolls the heat from the nearby wood heater to circulate it through the room. This oblique corner with its two long windows is a nice space in which to relax and read. It feels separate from the rest of the room and puts us more in touch with the outdoors (refer back to 9-19).

A Cordwood Wall

And now we come to the experiment that failed—the east section of the south wall. Here we have a cordwood wall made of bone-dry cedar rounds which sat in the house for six weeks in 100-degree weather. Even though they were aged and dried they still managed to check and crack within their cement frame. I took extreme care every step of the way in making this wall. I even dry-mixed the 1-part lime, 2-part Portland cement, 3-part sand mixture before adding water, to keep it from shrinking. But the cement still shrank. Even with every precaution exercised, before long the cedar rounds were loose in the cement.

This wall took forever to make. I could only go 18" at a time because so much mortar was needed between each round. Then I had to wait for that portion to dry before going on to the next. The wall is pleasing to look at, but it doesn't have any insulative value because concrete does not hold in heat. When I look at the wall now, I say to myself there is a month's worth of firewood that we could have used.

This cordwood wall has a window and a door. The window's frame was set into the mortar and seems to be solid in it. The door frame was built as a box and was also set into the mortar.

Its sides and bottom are full-dimension, 2 × 10 bridge timbers and its top is a curved jack-pine nurse log which extends beyond either side to grip the concrete. The door is double 2 × 6 tongue-and-groove cedar. It has no strap hinges and is held together with headless 4" nails, which were driven in diagonally along the seams between the boards. It has proven to be a good, solid door (9-23).

9-23 *The solid door set in the cordwood wall.*

Site Visit Update

On returning to this site several years after the house was completed, we noted a few changes in the house. The major development was at the west wall. Kathrina had extended this wall out a few feet to provide herself with a larger kitchen area and to allow a space for an indoor bathroom. On the outside of this wall, she put up a shed-roofed woodshed. Kathrina had also spent much time landscaping the area around the house to make the whole site more beautiful.

The loft area had originally had three sections that were defined by rectangular areas. The first section, coming up from the stairway, had been their daughter's sleep and play area. The area directly behind hers was a small storage space. There was a partition between that space and the next. Beyond the partition and the curtained doorway was their 10 × 12 bedroom. When we revisited, the dividers had been taken out of the loft area to convert what had previously been the three smaller sections into one larger bedroom space. The window placement on the main level had also changed a bit to bring more light in along the south wall.

Much of their designing of the house had been oriented toward saving money, but they definitely did not cut corners on any of the structural materials. In fact, much of the house was overbuilt. The planning process was actually a push-and-pull between form and function. Glenn and Kathrina said that it was sometimes difficult to find a balance. All in all they did very well except for a few mistakes: the cordwood wall and the separate crossing beams. As Glenn said, "The experience of building our own home also built something in us. It gave us a confidence in ourselves and other people."

Cathedral ceiling over the living room.

But the major changes we found on revisiting the site were not in the recorded details of the homestead, but in the absence of the people who made it happen. The builders were no longer living in their house. The homestead had been put up for sale. We were able to get together with Kathrina, who had just returned from a vacation. She said that the lovely, but secluded valley was just too difficult a place to make a living, except in jobs related to the primary local industries of logging and mining. Her previous partner, the man who was looking for the home he never had, had gone away in search of it.

We have seen many people come and go, and many couples broken up. It is not for everyone, and that's why these areas are so secluded and unspoiled. It is a wonderful experience for those who are willing to deal with the daily struggle and hardships which come with living in harmony with nature.

CHAPTER 10

POST & BEAM, WITH HALF-TIMBERING

INWOOD

As the Surroundings; So Shall It Be

The inner journey to come to terms with the self may take on a very outward expression and lead to union with another self. Such was the case with Dick, whose journey led to a homestead, and his wife, Jimi. Dick worked for many years at an office job in his native country, Germany. He soon became very restless and realized something was missing in his life. He began asking himself questions like: "Was this body designed to sit all day at a desk and push papers around?" Dick became aware of himself as a human animal who was meant to be outdoors, using his muscles as well as his mind to sustain his existence. It is that awareness of self as human animal that was the important factor, as Dick tells it, in changing his whole way of life:

I picked up whatever literature I could find about living in the country and surviving on a homestead. My dream was to meet all my needs in such an environment without having to waste many precious hours each day working in an office.

My first step toward my dream was to travel around and find the place I wanted to spend the next several years developing. It had to be a place that allowed me enough personal freedom to experiment with my ideas and reap the benefits. Though there is nowhere in this world that one can find such total freedom, I am happy to say I stumbled upon an area which is a satisfactory compromise. And here is where I met the beautiful, hard-working woman who shared the same dreams and soon decided to share her home with me as well.

Finding Our Homesteading Site

Our homestead is located in the foothills near a range of high mountains. It provides us with good soil, plenty of fresh water, varying terrains, and privacy. It reminds me of many areas in the Alps which I enjoyed visiting. In fact, every day as I was planning our homestead I used the information I learned from Alpine farmers. Those farmers always built their homes and the animal quarters on the hillsides, leaving the flatland open for farming and gardening. The grazing fields were also on the slopes, so the nutrients of the animal manure would wash down onto the produce fields.

The barns were dug into those slopes to provide the animals with warm, earthen stables that were beneath ground level on the uphill side and exposed on the downhill side.

Building into a Hillside

It is important to build only into the slope of a small hill when that hill's crest can be covered with such a straddling roof. If a structure is built into the bottom or at a lower part of a large hill or mountain, the hole for that structure will usually create a spring that will penetrate any concrete basement unless its walls are thoroughly tarred and have a water barrier of gravel or clay tile around their footings. Below is the example of an Alpine barn built into a hillside.

Of course such stables needed to be well ventilated. Another advantage to this design is that hay and grain can easily be unloaded into the upper loft which is level to the ground on the uphill side.

Locating the House

Our house is also built into a small hillside and has very good drainage on either side because it is sheltered by the long, overhanging roof which straddles the crest of the hill. It has a full 27 × 27 basement which was dug out by a Caterpillar™. I wanted such a basement to use as a workshop area and as a place for a root cellar, where we could preserve some of our garden—and field—produce for the winter. A refrigerator just could not keep all that we needed to store. Besides, we did not want to have to depend on expensive electricity.

If there is time and means, it is a very good idea to build the root cellar under the house; then there is only one roof to worry about.

There is no need for additional insulation above the cellar because very little, if any, warmth travels down to it from the living section on the upper level. If the root cellar is built into the slope, like the animal stable, it should be deep into the ground on the uphill side and level with it on the downhill side, enabling the gardener to simply wheelbarrow the produce in through the front door (10-1).

Our Root Cellar Design

In our design, the 20 × 27 workshop is on the downhill side of the 7 × 27 root cellar, protecting it from the weather and insulating it. The long, overhanging roof which straddles the crest above also protects the cellar because it detours the runoff, preventing it from collecting around and penetrating through the rammed-earth walls of the basement area. Even with this roof, the root cellar still retains all the natural moisture of the earth, just as an ideal garden does, because it is underground.

10-1 Utilizing the natural hill contour for our house.

2"x4" BRACES ARE DRIVEN INTO GROUND & KEPT FROM SPREADING WITH WIRE OR 1"x SCRAP BRIDGING THEM

OPTIMUM TAMPING TOOL IS **3"** METAL SQUARE WELDED ONTO LENGTH OF PIPE

10-2 *Rammed-earth forms.*

Putting in the Footings

We started by putting in a form for the footing around two sides of the perimeter of the basement. The form was made with 1 × 6 boards, two-high. These were braced at the corners and at 41 intervals with 2 × 4 uprights that were buried 1' into the ground. They extended 8' high for the full-length walls and were held together at the top with twisted wires (10-2).

Using Rammed Earth

The retaining wall around a basement which is set into a slope can be made of rammed earth (soil cement) since there is no danger of runoff to wash it away. Rammed earth is an inexpensive soil mixture, usually made up of 60 percent sand and 40 percent clay-type soil. It is held together with about 7 percent Portland cement. If rammed earth is used for fill between heavy post-and-beam walls, it can contain clay, straw, small twigs, even sawdust, and it will require just a small amount (no less than 7 percent) of concrete to cement it all together. A wall of this sort should be protected by a roof overhang of at least 2½' to prevent direct moisture from eroding it.

Rammed earth is more economical and insulates much better than an equal amount of concrete. Its thermal quality makes it remain cool in summer and helps it to retain heat in the winter. A 10" thickness of rammed earth, 60 percent sand, and 40 percent clay with 7 percent Portland cement as a retaining wall can easily support a single-story dwelling with a heavy snow load. We used this standard mixture for our basement walls.

Building the Cellar Walls

The rammed-earth mixture is a drier one than regular concrete. It should be moist enough to mix properly, but be crumbly to the touch. It should not slump when it is worked a bit by hand. When the mortar was the proper consistency, it was shoveled into the footing form. It was tamped down with an eight-pound sledgehammer until it pressed into every part of the form and the excess mortar oozed out of the corners. It was then left to set, with pieces of rebar sticking out every 18" to join with the retaining walls (10-2 and 10-3, step 1).

We began building the forms for the north and south walls, and realized that we would have a problem securing them above the footing slabs. But we figured that because of the dryness of the mortar, not much would ooze out from under the forms when they were tamped down. The 1 × 6 boards were raised to 36" at these walls. They, too, were braced at every 4' with 2 × 4s and this bracing was supported by the longer uprights which framed the footing forms. To tie the walls together, we placed bent, hewn timber uprights at each corner over the footings. These uprights also acted as nailing posts for the form ends. Their bends lean in toward the building to give the walls added structural strength. I raised the forms 36" because this height is a comfortable one for the first tamping and it is also where the windows were to be started on the south and east walls. The north wall became a full wall without windows (10-3, step 2).

By the time I got around to building the form for the west retaining wall, I decided to try a different style. I built the forms so the inside of this cellar wall would slope like a dam. It would be 10" wide on top and slant to a width of 24" at the footing. This wedge—or dam-shaped—wall is much stronger than the ordinary straight wall and is easier to make. It does not have to be supported on a footing because its thickness is relative to the amount of back pressure it might receive (10-3, step 3 and detail).

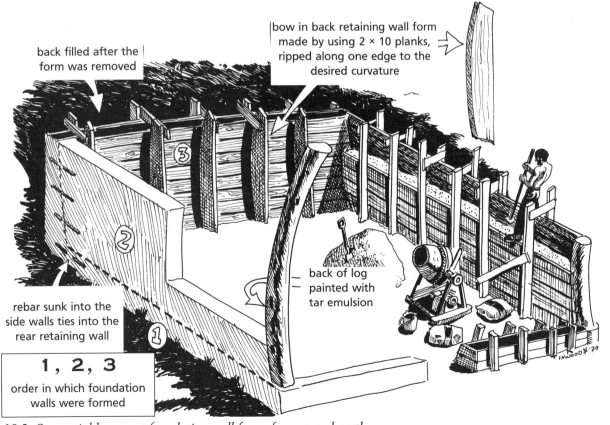

back filled after the form was removed

bow in back retaining wall form made by using 2 × 10 planks, ripped along one edge to the desired curvature

rebar sunk into the side walls ties into the rear retaining wall

back of log painted with tar emulsion

1, 2, 3
order in which foundation walls were formed

10-3 *Sequential basement foundation wall forms for rammed earth.*

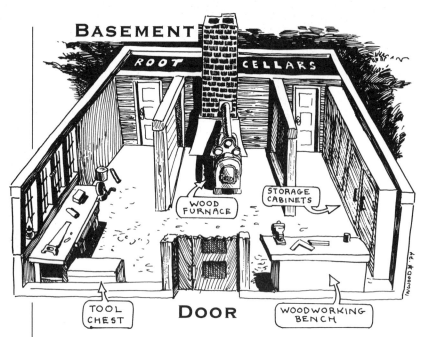

10-4 *The layout of the basement.*

Placing the Windows

After the rammed earth was tamped in and the completed retaining wall was left to set, the 8× timber windowsills were notched into the end posts over the 3' wall sections of the south and east walls. An 8× upright support was placed between each window space to frame it in. These uprights also acted as structural posts for the top wall beams which were notched in above them. Five windows were then put into the south wall, and four windows and a door went into the east wall to bring in plenty of light to the shop area. Workbenches were built under these windows and other woodwork conveniences will soon be added.

Workshop and Root Cellar Floors

I did not want to put a cement floor in the workshop because I do not like to walk on such floors. For the present, the floors in both the workshop and the root cellar are dirt with a few wood chips mixed in. I was thinking that I might sink some joist beams into porous gravel and nail a rough 1× floor over them. The gravel would provide drainage between the joists and prevent them from prematurely rotting (10-4).

The two root-cellar sections are separated from the workshop area by an 8"-thick, insulated double wall. The insulation used between the walls is oat straw which has been bathed in an asphalt emulsion. This emulsion is a very effective and long-lasting mixture of three fungus-retarding agents: asphalt, lime, and water-glass silicate. I submerged the straw in the emulsion, left it in the sun to dry, then pressed the treated straw in between the walls with my fists.

Though the walls of these cellars remain dry, they receive enough moisture from their soil floors to keep them cool. For proper circulation, they have air vents near their ceilings to allow the warm, rising air to escape. These 8 × 8 × 16 cement blocks are built into the north and west walls. The cool air comes in from the workshop and pushes the old, musty air out through the high vents. Root cellars need this type of vent system to prevent mold and fungi from forming in the otherwise stagnant dampness.

Setting the Floor Joists

After the basement walls were finished, 28'-long fir joists were put in over them. They spanned between the east and west walls. The joist ends that rested above the west wall were tarred and cemented onto that wall with the rammed-earth mixture (10-5). This provided a flat surface for the wall plate and floor.

10-5 *Floor joists set into the foundation wall.*

Half-Timbering

On the uphill side of the slope we can walk from ground level, through the woodshed, and into the living section. Here again, I used some half-timbering techniques I learned from the Alpine farmers. Our walls were a post-and-beam braced frame construction with a modified rammed-earth mortar as the filler. The triangular bracing for these walls is a variation of the half-timber work used in this type of construction in Germany.

The posts were made from cedar logs which I hewed to 8" square at the site where they were cut, so the horse would not have to drag any excess weight. 1 used cedar—it is the most porous of the local woods. Being porous, it is rot resistant, light in weight, and also very insulative. I hewed these timbers by first chopping a score cut against the grain every 1' or so with an ax. If the wood had a very straight grain, which most large cedar logs do, the score cuts could be spaced farther apart. I used a coarse adz or a broadax and made them roughly square. At the building site I finished the 8" squares with a shipbuilder's adz.

10-6 *Typical half-timber configurations.*

The posts were spaced along the south wall according to the width of the windows we had. We bought 94 old 4 × 2 and 3½ × 2 framed windows for 2 dollars each. We wanted at least four of the 4 × 2 windows along the south wall to bring in the sunlight throughout the year. There is something very romantic about waking up on a cold winter morning to the bright sunshine reflecting off the white snow-covered landscape. It really helps to start the day off right. And to me light is worth more than warmth. I spend a lot of time outdoors and enjoy it when the outside can come inside by way of large window spaces. The Japanese say that light is very necessary for comfort. Light spaces bring about inner happiness.

After the posts were toenailed onto the bottom wall plates, they were braced with slightly curved diagonal timbers. These braces were hewed from bent cedar pieces to add an aesthetic touch to the walls. In European post-and-beam architecture there are sometimes many bracing designs used to break up the monotony of similar diagonal patterns. Three common patterns are referred to as *Der Mann, Der Womann* (or *Die Frau*), and *Der Wilde-mann* (10-6). Our design was much simpler, the aesthetic beauty being in the curved pieces that I hand-hewed (10-7).

10-7 *Curved pieces used for half-timbering.*

Using the Root Cellar

The root-cellar sections are divided by a rammed-earth wall. On the north side of the wall there is a shelved area for the storage of canning jars, crocks of sauerkraut, sacks of potatoes, a barrel of eggs, and more delicate produce like apples. Apples are not supposed to be mixed with the odorous vegetables like cabbage and onions because they will end up tasting like them.

At first, we preserved the eggs by mixing a solution of water-glass silicate into the water in the barrel. An old, nearby farmer told us of a simpler method that we now use. He mixes lime with salt and puts the two ingredients into the barrel of liquid. The mixture produces a diluted, mortarlike substance that coats and seals the eggs, keeping them fresh for several weeks at a time.

The south area of the root cellar has a 2½'-high bin that is filled with sand. We bury carrots and beets in between the layers of sand. This preserves them throughout the winter as well as if they were still in the ground. The various crops like cabbage and brussels sprouts were harvested with their root systems attached and were replanted into the moist earthen floor. This method of retaining freshness works well because the plants' roots think they are still in the soil and continue to supply the plants with life-sustaining nutrients.

There are four holes, 14" deep, in this south cellar for milk. We placed old flue linings in these holes and put in the containers of milk. The milk keeps cold enough in these linings to stay fresh for several days. The milk even feels cold to my teeth after it has been in a hole for many hot summer days.

BINS OF SAND FOR ROOT CROPS

VENT

SHELVES FOR CANNED GOODS

VENT

TREATED STRAW INSULATION

CERAMIC FLUE LINERS SUNK INTO EARTH

Filling In the Half-Timber

The windowsills and the top beam were not put in place until after the rammed earth was tamped in. They would otherwise have been obstacles during that process. To prepare the posts for the rammed earth and to prevent air spaces from forming when the mortar dried and contracted, I attached 1 × 1 strips of board to the outside and inside edges of the posts. An inside wall form of plywood the height of the windowsill was then nailed to the posts, and two 1 × 6 boards were attached to the outside (10-8).

A mortar using rammed earth consisting of 5 parts sawdust, 5 parts sand, and 1 part Portland cement was mixed very dry (moist to the touch but crumbly) for the walls. People said this mixture wouldn't last because the sawdust would soon rot out, but I remembered reading about sawdust-and-cement floors in 1895 Victory-type ships. It worked for those ships; why couldn't it work for my walls? It in fact does work very well, probably because the Portland cement contains lime which prevents fungus from forming on the sawdust. This mixture was

10-8 Half-timbers and rammed-earth form setup.

pushed between the forms and tamped down with the sledgehammer (10-9). Eight inches of this mortar using rammed earth gives more insulation than an equal thickness of regular cement. It is more porous and contains many tiny dead-air spaces like a hollow cinder block.

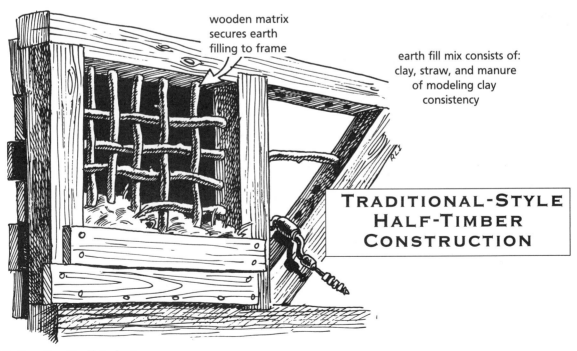

10-9 Details of half-timbering.

10-10 *The south wall exterior.*

10-11 *View of the southeast corner.*

It is durable enough for filling in between posts and beams, because it does not have to carry any structural weight, and will last quite a long time if a certain precaution is taken—this being that the roof directly above the wall have an overhang of at least 2½" to prevent direct precipitation from eroding it (10-10 and 10-11).

We are very happy with the way the south wall came out. It is aesthetically pleasing and it gives us a very fine view. There is, of course, plenty of light coming in from its 16 feet of window space (10-12). In fact, just below the windows inside the house we have a wide sill for starting plants or sprouting grain and seeds. We even have a continuous oat sprouter, made from a hollowed-out log on a slight slant. It sprouts oats by the bucketful for chicken feed, so we have eggs with dark orange yolks in the middle of the winter. This sprouter is warmed by a couple of hot bricks, exchanged twice daily and reheated on the woodstove.

The southern half of the west wall is also rammed earth filled half-timber. This wall is level with the crest of the hill and is protected by a long overhanging roof that covers the woodshed in front of it. The entrance to the living area is located here, under the 14' overhangs (10-13).

10-12 *South wall interior; plenty of light.*

10-13 *Entrance on the west wall.*

The northern half of the west wall, and the north and east walls are wood-frame construction with 2 x 4 studding and cedar 1× sheathing. They were insulated with asphalt-emulsion-treated straw as was the inner wall to the root cellar. This treated straw is proving to be a very good insulator. It provides the walls with a lightweight, porous sealer that contains many dead-air spaces which effectively keep out the cold and retain the heat (10-14).

Building the Chimney

For our chimney we made a concrete slab above the rammed-earth wall which divides the root cellar compartments. We used two commercial 8" × 8" flue linings and mortared in red bricks around them, filling in any spaces that were between the bricks and linings (10-15). Near the bottom of the chimney we left one brick loose in front of the lining opening to clean out the creosote. To make sure we were secured against chimney fires, we wanted a solid brick chimney instead of just having

10-14 A sleeping area.

stovepipe going out through the wall. Many people I know and have heard about have lost their homes due to creosote buildup that finally caught fire. The fire then ignited with either their cedar-shake roofs or framed ceiling.

10-15 Chimney construction and a schematic drawing of multiple heater hookup to the single chimney.

Structural Integrity

Throughout the open living area there are a few 6 × 6 upright posts which brace the horizontal rafter supports and hold up the roof (10-16). These uprights relieve the roof pressure on the walls and prevent them from spreading under the weight of a heavy snow load. In the center there is also a 22'-long center post which spans from a pier on the shop floor to the peak of the roof. The upright supports are spaced approximately 9' on center, bracing the peak and going north and south across the east floor. Since the roof peak is off-center, there is no need for upright supports on the west side because the rafters span less than 11' between the peak and the west wall.

Notched in above the posts, going north and south, are the 6 × 6 horizontal rafter supports.

10-16 Basic post-and-beam layout.

They are braced to the uprights by diagonal wind stiffeners. These wind stiffeners are curved pieces of log that add another aesthetic touch to the interior of the house. Their structural purpose is to prevent the walls from parallelograming or collapsing because of unexpected heavy winds. All the natural forces that

10-17 "Wind bracing" of curved timbers.

want to destroy a structure attack the roof, except for the wind. Wind has been known to destroy many buildings that would otherwise be sound but lacked bracing against its unexpected force (10-17 and 10-18).

The center ridge beam is not one continuous timber but two separate pieces. These pieces were spliced with a side-lap joint and were bolted together. They were then supported from underneath by a short beam that spans between the two nearest uprights. This support beam is braced by two diagonals, securing it to the posts. The ridge beam spans 3' beyond the north and south walls, providing them with plenty of overhang for protection (10-19 and 10-20).

10-18 Curved timber supports.

Spacing the Rafters

Because I was working with poles 5" in diameter and even larger, and because I did not plan on using store-bought insulation for the roof, I spaced my rafters roughly 28" on center. This rafter placement is sufficient to carry a heavy snow load since the rafters are braced in the center of their span by the crossing support beams. The rafters on the east side of the building are pine and larch because these types of wood have very little taper. They span from above the center crossbeam to 5' over the east wall. This overhang protects the entranceway below and detours the runoff so it won't come near the basement retaining wall.

The rafters on the west side are cedar because they only span a short distance from the off-centered peak to the west wall. Since these rafters overhang 14' beyond that wall to cover the outside woodshed and shield the crest of the hill from runoff—they have to be more weather resistant than the others. Cedar, though it usually tapers drastically, is the most weather resistant of all the local species of wood. Since these rafters only span a short distance inside the house, their tapers are not very noticeable.

10-19 Lap joint on the center beam.

10-20 Beam support in the kitchen area.

10-21 *The built-up roof.*

Roofing

Our subroof is a double thickness of slab boards which are on the average about 6" wide. The second layer laps over the sides of the first the way roof shakes overlap (10-21). The boards of these two layers are spaced half their width apart to create dead-air corridors between them. When these corridors are properly sealed off, they effectively insulate the roof because they are not exposed to outside weather. And since the air is trapped in these areas, much of the rising heat from the house cannot pass through them. It is locked, instead, between the boards and is not lost through the roof. Of course there is some heat loss, but not enough to prevent our house from staying toasty when our woodstove is going.

Above the two layers of slab boards there is a sheet of aluminum builder's foil, shiny-side-down, to reflect the ultraviolet heat rays which have come through the air spaces. This foil barrier holds in much of the otherwise escaping heat and is well worth its nominal price. A continuous layer of 1× boards was then nailed over the aluminum foil to provide a flat surface for the finished roofing of rolled 90-weight asphalt paper (10-21).

This style of subroof gives us about the same insulation as would 3½" of fiberglass and is far less expensive. But even with 3½" of fiberglass insulation, there would still be some heat loss, resulting in the snow melting on the roof and icing up at the eaves. We have this problem now. When the snow melts and collects on the eaves, the mass of ice will travel upward by capillary action and back up under the eaves, thus entering into the house and dripping through the subroof. To prevent this ice buildup, we covered our eaves with an 18"-wide flashing of aluminum. The ice slides off this flashing instead of building up over it.

We have a skylight built into the roof over the kitchen area. This skylight was easy to install. It was framed much like a window casing, except more care was taken to seal this frame so no water vapor would seep through. A very good way to seal such a frame is to cover all the joints with tar. Also make sure that the window you use is of a substance that will not shatter or break under a heavy snow load. We used tinted, corrugated plastic. It is working fine and is much cheaper than a safe thickness of glass.

As a finishing touch to the roof, my wife hollowed out a thin cedar pole to be used as a trough at the edge of the north eave. This ingenious device keeps water from randomly dripping off that eave and splashing on whoever is walking under it. It also controls the flow of the melting snow and allows us to collect it in a barrel for domestic use when our water system freezes—which it does occasionally in the dead of winter.

Site Visit Update

When we visited this site several years following the completion of the house, Dick and and his wife, Jimi, were very comfortable in their little abode and especially pleased with the light-giving south wall. In fact they had not gotten around to curtaining it off with the woven drapery Jimi had produced on her loom, choosing the light instead.

Dick told us that if they had any regret over the design of the house it would be in the roof. If they had it to do over again, with the proper amount of money, of course, they would have put in at least six inches of fiberglass insulation or its equivalent. They thought this might control the heat loss and keep their house even toastier throughout the winter with the minimum of cordwood-cutting energy. "But then again," Dick said, "cutting wood keeps one healthy during the long dormant winter."

Skylight over the kitchen area.

Even at that time, Dick and Jimi said they were finding, through the experience of the last few years there, that trying to maintain an almost self-sufficient homestead was a full-time job and sometimes necessitated more physical, mental, and emotional energy than they were willing to put out.

Several years later we went to visit the site again and to talk with Dick about some projects he was working on. The house had changed very little, except for the fact that nobody was living in it at that moment. Jimi had gone elsewhere to live, and Dick had moved into another house on the property.

Dick said Jimi had left because she felt she was spending too much time in the effort to be self-sufficient and not enough time practicing her craft of weaving. This couple had been everybody's inspiration in the struggle for self-sufficiency. Whenever anyone visited them, they were working, from the break of day until late in the evening. That turned out to be the problem.

CHAPTER 11

LOG POST & BEAM, WITH HAND-MILLED PLANKS

INWOOD '73

In Accord with the Time

Sometimes we know when the time has come to address our inner needs because we feel it from within, and sometimes it is our circumstances that tell us that now is the moment to be in accord with the time. Something like this is what happened to Roger.

In retrospect it seemed as if he had always had a longing in his heart to go back to nature and, once there, to become self-reliant. He felt he had had to compromise these yearnings and find a creative outlet within the environment in which he lived. This creative outlet was painting. He spent several years in colleges and universities, and at one time had a strong ambition to become a university art instructor. But eventually he found himself without a job and these circumstances told him that it was time to do the two things he wanted to do most: start his own art school in order to share some important ideas he had about art, and go out into the woods and hack out an existence for himself and his family. He founded an arts and crafts school and taught at it for 22 months. The local community was supportive but too small to keep the school going. So he and his wife, Jane, as Roger tells it, gave up the art school and devoted themselves to developing their homestead:

The first few months that we lived on the land seemed like an extended vacation from our former rat race. We found solace in nature and in hard physical work. We cleared areas and set up a temporary camp. We spent very little money and kept ourselves busy doing what needed to be done. We made rough plans

11-1 *Peeling the bark off logs.*

for a woodshed, an outhouse, and corrals. The building site that we picked for our house was relatively level. We agreed not to employ any heavy equipment on the land. We even park our car near the road to keep from disturbing the natural setting.

The Idea of Building a House

Though I had previously worked as a laborer on a couple of ranches and did log work while employed by the U.S. Forest Service, we were somewhat inexperienced and idealistic in our approaches to the new land. I had once made a giant monkey-bar set out of logs, but I had never built anything like a house. Still, I had a pretty good idea of where to begin from having read many books which taught some basic techniques, and having a memory full of building ideas that went all the way back to my childhood. I wanted to build a house of my own design and imagination with only a few tools and without any conventional materials except for nails and wood. I knew that with practice I could eventually develop my own building techniques and be satisfied with my achievements.

It didn't take very long for the plans to begin materializing. I soon recalled much of my previous knowledge, and I remembered the way the Forest Service used to peel logs for the quick structures they built. They would cut the log to size, and with a sharp ax cut off thin strips of bark on three sides of the log (11-1). This allowed the moisture to escape from the peeled areas and also controlled checking. The remaining three strips of bark would easily peel off after the logs dried out and shrank. This would take anywhere from one to two years. Then, when the seasoned logs got a good soaking from a heavy rain, the bark could easily be removed. This method also produced a nice color effect. As the peeled areas aged, they turned gray. The protected areas stayed a golden to rust color until the bark loosened. The log, when fully peeled, looked wonderfully rustic.

I found the chain saw to be my most valuable tool. As I knew from previous experience, nothing could surpass its efficiency and speed in cutting and bucking firewood or felling and limbing trees. While it is a machine and, like most machines, is sometimes temperamental, with experience you begin to learn what it can do for you. It also costs a bit to maintain, but every time I rip through logs to make my own boards and cut poles to the size I want, I realize that I could not do these jobs by myself any faster or cheaper with any other tool. However, just as a matter of personal taste, I use an ax for limbing and notching. It may take longer, but there is a certain satisfaction in using an ax and it doesn't cost anything in gasoline and oil.

Working Alone

Since the construction job was primarily my own, and because we could not afford hired help, I had to design a method of building our house in which I could handle all the materials by myself. Though my wife was on the project with me, she was busy with housekeeping chores, gardening, animal maintenance, and civic activities. I didn't want to be calling on her every few minutes to help me fit something in place or assist with other awkward jobs. The building had to be a one-man effort with lightweight and easy-to-handle materials.

larger rocks at the bottom

11-2 Stone foundation posts.

The House Site

The site we chose for the house was on a slight slope overlooking our garden and the pasture in which our two-year-old colt was tethered. I compensated for the slope with fir pillars of varying lengths which were set on stone foundations. Fir was chosen because of its strength, weather resistance, and ability to hold nails.

The pillars were very short at the top of the slope and became gradually longer toward the bottom (see the completed house drawing on page 206 and 207). Each pillar was peeled on three sides, and each rested on a pile of rocks which went roughly 2½' down into the porous ground. For added drainage and strength, I placed larger foundation rocks in the bottom of the hole, and smaller ones going towards the top (11-2).

The Design of the House

The rear kitchen and dining room area were built on the same level into the slope. As the terrain dropped away, storage space was provided for under the front unit (11-3).

The many-sided rear section gives us the room we need for cooking, dishwashing, and dining. It lacks the monotony that a traditional, four-sided room can have. I originally planned

11-3 Crawl space storage opening.

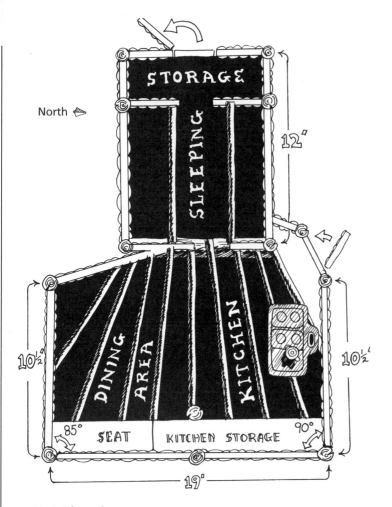

11-4 Floor plan.

to have seven floor joists of various lengths fanning out from a 9' beam in front, to a 19' beam at the far rear, going into the slope. The distance between the two beams was 12'. These beams were notched over the five vertical posts beneath and they were each hewn level. Even at that point I could tell that the space wasn't going to be adequate, so I added two 10½' beams which were almost at right angles with the 19' beam (11-4). Another floor joist was added to either side to secure the beams and lengthen the floor support. On the east side of the area, an 8' beam was notched to the front of the 10½' beam and was connected to the front beam. On the west side I added two other beams to include space for a doorway and a stairwell. I then added another 2' area into the slope behind the 19' beam for seating space, storage, cupboards, and counters.

The 9 × 12 front section was a bit simpler. It was raised on six upright supports. The two uprights in the rear also support the 9' beam in the kitchen area. Two other uprights are in front of these, forming a square. The other two are in front of the others. They border the 3 × 9 closet area. This section was framed with log floor beams, and three joists were added for more support—two running lengthwise on either side of the doorways in the 9 × 9 section and one going across to frame that section.

Putting In the Flooring

With the pillars and joists in place, it was time to work on the subfloor. I went around to several of the local mills and priced some low-grade 2 × 10s and 2 × 12s, but the cost was beyond my means everywhere, so I decided to make my own boards.

Since we live in an area that has cold winters, we wanted to make sure we had a well-insulated floor. We covered the subfloor with a vapor-barrier layer of black building paper and spaced 1½" pine saplings every 16" across the paper. 1¼" boards were then placed over the pine saplings as a temporary finished floor. I later spaced more pine saplings over it, and added a final board floor made of fiber. Needless to say, with all these layers we have no problem with cold or dampness coming through the floor (11-5).

Raising the Walls

When I was a young boy growing up in Idaho and Montana, I saw many old lambing and pioneer sheds. They had post-and-beam walls which were sheathed or paneled with rough lumber or vertical slabs. They sure seemed to have been around for a long time. I liked that method of building, so I incorporated it into my house, using half-rounds for siding. I fur

MASONITE

1¼" PINE BOARDS

SAWDUST

1½" PINE SAPLINGS
AT 16" CENTERS

BUILDING PAPER

11-5 *Built-up floor.*

ther modified this style to give the house proper insulation by adding a few more layers of boards. This added strength and helped to keep the heat in.

I set up and nailed in five posts on either side of the front area and a post on either side of the doorways of the 9' sides. Beams were notched and spiked across the tops of these poles to brace them and tie them together. Diagonal poles were then added for more support (11-6).

The sections without windows had diagonals spanning from the bottom of one corner to the top of the opposite corner.

11-6 *Log post-and-beam style of pole framing.*

Ripping My Own Boards

First, I felled a tree. I left it where it was while limbing off the branches from the butt up to the length I wanted the boards to be. The tree was dropped across a stump or blocks, so the butt of the tree stuck out parallel to the ground. The lower branches were then trimmed off, and the upper branches were left intact to prevent the tree from rolling while I chain-sawed. Standing along the side of the tree, I started my chain saw, and began cutting off one of the outer slabs. I used a downward motion, like one used for bucking cordwood. I didn't use any device for measuring the thickness of the cuts—I just eyeballed them, and before long the boards were coming out reasonably straight.

After each board was made, it was detached from the log. The first ones were quite uneven. By doing some hewing, though, I managed to make them usable. With practice, I developed the technique of ripping my own boards. I learned to keep my chain saw very sharp and to file the rakers of the chain lower than usual. That enables each tooth to take bigger bites out of the wood. If the rakers are very low, though, the chain grabs the wood too much instead of sawing through it.

Most of my boards are about 1¼" to 1½" thick. They are of white pine and cedar because these are softer woods and are easier to cut through. White pines in our area don't have much taper and are very straight, so long boards can be cut from them. They would produce boards that were the same width from end to end if my cuts were straight.

CHAIN SAW SHARPENED FOR RIPPING

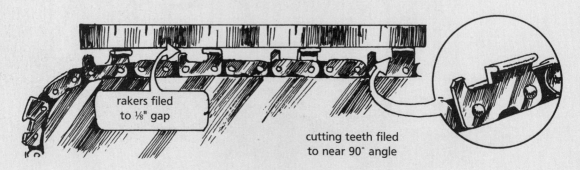

rakers filed
to ⅛" gap

cutting teeth filed
to near 90° angle

A Making lumber with a chain saw.

B Trimming off the outer slab wood.

C Ripping the first board.

D Cutting board off the log.

INWOOD 74

The sections with large windows didn't have any diagonals. The headers and sills of those windows provided horizontal support because they were notched solid into the uprights. The sections in the far front have smaller windows which are also framed into the uprights. There are additional braces below the bottom sills of those windows to make sure the walls won't go anywhere.

The same basic plan was followed for the kitchen–dining-area walls. What differed was the placement of the diagonal bracing. In sections without windows, instead of the braces going from the bottom corner to the opposite top corner, they only went from the bottom corner to the middle of the opposite pole. Though this method was sufficient and used less material, the method used in the front section was structurally far superior. It could sup-port more tension without giving way because the diagonals were wedged into opposite corners and were braced by them. The larger windows in the rear section have V-braces under them. These consist of two poles that meet in the center of the floor beam and span to opposite posts under the bottom windowsill, providing strong support (refer to 11-6).

Building Out the Walls

I was now faced with the problem of how to make the walls thick enough so I would not need store-bought insulation and yet still give them a finished look. I came up with the idea of using peeled half-rounds. I ripped 6" to 10" logs, peeled them, and spaced them upright against the outside of the post-and-beam frame, then toenailed them into place. Small quarter-rounds were then ripped and placed between the half-rounds to fill in the cracks (11-7).

Many 5"- to 6"-diameter cedar saplings were then ripped in half for an inner layer of sheathing. These half-rounds were nailed side by side, and quarter-rounds were later added between them to seal off the walls. This inner wall decorates and adds to the insulative qualities.

Each season the quarter-rounds can be wedged deeper into the spaces between the half-rounds, as both layers dry with age. The tighter they are driven in, the greater the wall's ability to seal the dead-air spaces between the slabs. The insulative quality of the wall is excellent when it is properly sealed, and this method is not costly. To finish off most of the walls, many more poles were ripped and their half-rounds were set upright side by side along the inside of the post-and-beam frames. They were then nailed to that frame.

1/4 ROUND CHINKING

ROUGH CHAIN SAWED 2" BOARDS – 4" APART

SLAB LAYER-ING IS RE-PEATED ON INSIDE WALL

BUILDING PAPER

VERMICULITE INSULATION

ROUNDED OUT-SIDE SLABS

BUILDING PAPER

11-7 Built up wall.

11-8 *Diagonal braces supporting eaves.*

Fitting the Ceiling Joists

I made sure to cut the ceiling joists 6' longer than the end of the walls to allow for 3' of eave overhang on each side (11-8). These joists were then notched into the upper log of the double top plate. They act as floor supports for the loft and prevent the walls and roof from spreading. The longer the eaves, the more the walls are protected from the weather. But to have long eaves, you must make sure to brace them properly because there is a great amount of snow and ice that builds up on this area. I not only extended the ceiling joists to the end of the eaves, I also notched in diagonal braces from the upright posts to the ends of the joists, for additional support.

Long eaves are a disadvantage when the house they are on is surrounded by a forest. In colder seasons, the long eaves will tend to prevent the warm sunlight from shining on the walls and entering the windows. In hot weather, though, this is an advantage.

The Loft Space and the Roof's Slope

The end ceiling joists also act as end logs to begin the loft area. The loft is the small area above the piano and the children's room which we use for our sleeping quarters. It is 5' high at the peak and is four logs and one rafter high on either end (11-9).

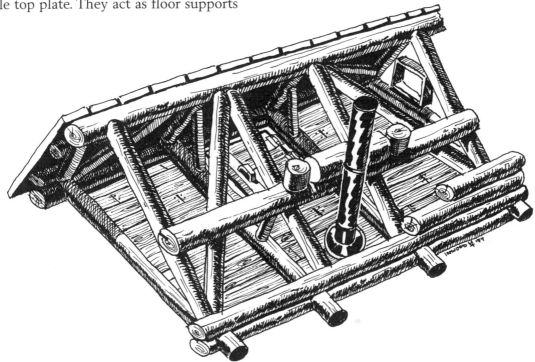

11-9 *Roof frame.*

Making Roof Shakes

To make your own roof shakes you need several log bolts. Each should be between 18" and 32" long, depending on how long you prefer your shakes; it's all a matter of personal taste. I like to use 21"-long shakes because they cover a substantial area and they can be overlapped nicely to prevent leakage. For me this length is easier to make than the usual longer ones, because our shake trees are young and small. They have twisted grains and many knots.

To find ideal shake material, you should go where a logging company has logged an area rich in first-growth cedars. There you will find many high stumps that were left after the slaughter. Such stumps, which are over 18" in diameter and have at least 6" of radius before the center rot, are an excellent source of shake bolt material.

To make these shakes, I take a mallet and froe and split the bolt into several sections. A section is placed on a stump or log round, then the bark and outer layer of soft sap-

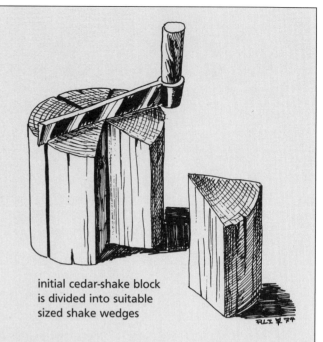

initial cedar-shake block
is divided into suitable
sized shake wedges

wood is trimmed off. I cut out half of the top of the working stump or round to make a safety ledge. The half that remains acts as a backstop to provide better control of the shake sections as they are being worked on. The next step in making the shake is to trim off any portion of heartwood that is dry-rotted. With a froe and a hard wood mallet, the shakes are then split off the bolt section.

Trimming layer of sapwood.

Trimming off dry rot.

Splitting with mallet and froe.

The bolt section should be turned end-for-end each time a shake is split off. This develops the taper effect of the shakes.

Because of the poor quality of our shake trees, I had to make thick, 1"- to 1½"-wide shakes. I'm beginning to like heavy shakes, though. Most homemade or commercial shakes are half that thickness. Heavier ones are more durable and are better insulators. Shakes are cheap if you make them yourself and they are, to my eye, the most beautiful of all roofing materials.

To lay the shakes on a roof, you start from the eaves and nail down the top ends of a full row of shakes to the accommodating nailer. To do the second row, you start a third of a

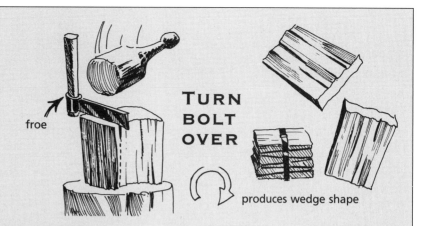

froe

TURN BOLT OVER

produces wedge shape

shake's length up until you complete that whole row, then repeat this procedure. Note that each row covers a large portion of the row below it. This ensures a 100-percent leakproof roof. This method is continued until the roof is finished. At the top of the pitch, a ridge cap of aluminum or some other material is placed over the highest shakes. It ensures against leakage at the peak of the ridge.

Splitting off a shake.

Tapered shake.

11-10 Gable with diagonal supports.

11-11 Shake roof showing the aluminum ridge cap.

The loft gables are made up of three horizontal logs which were round-notched to one another, and several smaller stockade rounds which follow the roof's slope (11-10). At each end there is a window for light and ventilation. These windows were designed to be large enough for us to crawl through in case of fire.

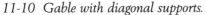

1"x NAILER STRIPS

EACH LAYER COVERS AT LEAST HALF OF PREVIOUS SHAKE

START FROM THE BOTTOM

SHAKE ROOF

11-12 Applying shakes to the roof.

We covered our roof with homemade wood shakes (11-11 and 11-12). To make the roof's slope, I simply extended two poles over the gable ends and met them at the peak in the center. This gave the 5' peak. We didn't need a higher space because, after all, we were just going to sleep in this area. To raise the peak would give us more space to heat and a greater chance of heat loss. We wanted the ends of the loft to be a bit higher, so we raised them by adding a 5"-diameter log on either side above the eave supports.

A second set of roof rafters was put up at the rear of the loft and a 24' ridgepole was nailed to their joined tops. Two 24' purlins were notched in across the center of the rafters. This framework was then cross-braced in many places so it could support the shake roof and a heavy snow load.

Included in the roof supports is a set of two angle braces that hold up the 8' front extension (11-10). Roofs are often the first section of a structure to go. They are exposed to all the weather and have the greatest tendency to rot and weaken; therefore they should be well made.

11-16 Homemade door latch.

11-13 Kitchen door.

11-14 Inside of kitchen door.

Instead of laying rafters for the roof, I decided to rip extra-thick boards and span them from the ridgepole to the eaves. These boards take the place of rafters and provide the finish roofing with super-strong supporting nailers. These nailers are made of fir because it is almost as weather resistant as cedar and is as strong and durable as any of the other evergreens. It also holds nails much better than cedar.

The Front Door

My next job was to hang a door.

Our massive door was made out of fir boards on the outside and cedar half-rounds on the inside (11-13 and 11-14). Between the two layers is a vapor barrier of building paper and a layer of 1×s spaced a few inches apart to create a dead-air space for insulation (11-15). The door was finished off with a locking bolt on the inside which was secured in place with 8" lag bolts (11-14 and 11-16). With that, the house was sealed off from the weather and was ready for us to move in.

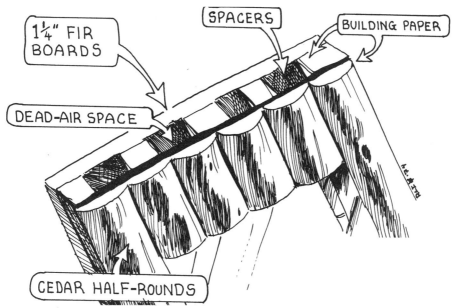

1¼" FIR BOARDS

SPACERS

BUILDING PAPER

DEAD-AIR SPACE

CEDAR HALF-ROUNDS

11-15 Door construction.

11-17 Kitchen cabinets of half-round logs.

11-19 Rounded cabinet made of half-rounds.

Finishing the Interior

The interior work that followed was realy enjoyable. From leftover cedar and other wooden half-rounds that I ripped for the purpose, I made cabinet doors (11-17, 11-18, and 11-19). Using small birches, I designed dining-room chairs (11-20) and a dinner table (11-21).

I wanted everything in our house, except for stoves and cooking facilities, to be handmade, nothing store-bought. I had little choice in the matter actually, because of our financial situation.

11-18 Another view of half-round logs in kitchen area.

11-20 Homemade chair.

11-21 *Homemade table.*

11-22 *Free-standing pole fencing.*

Time for Other Projects

After we had a suitable roof over our heads and warm living quarters, I started working on other necessary projects. One such project was to make a bordering fence around the horse's pasture. Because our ground is very rocky and is difficult to dig fence posts into, I built a jack fence instead of the typical post-and-rail fence (11-22).

To begin this fence, I first cut a few hundred poles to length and brought them to the site. I took two short poles, about 6' or 7' in length, and notched them together near their tops to create an inverted V-jack. These jacks were spaced every 16' or 17' apart to receive the horizontal poles which were notched and joined to them. The legs of the jack prevent the fence from falling forward or backward. A diagonal brace, running from the crotch of one jack to the bottom of the leg of the next jack, was put in at every fifth section of the fence to prevent any part of the whole structure from collapsing lengthwise. The braces were placed on the opposite side from the horizontal poles so as not to interfere with them.

11-23 Goat corral.

A jack fence also has one line of poles running horizontally at the bottom of the jack legs on the back side of the fence. This prevents the leg of the jack from being accidentally forced sideways, thus undercutting the support. The horizontal poles on the front of the jack are alternated, butt, tip, butt, tip, to balance out the weight on each jack. Also, the jack leg on the uphill side is shorter than the one on the downhill side to maintain balance.

The front of the fence, the side with most of the horizontal poles, should be facing the livestock. This side can withstand the most pressure. The poles, otherwise, are subject to being forced off the jacks when the fence is rammed by a frisky animal. This design, of course, is reversed when the fence is being used to contain goats or sheep, because these nimble creatures are apt to climb the progression of horizontal poles (11-23).

Our Well
Perhaps something should also be said about our well. I dug a 10'-deep hole, going below the water level, down to a bedrock base. This hole is 6' in diameter and is lined with a hefty boulder cribbing which encircles the well opening. The boulders for this cribbing were carefully chosen so they would remain secure when stacked. This kind of cribbing will never deteriorate and will never pollute the water (11-24).

The well is bordered above ground by a 2½'-high rock wall to minimize the danger of animals and humans falling into it. Boards are covering the well until I can make a hinged cover for it. The boards are a precaution against children climbing over the wall. The well was then enshrined with an unusual, rather Asian-looking, shake roof to shade it in summer, keep leaves from falling into it in autumn, and prevent snow from dropping into it in winter. This roof is substantial and has a certain aesthetic appeal.

A Pagoda-Style Well Roof
My idea, though not entirely clear at first, was to incorporate a shake pattern into the well's roof. From previous experience I found that shakes can have a somewhat sloppy look, especially around the eaves. I wanted to compen-

11-24 Our concept for the well.

sate for the "loppy-eared" look that I had been getting with the heavy shakes I was using. By building up the roof's eave support a little higher than would normally be the case, the first shakes went on in a near-horizontal position, but not horizontal enough to cause leakage. I found to my great surprise and satisfaction that the lower end of the second row of shakes came to rest, not on the upper part of the previous row as was usually the case, but near the center of those first shakes.

In using this design, I realized that I had discovered something about the way the Asian pagodas were made. I studied how I could develop the idea throughout the roof. It looked simple—and proved to be. It was all a matter of common sense, but it took an eye for shaping to make the roof to my own taste. I couldn't wait to get each row of shakes on and see the effect. In order to fit the inner logic that was unfolding before me, the shake nailers had to become steeper as they went up. There was a functional reason for this design as well. The more pointed the roof peak, the better it would shed the water, like the bow of a ship. The final step was to place an inverted, hollowed-out log over the crack formed at the apex of the roof (11-25 and 11-26).

11-25 Creating the Asian curved-roof effect.

11-26 Pagoda-style shake roof.

Site Visit Update

Roger and Jane had spent several years of hard but gratifying work to create this homestead for themselves and their young children. They had also built all the necessary outbuildings, including a five-ton capacity hay shed, a woodshed, a laundry house, a bunkhouse, and a chicken coop. They had cleared over an acre and planted pasture grasses and legumes for the animals to graze on. They raised animals and fowl; planted a full garden each year for vegetables and fruit; cut their own firewood and cooking fuel; and did a bit of seasonal hunting.

In short, if anyone had found a new way of life for themselves, a life that sprang from their inner needs, in harmony with nature, it seemed that Roger and Jane had.

Four years after the house was finished, we returned to this homestead, and to our great surprise there was a "for sale" sign on the property and renters occupying the house. We asked the occupants about the builder and his family and they told us that the family moved away over a year ago.

The homestead they left behind, however, told a story of a continual sense of keeping in harmony with their needs—building an addition to the core house, putting on porches, and creating storage space. As the renters told us, what had proved elusive to Roger and Jane was the ideal of self-sufficiency. Roger could not find suitable employment in the nearby area. As the times required, he had to look elsewhere for work. He was able to turn his experience into his source of livelihood—getting a job at a university as an instructor in log construction and building techniques. He was also building another log house not far from the university.

Rather than the previous, multi-layered, hand-ripped board walls, Roger decided to construct the addition's walls in the more traditional manner of full-round logs.

The huge addition dwarfed the original core. It provided the added bedroom and living area spaces they needed. This extension was built onto the front of the existing structure, utilizing the previously inaccessible front door as the entranceway into the living room (refer to 11-10, page 218).

Four years later, Roger and Jane had built this two-story gambrel roofed, full-round log addition. The original core house is just visible in the right third of the photo, behind the new structure.

The addition was leveled on the slope above foundation posts. This structure protrudes high off the ground in the front, providing a large storage space under the main floor. An enclosed porch extends out beyond the north and east walls of the living area, protecting them and providing a sheltered outside space.

The interior of the addition is two full stories. The lower floor is one large living area from front door to rear hallway. A freestanding, stone fireplace heats this space and the children's bedrooms above. Near the hall entrance there is an enclosed stairway up to these bedrooms.

In Accord with the Time

Self-reliance can mean many things, and having the inner sense to know when changes must be made is certainly one of them. This homestead still stands as a result of Roger and Jane's labors. Bob Inwood revisited the site in the summer of 1999, and took the detail shots on this page. Perhaps Roger said it best when we last talked with him, "As anyone knows who has made something more or less original and usable with his or her own hands, such results give an incomparable inner satisfaction."

Above are details of the core structure diagonal supports and the well roof. Below are details of a door and a section of the proch on the addition, photographed in the summer of 1999.

CHAPTER 12

LOG POST & BEAM, WITH CURVED-POLE ROOF

A Sheltering Arch

Harry and June had come to live on an old homestead and build their own house, as described in Chapter 5. With their primary shelter, the house, finished, it was time to think about the other buildings they needed. The goats and horses were comfortable in the small old barn, but there was not enough space in there to store all the hay that was needed for them. It looked like it was going to be a fine year for crops and they knew they would probably get a few tons of hay from their fields. Since the weather in the area is so unpredictable, Harry knew he could not just leave the freshly cut hay out in the fields to be sun-dried; more likely than not an unannounced rain would come down and ruin it all. What he really needed, as he tells it, was to have a storage place ready by harvest time:

I considered different building designs. I wanted a large, open structure that would be both a storage and a drying area. It had to have an enclosed loft large enough to store at least 10 tons of baled and loose hay. There were also a lot of tools and equipment around that had no definite places of their own. We needed a place to house all the animals from the weather.

A Barn

I decided to build a huge, barn-type shelter for everything that needed a home. A 20' × 48' area was prepared and ten concrete piers were poured. We spaced these 12' apart on the 48' sides. Steel pins were then stuck into them to accommodate the hewn 12"- to 14"-diameter

12-1 *Post-and-beam barn structure.*

sill logs which were to stretch along those sides. These long sills are the bottom beams for the 11' upright posts which frame the first story. The posts were spaced 12' on-center above each pier and were notched into the beams. A 48' top plate beam was then notched above the posts and the posts were braced in place (12-1).

Wherever beam logs came together over an upright post, that post was shortened and a 24"-long log piece was notched in above it to reinforce the joint. The log piece was then spiked to the post and each of the beam sections (12-2).

12-2 *Log piece notched below adjoining beams.*

A Shed-Roofed Addition

This area immediately seemed too small, so we widened it by building onto the north side a 12' shed-roofed addition, making the barn's width 32'. The new 8' outer wall was framed in the same manner as the other two long sides. Its rafters were spaced at 24" centers, spanning between the beams on either side. We spaced nailing strips across the rafters, and a finished roof of cedar shakes was put on. Thin poles were later run horizontally across the 8' upright posts and scrap 1× sheathing was nailed to them to enclose the shed area. This sheathing shielded the area from direct moisture but did not close it off from the crosscurrents of wind which allow for good air circulation. This section became ideal for hay drying (12-3).

Hay-Drying Racks

To make the racks for the hay, I simply ran smaller 7' rails along each 11' post of the inner wall and attached them at top and bottom with 4" spacer blocks. Long spikes, spaced 18" apart, were driven through the rails and into the posts. These spikes act as rungs for the horizontal poles which cross the posts (12-3, inset). I then extended five tiers of poles between the 8' and 11' side walls.

SPACER BLOCKS

HAY-DRYING
RACKS

SPIKE
RUNGS

12-3 *Shed-roofed addition.*

Their ends rested on the crossing horizontal poles of each wall (12-3).

During harvest we spread out the freshly cut hay on each tier. When one tier was filled, the poles for the next were put in place. Fresh green hay was then spread out on that tier, and so on until about an acre of hay was drying over the five racks. After the hay was dry enough to store, the poles were taken down and this 12' × 48' section was turned into a winter storehouse for supplies and equipment.

The Hayloft

We then constructed the loft area for storing the hay. A 48' log beam was placed over the ends of the shed roof rafters at the 11' inside wall. The 8" hewn-log ceiling joists spanned from above that beam to 2' beyond the top beam on the south wall. These 22' joists were spaced at 24" centers above the side walls. The 2' that went beyond the beam allowed for a roof eave which would prevent rain and snow from getting into the open area below. The north side was protected by the shed roof that would be overlapped by the north loft roof eave.

I wanted the loft roof to have steep sides for better drainage. The better the drainage, the less chance of rot, because the moisture would not collect on the roof's surface. If the roof has a steep pitch, snow slides off before the load becomes too heavy. I also wanted the roof to be wide enough to accommodate the several tons of hay our animals would need throughout the long winter months. The common gambrel barn roof interested me, but I wanted a different design, one that would give even more storage space over the 20' × 48' floor area. I remembered the old, navy Quonset huts I had been so familiar with. Surely there must be a way to utilize that design when working with logs.

A Curved-Pole Roof

I constructed a framework of log roof braces over the rough, 1× loft floor. The first section was 48' long, 14' wide, and 8' in height. The sides were supported by uprights spaced every 12', directly over crossing joists. Also at every 12" a crossbeam was notched above the uprights to keep the long framework from spreading.

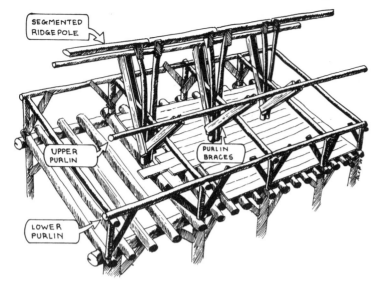

12-4 *Curved-roof brace support system.*

12-5 *Basic structure of the curved-pole roof.*

12-6 *Interior view of the roof construction.*

When I was done with this framework, I came down from the loft and examined the framed area. I decided to have the peak of the roof another 4' above it, making the whole barn 24' tall. In order to do this, I raised a sectioned ridgepole that extended 3' past either end of the frame (12-4). It was braced at 12' intervals by double 12' uprights which spanned between the joists and the peak. These uprights straddled the cross-beams at their centers. They were doubled because each was bracing one end of the four poles that made up the length of the ridgepole.

The 48'-long upper purlins were then put in place halfway between the ridgepole and the lower purlins (the lower purlins are the 48' sides of the rectangular roof framework). These purlins also followed the proposed arch of the roof. They were braced by short, diagonal boards which straddled each of the cross-beams (12-4, 12-5, and 12-6).

Bending the Poles for the Roof

With the roof-support frame finished, it was time to put my experiment into action. I found a thick stand of young fir trees and thinned out over 50 saplings which were about 3" in diameter at the butts. We cut 16' sections with no large knots from them and these were immediately peeled. The saplings were then put into water to soak for a few days. While they were soaking, I augered a 2" hole near each end of every other log joist.

When the saplings had soaked until they were flexible enough to bend easily, I took one of them out of the water, trimmed its bottom end to 2", and stuck it into an augered hole. That end was spiked into the joist (12-7).

The sapling was then bent over the roof frame, and a piece of rope was tied to its top end. That end was pulled down above the ridgepole and the rope was tied to the joist end on the opposite side (12-8). The sapling was positioned and nailed to the purlins and the ridgepole.

I repeated this process until the rafters were spaced 48", or two joists, apart on either side of the frame. A pair of longer rafters at either end of the roof were attached to the top wall-beams and were bent forward over the ridgepole to brace the overhangs.

12-7 *Anchoring the bottom end of the roof rafter saplings.*

Double-Rafter Poles

For added strength, I decided to put another set of rafters over the ones already in place. To ensure a snug fit, the undersides of the top

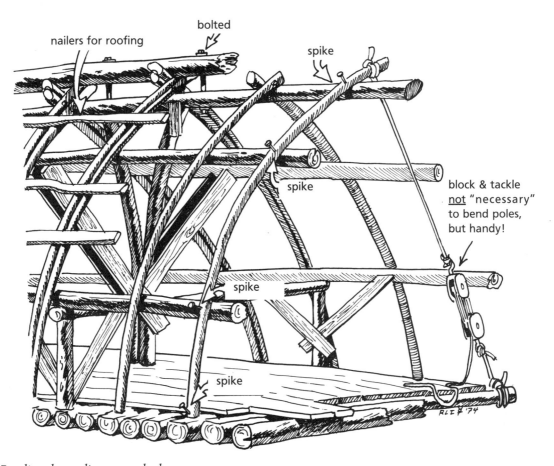

12-8 *Bending the saplings over the brace.*

rafters were grooved out about 1" deep so they cupped over the bottom ones (12-9). The grooves were made by a chain saw with guides on either side of its roller-tip bar (12-9A and 12-9B). The guides were attached to each side of the bar by a bolt which came through the roller-tip opening (12-9C). The diagonal guides straddled either side of the pole, allowing the chain saw to cut a 1" groove in it.

To make the groove, I dogged a pole across two logs, stood over it, and cut along its length at a slight right angle. I then made a left-angle cut deep enough to meet the first cut and removed the piece in between. These top rafters were nailed above the bottom ones and the rafter ends were cut a few inches after they met the ridgepole, allowing each set to cross at the peak.

The Second Ridgepole

After the rafters were all in place, a second ridgepole was put in over the crossing ends to sandwich them in. It was spiked to the rafter ends and bolted to the bottom ridgepole with ⅜" bolts at 6' intervals. The ridgepole sections that stuck out beyond the end rafters were reinforced by a third piece that was wedged in between the top and bottom ridgepole ends. Before that third piece was bolted in, two holes were drilled into either end of the bottom pole to accommodate two U-bolts from which large pulleys would hang.

Cedar Shakes for the Roof

Next came the nailers for the cedar-shake finish roof. These nailers are 3"- to 4"-diameter poles which I hewed on two sides with a sharp broadax, making flat surfaces for the shakes to be nailed to. I prefer to do my hewing in the winter. For some reason all types of wood split faster and cleaner when they are frozen.

I used the snakiest, most crooked poles for the nailers because it is not necessary for shakes to be nailed to a straight strip, as long as they have a nice flat surface. These nailers were spaced anywhere from 18" to 20" apart for the 26" cedar shakes. Because of the steep roof pitch, it was not necessary to put the nailers any closer, since the shakes do not have to overlap as much as they would on a roof with a less steep pitch. This spacing also saves on shakes.

The homemade shakes were attached to the nailers. The gable ends of the loft area were then sheathed in with 8'-long slabs which were being discarded by a local railroad tie mill . I framed double doors on the front gable, through which hay bales could be brought in. On each gable, a ventilation opening was left directly under the roof overhang to prevent the stored hay from mildewing.

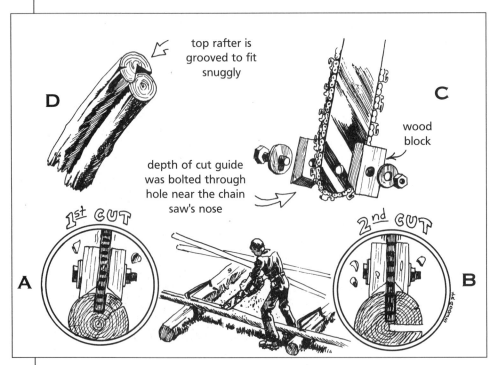

12-9 Double-rafter poles.

Site Visit Update

Just like the house, Harry and June's barn was built slowly and carefully. We visited the site regularly as described in the "Site Visit Udate" for Chapter 5, after their house was completed (see pages 118 and 119).

They took great pride in their work. When we visited the year after the house was finished the barn was still being built. The cost of constructing these structures was very low since they made most everything themselves. They couldn't set any price on doing things for themselves, but Harry said that every time they cleaned out a notch or put a log into place, it brought them pleasure.

Adjacent to the barn, Harry was constructing another log shelter. The walls were over 10' high on the downhill side and were just as tightly notched together as the logs in his house. At first we thought he was building a guest house or a house for one of his children; but why so close to the barn? Then we found out that this massive and elaborate structure was being built for his chickens, lucky birds.

Whenever we visited—after 8, 12 or almost 30 years—the homestead, including the barn and barnyard, was impeccable. Harry and June said that their buildings have to be beautiful as well as practical; the gardens and fields have to be neat and straight; the landscape has to be trimmed and well cared for. As Harry said, "Even our fences have to accentuate the natural beauty that surrounds us. Our homestead is a reflection of our own personalities; we respect it as we respect ourselves."

The barn, with chickens, visited in the summer of 1999.

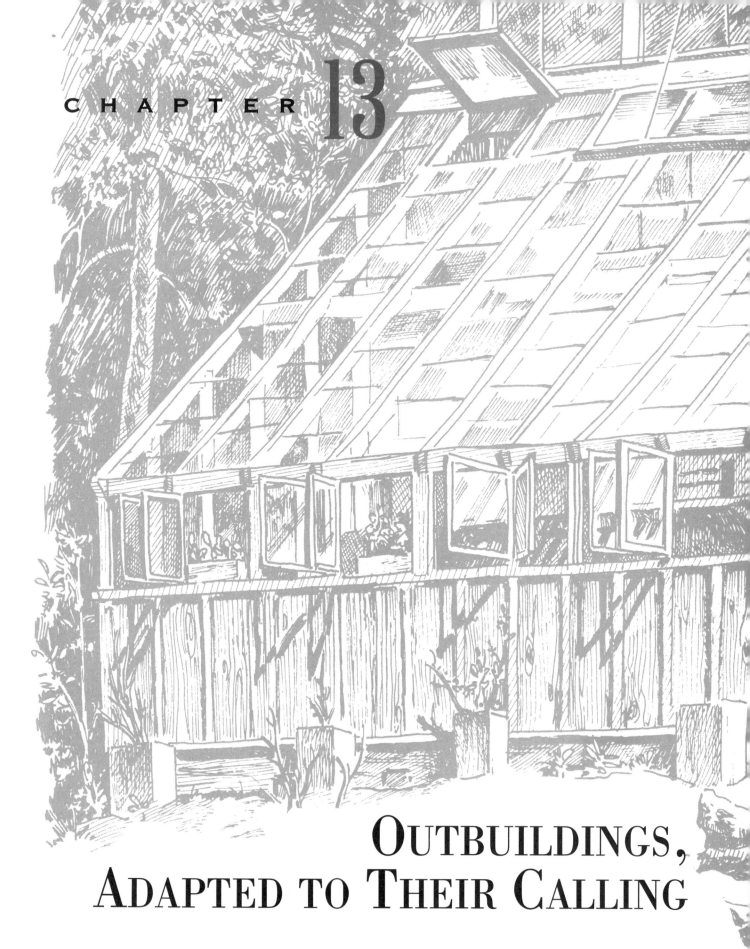

CHAPTER 13

OUTBUILDINGS, ADAPTED TO THEIR CALLING

Wood-Frame Greenhouse

After Christian Bruyère and his wife, Margee, built their barn, they built the main house for themselves, their son, and their extended family. As the seasons came around to spring, their next major concern was to prepare an area for a garden that would feed them. As Chris tells the story, this was not an easy task:

The ground we were working with started out at about 50 percent gravel and 50 percent light sand. There was barely enough soil to stain your hands when wetted down. We had a shredder so we went to all the neighbor's yards and collected their leaves and shredded them. The leaf shreddings decomposed well. Soon we didn't even notice them in our garden, except for the presence of a new fiber in the ground. We also searched and scrounged the nearby hillsides for topsoil, and within a few months we developed the garden plot into workable soil.

The first year on our land was one of unpredictable weather. It was rainy and cold all spring, and even in summer there wasn't enough direct sunlight to sustain a lot of our crops—especially since the soil needed so much attention. Due to this factor, and instead of dealing with the direct weather, we wanted to expend our energies into developing a controlled-environment greenhouse. Here we could bring up most of our vegetables in flats and then transplant them after they had a proper start. This way we'd also have more than a month's jump on the other people in the area. It is risky to start most crops in the ground until June in our area because of late spring frosts which annually take their toll. We just start them in the greenhouse, thin them out right in the flats, and then transplant them into the ground. There wasn't anything that just didn't take off right away in the greenhouse. This was very encouraging. If it grew half as well outside, we'd have excellent crops.

We didn't lose any of the greenhouse-started plants. It was not like having hit and miss rows of plants; we controlled exactly what we wanted. We put in 137 tomato plants that year without losing one plant. And that was true of all our transplants—they went right on growing rapidly. It was definitely worth the effort in putting our energies into this type of controlled environment. I wouldn't do it any other way except maybe add a greenhouse to an already existing dwelling house so that the greenhouse could get the heat exposure from the dwelling all year round.

The Greenhouse Site

The site for the greenhouse was an electrical power line clearing with good southerly exposure. It gets the morning sun as well as an uninterrupted exposure throughout the day. We leveled off the top of the clearing and dug corner holes outlining the 12' × 16' area (13-1). Other holes were dug at 4' intervals along these periphery lines; we creosoted cedar posts which were then put into the ground in them. We chose a size that would allow us to

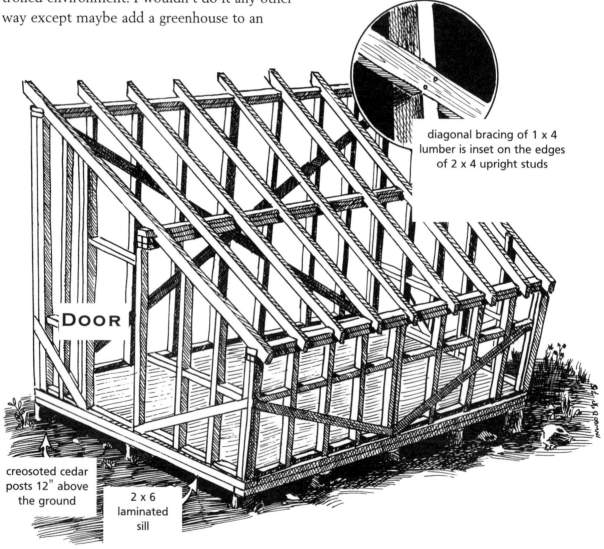

diagonal bracing of 1 x 4 lumber is inset on the edges of 2 x 4 upright studs

DOOR

creosoted cedar posts 12" above the ground

2 x 6 laminated sill

13-1 Wood framing for the greenhouse.

13-2 Conventional stud wall with cedar sheathing inside and out.

Labels in figure:
- rough-cut cedar sheathing with 1 x 4 batten boards
- 18-pound building paper
- 18-pound building paper
- 4-mil plastic vapor barrier
- interior cedar sheathing
- 3½" fiberglass insulation

keep fragile plants, such as peppers and cucumbers, in it throughout the entire growing season. Fortunately I had a transit to make sure these posts were really level. Cedar sills were then cut and placed above these posts. They were just above ground level. I figured that creosoted cedar on porous soil such as this was good for at least 40 years, so why worry about a concrete foundation for such a lightweight structure.

Framing the Walls

A conventional stud wall was built over the sill in front and on the sides up to about 30", to the bench height (13-2), leaving a space on the west wall for a door. We're short people, so we prefer that height. The windows and glass began at this level. Cedar was also used for the sheathing inside and out, with 3" batons between each of the vertical boards. 3½" of fiberglass insulation was put in between the studs with an 18-pound building paper backing on either side. A 4-mil plastic vapor barrier was then stapled in over the building paper.

The high 12' back wall was constructed in the same manner. This tall back wall provided us with the necessary pitch and gave us total exposure to the whole greenhouse by making it possible for us to use a shed-roof design rather than a hip design. If the roof went up and back down as it would in the hip-roof design, the storage space on the walls would have been cut down considerably. You need a lot of storage space in a greenhouse for fertilizer and soil preparations such as bone meal and for peat moss. Also, the high north wall provides protection against the cold northern winds and weather.

Even with the sheltering north wall and the shed-roof design, there has been no problem with plants leaning toward the south, not even in early spring when the arch of the sun is farthest away. The deflection seems to be pretty even in the greenhouse throughout the growing season. If this problem should arise, it can be easily remedied merely by turning the flats around. This will force the plants to grow back the other way.

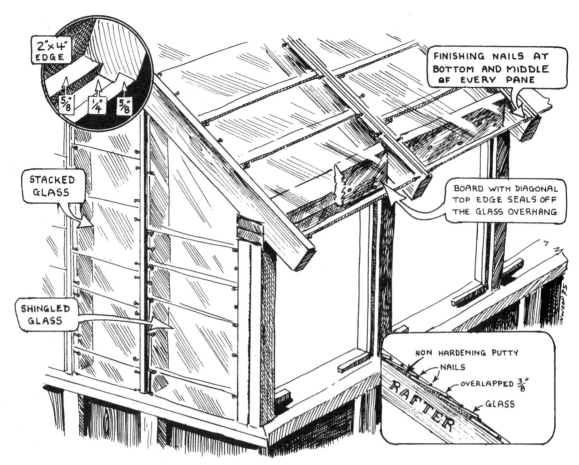

13-3 Details of glass installation.

Much Depends on the Glass

The spaces between the side-wall studding depended upon the width of the glass used. We scrounged around and finally found a man who wanted to sell all his used glass pieces. We made him an offer for the whole lot and brought the assortment home. We found the widest width we could use, saving the most glass. We cut all the glass to that 21-inch width. The height didn't matter. It could be as long as possible. Our pieces ran between 2" and 20". The longest pieces were saved for the roof because of the greater spans.

We were dealing with double pane and thicker glass, which was really a hassle to cut, but before long we became quite proficient in glass cutting. Some of the glass had extreme tensile strength and didn't cut properly. To cut such miscast glass at absolute right angles was nearly impossible because it has a tendency to break away on your line, undercutting itself. If

you stack glass with this kind of break, it leaves a small opening between panes, causing weather to come through. Where I made good cuts I just stacked the glass vertically, edge to edge between the grooved studs, then nailed and puttied them in. Where the cuts weren't so straight we put a ¼" to ⅜" lap on it just like a shingle. We put in one finishing nail on each side underneath the glass being lapped, one partway up to hold it in place, and one just below the top of that piece to accommodate the above lapped piece and set in the putty. There was no leakage on the side walls and only a small amount of leakage from the over-head glass where the putty has cracked.

The side wall 2 × 4 studs were rabbeted on the outside end to give them a ¼" tongue, just enough to keep the pieces of glass from touching each other on either side of the tongue to accommodate the glass. These laps were set in deep enough to allow a little space between the outer edge of the studs and the glass so nails could be driven in and putty could be spread (13-3). A space narrower than 21" was left near the end of each side wall to take the smaller pieces which we had left over. This prevented wasting our resources and allowed us to not have to compensate for the exact size of panes plus the distances between each panel in figuring out the overall length of the side walls.

A Greenhouse Dutch Door

A Dutch door is an excellent door design in a structure such as a greenhouse where you want to allow the maximum ventilation on hot days, but without letting animals in. The Dutch door keeps the dogs out, but since there is no screen protection, the cats still come in, walking across the flats, seeing how all the little plants collapse underneath their feet. They also have a tendency to use the flats as kitty boxes, scraping the soil, disrupting the seedlings, and doing their thing in it.

For a necessary artistic touch, I made a stained-glass window for the upper section of the Dutch door. The door provided the greenhouse with a softness that it wouldn't otherwise have had with its rigid glass and wood-framed composition. This was also an excellent way of using some of the scrap pieces of glass we had left over. It further tested my skill in cutting glass. But the came around the pieces was too small—a mistake. Consequently, I had to back it with unsightly welding rod for additional support. This door was hung on hinges to the double 2" × 4" stud which bordered it (13-4 and 13-5).

Making the Window Frames

For the front windows I constructed light-weight frames, 21"-square, out of 1½"-wide by 1" material (13-6). I wanted to keep them narrow so they wouldn't throw off too large a shadow. In doing so I sacrificed strength for transparency—which was a mistake. The

13-4 *Hanging the Dutch door on the greenhouse.*

13-5 *The stained-glass upper section of the door.*

frames should have been stronger to hold the heavy glass. They were grooved on the inside all around to snugly accommodate the glass pieces and were tenon-jointed at the ends. Handles were put on the lower sill pieces for

13-6 *South windows allow ventilation so the greenhouse doesn't get too hot.*

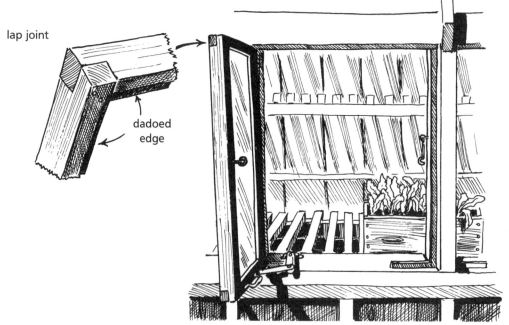

lap joint

dadoed edge

13-7 Window frame detail.

ease in closing and eye screws were fastened for locking. I also installed locks at the bottom to hold the windows open so they wouldn't bang shut during a gust of wind. Thin-cull cedar strips were then attached as stops, leaving the area between the ends of the sill open to conserve on materials (13-7).

There are eight windows along the front wall going from one end to the other. I used a lot of windows here for ventilation because I didn't want to have to whitewash all the glass in the greenhouse to prevent the plants from burning on hot, dry days. As long as the soil in the flats is kept moist, the ventilation prevents the plants from burning. We watered first thing in the morning and an hour before the sun set each day, saturating the plants until a puddle formed. Then as soon as the temperature dropped, we closed off the greenhouse so it would retain the heat.

Placing Rafters

Directly above the window spaces we put in a wall plate of double 2 × 6s laminated together (refer to 13-6). The lower rafter ends were cut flat at the bottom to meet this plate. These rafters extend from the front wall to the back wall, spanning 14' with a double-laminated 2×

beam supporting them in the center of their span. This beam is held in place above the center studs at the opposing side walls. Here too, I feel the construction should have been more solid. This supporting roof beam should have been heavier and should also be braced in the center by an upright of some type. But we were running out of material and wanted to finish the greenhouse for use.

Even the way it is now, the 33-degree pitched roof held a load of almost 3½' of snow at one point last winter without sagging.

The tops of the rafters where the glass panes seat into them were rabbeted in the same manner as were the upright studs. All the roof panes were shingled above the rafters, starting at the bottom of each panel and working upwards with each just like you'd shingle a roof. They were held in place at the bottom with finishing nails and putty, the same as were the shingled wall panes.

Square glazing nails would be ideal for this job but we could work only with what we had. In fact, the roof leaked because the putty I used soon got brittle and cracked. I couldn't find any nonsetting putty, but I advise the use of this kind of putty for sealing in this type of roof. It remains soft and pliable

13-8 The three top vents allowed hot air to escape.

instead of hardening and cracking with age. I would have used cedar for the rafters because it is by far the most weather resistant of the local woods, but clear cedar in 14' lengths would have cost a fortune. I used fir instead, and coated it with urethane to help preserve it. Hopefully, this coating will allow it to last about as long as the cedar; but the urethane has to be replenished at least every other year for full protection.

Venting

Next, we made the three top vents which allowed the hot, rising air to escape as the cool, low air entered to circulate (13-8). These vents were framed in the same manner as were the front windows and were fastened to the top wall plate with hinges. The glass used was a heavy rippled, opaque shower-door glass. I used this heavy glass mainly to test my skill at cutting. Four long upright braces were then constructed above the high back wall and a 2 × 4 crosspiece was nailed in above to connect them. Three pulleys were suspended from this top piece for the cords that are connected to the bottom of the vent on one end to one of a series of hooks on the other. The hooks were spaced at different levels; the highest closed the vent; the one below it allowed the vent to be held halfway open; and the bottom one allowed the vent to be opened all the way. This lower hook was another mistake, because it held the vent open too far. Consequently, a wind came by and broke one of the panes.

The Interior Space

The interior of the greenhouse was also designed to fit our needs and was constructed out of the materials we had left, mostly cull cedar. The benches are 30" high along the front and side walls. They were very simple and economical to build, utilizing a lot of scrap. The inner ledges were nailed to the wall at the 30" height. Several 2 × 4 upright braces were then set up 24" from the walls to accommodate a front crosspiece at the same 30"-level. Then 1" slats were then ripped with a power saw and nailed at 1½" intervals across the two ledges. These racks held the starter flats which were filled with prepared soil. The flats were also made from the scrap cedar. They were 14" × 21" and 4" in height. Their bottoms were slatted with from ⅛" to ¼" space between each slat to allow them to drain down onto the dirt floor.

The Greenhouse Hot Box

The hot box enables us to start plants as early as February or March. We keep the primary flats there until the plants sprout their true leaves, then they can go out to the racks. The hot box is 2' wide by 4' long and is 34" deep. It is powered by a series of four 60-watt bulbs which are located at the bottom. This is a pretty minimal source of heat so the box was built as tightly as possible. It has two doors: a drop door on bottom hinges to feed the lower slatted shelf and a lifting lid on top, with framed glass to allow sunlight into the top shelf.

Even when the temperature outside was just below freezing the hot box maintained a good 70 degrees F (21 degrees C). It got us over that early-spring fluctuation of cold spells that keep snapping in, threatening to wipe out all the flats even though the plants have pretty well started. Now, in the warmer months, we just use it at nights for the beginning flats. We put the flats in, then turn it on. It holds the temperature at about 75 to 80 degrees F (24 to 27 degreees C). It's almost a better environment than is the whole greenhouse. In the greenhouse you have to keep watching the temperature, while the hot box always maintains a pretty constant one.

The hot box will take 8 flats, but we get a better circulation of the heat when we use just 7—3 in the bottom and 4 on top. The top ones are double tiered, two above the other two. As long as the plants are young, the top flats won't interfere with the growth of the lower tier.

To get rid of snow on the greenhouse we just turn on the hot box to start it melting.

lap joint

glass

layer of rough-cut cedar boards

four 60-watt light bulbs

Growing in the Greenhouse

The plants are started in the flats on the front- and side-wall racks (13-9) until they are developed enough to take care of themselves, then they are shifted to the back shelves and more seeds are started, taking their place on the rack. The back shelves are also slatted for drainage and economy of materials. They are braced against the back wall with diagonal supports which extend from that wall to the front crossing piece. The higher shelves are for the more self-sustaining plants like the maturing cantaloupes and cucumbers. To water them we just bring a ladder and spray them with a fine mist spray from a hose attachment. The cucumbers are set in deep flats along the top of the back wall. They just drape over the shelves and vine down.

When we close the greenhouse off it retains moisture so well that we get humidity vapor on every pane. I don't think I need to introduce another source of humidity or else it might begin producing mold. I sometimes get some surface scale, mainly because the soil is rich with compost and bone meal. But a little scale can't really hurt.

For our needs, this greenhouse is proving to be perfect. Sure, I suppose we could have got-

seed flat construction

13-9 Starting plants in flats.

ten by with several outdoor hot frames and cold frames, but it's not that pleasant in the spring to be working outside, doing your bedding plants and what not. And in the middle of winter the greenhouse is a pleasant, peaceful space to just go into and relax. It's always warm enough in there even if it is below freezing outside.

Sunken Greenhouse

After a few years traveling around, working where work was available, one day we found a place we wanted to call home. It was a beautiful spot, secluded, at the end of a road, with an old house on it. We bought the land very reasonably and immediately began fixing up the place. We became compulsive homesteaders, building and planting and raising and hunting.

This last year we decided we needed a greenhouse so we could have some control over our crops. Depending on good weather may work in some milder area, but in our region we are constantly threatened with late frosts and long periodic stretches of foul weather.

Finding the Right Site

We figured that the best place to build a greenhouse would be in a clearing with plenty of southern exposure, preferably with some protection from the cold north. Another way we could economize on energy and hold in the heat was to build the greenhouse into the ground. So, we dug a two foot hole for the structure so that it would be protected by ground moisture and by its warmth. Even when the temperature above the ground level is -20 degrees F (minus 6 degrees C), it will remain only 40 degrees F (4 degrees C) below the frost level. Everything in the ground keeps warmer and less fuel is needed to protect the starting plants through the early spring. We would have gone even deeper but we encountered huge boulders (13-10). As an added precaution, to prevent periodic cold spells from destroying our early efforts, we also heated the greenhouse with an efficient wood-heating system (13-11).

Such a heater should be foolproof. It has to be able to give off continuous heat through the late winter and into the early spring danger period, when a momentary frost could wipe out all your preparation work. It should be located somewhere along the north wall, so that plants to the north, farthest from the sun, can get the most heat. Our heater bums dry cottonwood very efficiently. You put a stick in and it burns to the last ash, going 24 hours or more without reloading. I designed it using an old wood heater door, welded onto an old sawdust burner firebox. It has a 12" galvanized "smoke pipe" which is connected to the firebox, extending the length of the greenhouse. This smoke pipe acts as a heat-exchanger unit, radiating the heat throughout the greenhouse with the help of an aluminum reflective shield that reflects it into the room. This unit is on a slight incline pitch from the firebox to the east wall, 4" in 14", so the smoke can properly travel through it and out the stonework flue

13-10 *The gentle hillside site with lots of boulders.*

13-11 *The loading box for the heating system.*

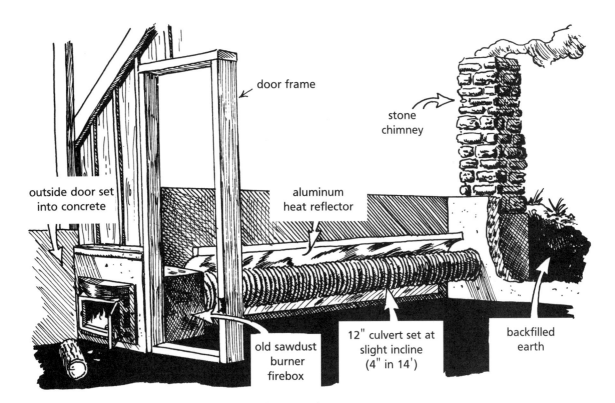

13-12 Details of the heating system for the sunken greenhouse.

chamber and stove pipe chimney located outside the east wall. This incline also allows the creosote to run back into the firebox instead of accumulating in the smoke pipe; but an even greater incline would have been better. The loading door is outside to prevent drastic temperature changes when refueling and to provide the oxygen from the outside instead of depleting the moisture content from the greenhouse (13-12).

Designing the Greenhouse

The outside dimensions of the greenhouse proper are 7' wide by 14'-4⅜" in length. The length was determined by the width of the glass panes, plus space between glass (tongue of rafters) plus ⅛" allowance for each pane (to be explained in detail later). It was important to me that the building be laid out so the glass would come out evenly—because the glass had been precut. This greenhouse has an outside porch area that extends to the west. The outer dimensions of the porch are 7' × 7', making it a 6½' × 6½' enclosure for protection from the weather when stoking the fire. It is also a shel-

ter for the firewood, keeping it dry throughout the year. This shelter was included in the design plans and was allowed for when we set up the forms for the concrete foundation. The actual construction did not begin until most of the designing had been completed. I even figured out the braces for interior benches and shelves so that iron pegs could be sunk into the setting concrete, instead of drilling holes into it later to accommodate them. All openings and interruptions in the walls had to be figured out exactly when building the forms, otherwise changes might have forced us into altering these spaces after the concrete was poured.

Pouring the Foundation

On a small job like this where the pouring of concrete was done by one person alone, the pour was very slow and did not require a solid form, especially since a lot of stones were used. You can save money by using all the stones the walls will take, providing you've put concrete between every stone to cement them together. The forms were made of 1" × 10" horizontal boards, braced by 2 × 4 uprights which were held at the proper width by spacers. They were wired together near the top and bottom to secure them in place. The wires of course were left in the concrete after the forms were removed. The south and west walls were poured first. Then the same form panels were used for the other walls, so as to conserve on materials. The whole job was more than I wanted to pour at one time, working by myself (13-13).

I began the concrete work by pouring a footing around the greenhouse. This footing was the height of the 1" × 10" which was used for the inside form. The outside form was a dirt bank, 12" away. A footing should be at least twice the width of the walls. My walls were to be 6" in width. The height of each wall depended on the slope of the land. The front, south wall needed to be 24", so a form was built to that height. This form extended from the east wall to 3' beyond the greenhouse proper to allow for a stepway at the center of the south porch wall. The west wall was the same height and the north porch wall was stepped up a few more inches, making it level with the ground. It had to be stepped up again to 48" at the beginning of the greenhouse to compensate for the sloping ground. It remained this height until after the northern half of the east wall. It was then stepped down to 24" to allow the southern light in. Here the form was built around the smoke pipe as the inner west wall form was built around the firebox, both already being in place. Two pilasters were added at equal distances of 7' along the back wall to protect it against eventual back pressure from the expanding ground in winter. These pilasters were 10" wide, diagonaling from the top of the north wall to 3' beyond it at the base. Each pilaster was reinforced with cross-welded metal rods for added support.

CONCRETE FOUNDATION

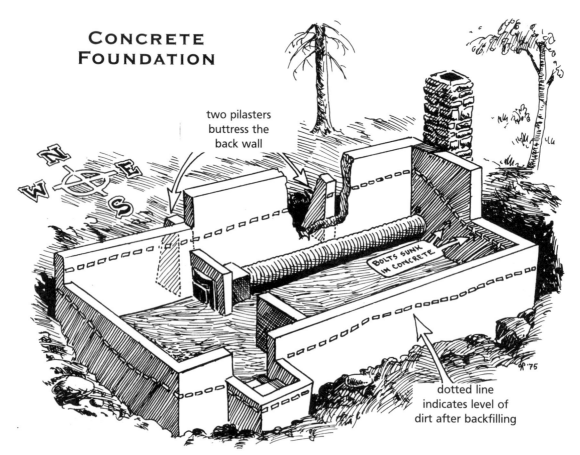

two pilasters buttress the back wall

BOLTS SUNK IN CONCRETE

dotted line indicates level of dirt after backfilling

13-13 *The foundation for the sunken greenhouse.*

Holes were then drilled into the forms to accommodate the bolts and pegs for the shelves and tray before the cement was poured.

I used a 1.5 mix of Portland cement and sand, putting in as many stones as possible. Cement was used instead of concrete blocks because cement allows moisture through the walls and concrete blocks have air spaces which cause the moisture to evaporate within them. Moisture is necessary to create humidity and should be allowed in whenever possible. I tamped the freshly poured concrete slightly with a stick to press it down and then hit the bracing studs really hard several times with a hammer to make it settle. You can see the air bubbles come up and the top of the concrete just level right off as you rap on the studs. After the concrete was tamped and leveled, bolts were sunk into the setting concrete to accommodate the 2 × 6 sills that would be resting above these walls (13-14).

Building the Framework

I used rough-cut material throughout the greenhouse to get the full 2" out of the board instead of losing ½" with the planing. The front sills overlap the concrete by about 2", shielding

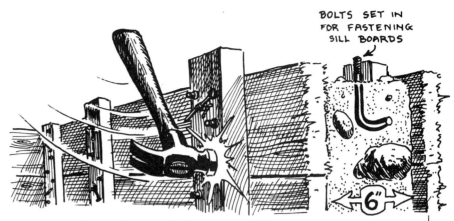

BOLTS SET IN FOR FASTENING SILL BOARDS

6"

13-14 *Pounding on form studs drives air bubbles out of wet concrete.*

it from direct runoff. These sills are tapered 12 percent on the outside edge to prevent runoff from entering into the greenhouse. The taper enables the runoff to drain down into the dirt outside (13-15).

Instead of working with the usual 16" to 24" center spacing with the wall studs and the roof rafters, I calculated the spaces so the distances between all the studs and rafters would be equal. I had to do this because all the glass I used was salvaged ¼" glass that was already precut at 12" widths. The glass was salvaged from a plate glass company. I got a great price on it, because most people can't use small ¼" pieces since sashes are not made for them. I bought all the plate they had from which 12"-width pieces could be cut—length did not matter. The company had to do all the cutting because ¼" is too difficult to attempt to cut

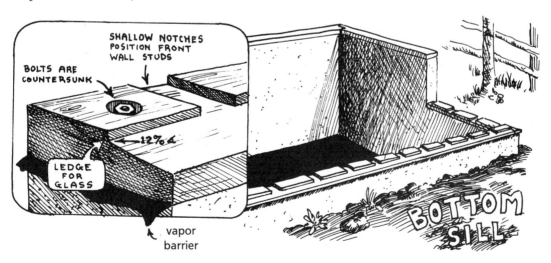

SHALLOW NOTCHES POSITION FRONT WALL STUDS

BOLTS ARE COUNTERSUNK

12%

LEDGE FOR GLASS

vapor barrier

BOTTOM SILL

13-15 *Details of the sills.*

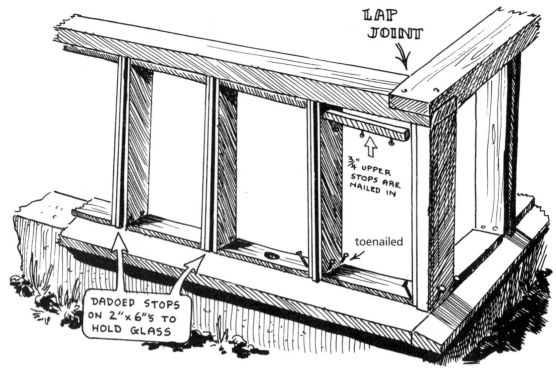

13-16 *Dadoed 2 x 6s designed to hold the glass for the low wall.*

without the proper facilities. I figured out 13 panels each with 12"-wide panes. This meant that each panel had to be 12" plus the space between the glass taken by the 1" stud or rafter tongue, plus ⅛-inch allowance for clearance on either side of the glass, plus 2" on each wall for the width of the corner 2 × 4—making the total wall length 14'-4⅜". Each of the studs and rafters was cut out of the rough-cut 2 × 6 stock, making them plenty strong at such narrow centers to hold any snow load, even if single-weight glass was used.

The pitch of a roof that is comprised of only rafters and glass should be quite steep, having at least a ½' or 3½' in each 7' pitch, so as to allow the accumulating snow to slip down off the panes.

Building the Short Wall

The studs between the short wall windows were cut slightly over 24" in length to accommodate the 24" windows. They were rabbeted on the outside end so all the protruding tongues between the window laps were centered 1" high and 1" across. The widths of the laps were each approximately ½" depending

on the exact width of the 2× studs. The studs were placed at slightly over 12" centers and were capped with a 2 × 6 wall plate which was lap notched into the crossing side-wall plates at either end. The glass was then set in and framed with the ¾ strips left over from rabbeting the studs (13-16 and 13-17).

13-17 *The glass has been set in and framed.*

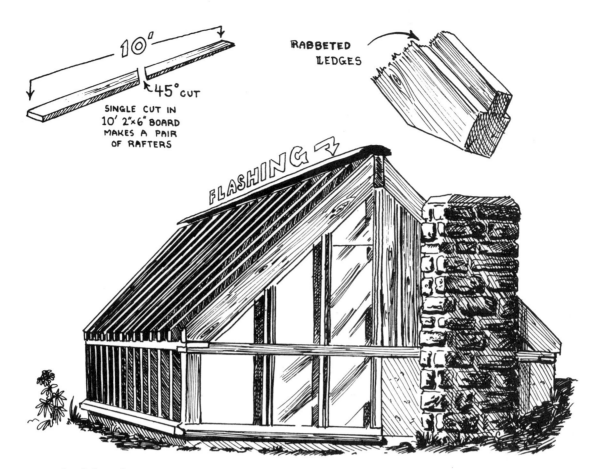

10'

45° CUT

SINGLE CUT IN
10' 2"x6" BOARD
MAKES A PAIR
OF RAFTERS

RABBETED
LEDGES

FLASHING

13-18 *Details of the rafters.*

Making the Rafters

Next came the rafters. I cut them in such a way that I got two out of every 10' board, using the same angled top cut for both sides. They provided the necessary pitch. These rafters were rabbeted in the same manner as were the front studs and were cut at angles top and bottom to allow them to seat as much as possible at the 2 × 8 ridge beam and the top wall plates. Since the rafter tongues between the panels were ¾" higher than the glass, planks could be put across them, resting on the wood instead of coming in contact with the glass and possibly shattering it (13-18).

Installing the Glass

The glass was now ready to be set in as shingles would be, starting from rafter bottom up. Before laying in these lapped panes, I first set a bed of putty down, using black caulking compound for this job, because it does not dry and crack as readily as does normal putty. Small metal S-clips were then nailed into the rafter bottoms on either side of the glass (13-19 and 13-20, on the following page). The length of the bottom pane was then measured and another set of clips were nailed in where the top of this pane meets the rafters. The bottom pane was then seated into the putty between the clips and the above piece was lapped about ½" to ¾" over it. At this overlapping a tapered wedge was set in above the rafter seats to compensate for the lap, allowing the glass to set snug into the putty. This wedge was feathered with a hand plane until it was the proper size.

After the bottom panes in each panel were seated in place, a measurement was taken of the space between the lower end of the glass and the top plate. This measurement designated the size of the bird stops, called this because they do stop birds from coming in.

13-19 *Rabbeted rafters allow for the installation of the glass.*

It is important to have a roof that allows the light to come straight overhead because plants will reach toward the light. If light comes in from overhead, plants will grow straight.

The north side of the east wall and the west wall, where the front door is located, were sheathed in on both sides with 1" cedar because these areas get very little direct sunlight. The front door has 6'-4" of vertical clearance, and was constructed of rough-cut vertical 1×s held together with a Z-brace. Thin baton strips were nailed on over the board junctions to seal them off. Above this door I installed a vent. The vent cover was hinged at the bottom with a strip of rubber, allowing it to open to the inside (13-21). Greenhouses should have good vents high up where the plants don't get the direct draft. High vents also help circulate the air and prevent hot air from collecting at the top, which eventually gets the greenhouse warm enough to burn the plants on warm days.

Just outside the vent area, above the doorway, a 2 × 8 crosspiece was nailed in place to accommodate the porch rafter bottoms. Uprights were set up above the outer west wall and a wall plate was nailed in across them for the outer rafter bottoms.

The opposing rafter tops then met at the ridge beam. Stringers for the shakes were

13-20 *Glass installed, showing the putty.*

13-21 *Details of the vent cover.*

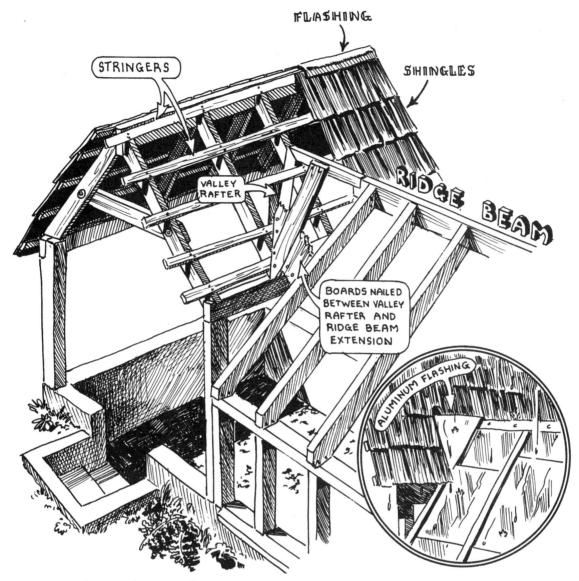

13-22 *Details of framing the two roofs.*

nailed in place and an inverted V-shaped plate was attached where this roof separated from the greenhouse roof. A small ridge cap was extended from the apex of that inverted V to the greenhouse roof peak. This area between the roofs was sheathed in and capped with aluminum flashing to prevent leakage into the porch area. Shakes were then split and put on the porch roof. Another piece of aluminum flashing was nailed in above the shakes at the peak, to seal the roof (13-22 and 13-23).

The wood heating system previously described works excellently in heating and producing humidity for maximum growth in the late winter and early spring. In fact, the

plants closest to it and farthest away from the southern sun grew much faster and healthier than those closest to the direct sun-

13-23 *Roof framing over porch from inside.*

13-24 *Lower back shelf and heat exchanger pipe.*

13-25 *Shelf with flats.*

light. This could be attributed to the hazy, overcast early spring weather during which time the direct sun seldom came out. For humidity, we simply set a kettle of water on the firebox and let it steam into the greenhouse. And if we wanted more moisture content in the air, we just hosed down the dirt floor and let it circulate throughout. Plants thrive on humidity and should always be supplied with plenty of it.

The bottom shelf along the back wall for the plant flats is supported over two pipe rails which were bracketed to the east wall and held up with a wire support at the west wall.

13-26 *Flats on the upper back shelf.*

The pipes were also braced in the center by upright pipes resting on concrete footings. The 2 × 4 blocks are spaced along these pipes and notched over them to hold the crossing shelf boards (13-24).

Another narrower shelf, also for the starter flats, was suspended above this lower shelf. It is held with blocks nailed to the side walls at either end and supported in the center by a wire bracket hanging from the above rafter (13-25).

The flats were made from the cedar shake scraps. They are 13" long, 4¾" wide, and 3" deep. The plants are

BOLT SUNK INTO CEMENT HOLDS MIDDLE BRACE PIPE

BRACKET BOLTED TO PINS SET IN CEMENT

CORRUGATED METAL FORMS TRAY BOTTOM. EDGES ARE BENT OVER AND NAILED TO SIDE BOARDS.

¾" PIPE

STRAP IRON

BRACKET WELDED TO SUPPORT PIPE

13-27 *The front tray.*

transferred to these flats shortly after they are started in the front tray, then they are transplanted into the garden. There are never more than two rows of plants in each flat—to avoid crowding (13-26).

The front tray is used for starting the plants, mixing the soil and growing plants that will not be transplanted into the garden until well after the last threat of frost. This tray extends from one end of the south wall to the other (13-27), held on by brackets attached to peg bolts. It is supported at the center by a crossing pipe rail which is encircling a peg bolt at the south wall end and is held up on an upright welded to it on the inside end. The tray bottom is of corregated galvanized roofing which lines the boards on either side and is turned up 1" at the ends to hold water. I had to split the ends every few inches on the ribs to make the bend.

Squash was by far the fastest growing greenhouse crop (13-28). It grew so huge even early in the spring that we had to take out a few panes and add a temorary plastic shelter to contain it well before it was ready to transplant.

All and all we are extremely pleased with the greenhouse and feel that our efforts were well justified. Even with the slightest fire from

13-28 Squash was very successful.

the wood heating system we can keep the tomato plants going until December 1, getting several quarts of ripe tomatoes. We even have enough to give to neighbors. Outside, most years, the frost kills the tomatoes before the first ones get a chance to really ripen.

Cedar Log Root Cellar

(by Kathryn Woodward)

Winter has become our season of plans. As a city child I had never bothered classifying the seasons except as they related to the school year or to the clothes I could con out of my mother, and later to how much I was cooped up with my children. In the country they are definitive. It was our second winter and we were planning the work for the following building season—the seven months when there is no snow, usually referred to as summer. Our land had been bush when we arrived, two couples and two children. We had spent the first hectic summer jointly building our water system, two cabins, an outhouse, a chicken house, a tool shed, a makeshift wood shed, clearing land for a garden, pasture, and orchard (13-29) and keeping our co-operative running smoothly. By fall, completely exhausted, we gratefully returned to our respective cabins. The first winter was therefore one of minimal plans, mostly for the expansion of what already existed. Our partners were designing themselves a new house to be built in slow stages and we were contemplating a wood and storage shed.

By the second winter James' and my most fundamental needs had been met and it was time to evaluate the accomplishments and weigh them against the dreams. We had had a basic premise when we made the move from city to country: to learn the skills for providing the essentials of human needs with our own hands and minds. The winter nights of talking accumulated as we debated the direction of our future energies, how much of ourselves we wanted to devote to the "place" and where did those nonessentials that have become indispensable fit into our new lifestyle. We were learning that neither of us wanted to live as at Walden Pond, that we both wished to find a satisfactory way to combine the best of urban and rural worlds. We discussed how a homestead grows in stages, each stage being a unit unto itself, dependant for efficiency on total completion of that phase. Keeping a cow creates the need for pasture, a hayfield, fencing, a barn (13-30). Truck gardening might involve further clearing, a tractor, sources of fertilizer, good transporta-

13-29 *Land was cleared for a garden and orchard.*

tion. We were on the last lap of stage one: shelter, water, garden, and winter fuel.

Did anything remain before we chose to tackle another stage? If we were going to the trouble of growing our own food and buying or trading for what we could not produce, were we obligated to provide these fruits of labor with adequate storage? We answered yes. Other people's basements and decrepit root cellars had proven wasteful. Storing jars in the house meant risking total loss by freezing if we happened to spend just a few nights away from home during a cold spell. The freezer, though a miraculous invention, is not useful for all foods and depends upon the benevolence of the power company. And so grew our plans for a root cellar as the building focus for the third summer.

13-30 *Keeping cows creates the need for pasture.*

Finding a Site for the Root Cellar

The placement of the root cellar was a foregone conclusion. We had always assumed that one would be built sometime. So during the first summer when we hired a backhoe for the water-line trench we had it scoop out a hole into the mountainside. We had little choice about the exact location of the hole. The flat portion of our narrow acreage butts up to the mountain slope and we merely chose a spot that was close to the two cabins, where the hillside is steepest and where there is no spring runoff. The snugger the building fits into the mountainside, the less work there is pushing dirt up against the walls for maximum insulation. Proximity to the house is a consideration which can be overlooked only in the summer when snow is a mere memory.

Another consideration is shade and sun. Our main concern is keeping the food from freezing in the winter, since we do not store much

during the two to three hot months. Therefore, we picked a site that would be shaded in summer by deciduous trees and shrubs whose leaves drop off, exposing the root cellar to whatever bit of sun manages to fight through the snow clouds.

The backhoe dug out a hole whose size ultimately proved to be a lucky guess, but it would have been far better to approach construction in the logical order—that is, plan the size of the root cellar first, then get a hole dug to meet the specifications. The hole should be about three feet larger than the outside dimensions of the building so that there is room to work, but should not be made any larger than needed. That will just add to the time or money to have the building backfilled.

Whatever books and pamphlets on food storage we could find were limited to either basement root cellars or outdoor ones, constructed of concrete. We were definitely committed to an outside root cellar. Two families would be using the structure and we felt that it would be better located on neutral ground rather than have one family disturb the other to get its food. We also considered that since fire is always a risk when heating with wood, it was advantageous not to have everything under one roof. And of course we had the hole.

13-31 The root cellar was designed to harmonize with its setting.

Choosing the building material for the root cellar emphasized once again the lesson that country people usually know what resource is most suited for their area. We were all set to build with concrete even though many of the book diagrams were of root cellars so elaborate they resembled bomb shelters and even though neither of us thought concrete a particularly attractive medium. But we had decided to forego aesthetics in favor of practicality—if the books said concrete, then it was concrete. Luckily, Jim found himself talking about root cellars to a longtime resident who warned that concrete was, in his opinion, the worst of all alternatives for this climate where there is so much rain and snow. Concrete retains moisture, doesn't breathe well, and therefore presents problems of ventilation. Without proper ventilation mildew develops and food spoils. Seepage of water into the root cellar will also ruin the food there. Our friend suggested three alternative building materials: rock (being more porous than concrete), frame construction packed well with insulation, or log construction. The rock medium was intriguing but is time-consuming and we have a fairly short building season. Therefore it was frame or logs.

Up until then all of our buildings had been built with dimension lumber utilizing some poles. We have few large trees on our land due to past logging and to a forest fire; with several mills in this area lumber is relatively cheap. And we had always been building against time. So while we were fast becoming proficient in frame construction we were totally ignorant of log building. But during our first summer we had picked up a bunch of cedar logs for a sauna that wasn't getting built. The length of the logs, strangely enough, exactly fitted the hole. They were just lying around, soon to decay. We said, "Why not? Let's try it." And our decision was made.

Once we decided to use logs we found the whole building taking on an almost spiritual tone. Providing a space for our own food with materials from the surrounding countryside and designing the whole building to harmonize with its setting became the principal expression of our joy to be living here (13-31).

We were now ready to get down to the business of constructing. To fit the size of the hole in the mountain and to accommodate the logs already cut we decided on a two-chamber root cellar whose outside dimensions were 10' × 14'. The inner chamber would be 8' × 9' and be separated from the outside room by an insulated frame wall. Using a frame wall eliminated the difficulty of interlocking logs and provided better insulation than the curved surfaces of logs. Since this wall must insulate independent of backfill dirt, no skimping should occur.

The height of the root cellar, 6'-2", was determined by the height of the tallest member of our family and by the number of logs we were able to get. It is best to keep the building as

13-32 Western red cedar.

small as the need warrants. Excess space increases building time, but more importantly, proper temperature control is difficult to maintain in a larger structure. The two-room construction is essential because it allows the outside door to be closed before opening the door to the main chamber, thereby keeping the exchange of air and temperature at a minimum. The outside chamber provides an excellent place to hang meat—and to store winter apples until the coldest weather.

For building logs we used Western red cedar (13-32), some of which were picked up at a road construction site; the rest came from an abandoned logging operation. Western red cedar is one of the most impervious woods to

13-33 *Laying out the forms for pouring the foundation.*

rot and dampness. When in the ground it is the number-one choice for this type of building. If cedar is unavailable just ask around for the best wood in your area for underground use and how it should be treated.

When choosing the trees to cut, aim for the straightest logs for uniform thickness. Uniformity of size will make notching much easier. A 6" diameter is the minimum thickness; 8" to 10" would be better. But for ease of handling, the size of the building and therefore the length of the logs should be taken into consideration. Trees which have fallen naturally or have been cut and are lying on the ground must be examined carefully. If an unpeeled log has been on the ground for too long, rot may start to work its way under the bark. If cedar logs are used they should be well dried, because their shrinkage is tremendous. But all logs should be dry and peeled before using.

When our logs were assembled at the site their progression in the building was planned out. Starting with the largest logs, we arranged them with an eye toward uniformity in the tiers and toward a steady succession from thickest to thinnest for the courses.

Actual construction was begun by cleaning and leveling the site. An unleveled site produces unlevel walls and therefore a totally wonky building. We went so far as to use a good level on the ground to assess our progress. Once satisfied, we built the forms for the footing, using 2 × 6 boards. The forms should be strong enough or well enough supported so that they are not pushed out of line when the cement is poured. We braced our forms with outlining stakes that were driven into the ground every few feet and nailed to their outside. To further prevent spreading, holes were drilled and wire braces were put in every 4'.

The footing itself must be solid and strong to avoid settling, to prevent shifting when the site is backfilled, and to ensure that stress is equally distributed throughout the total perimeter of the building. We decided on a concrete footing because it met these standards (13-33). Two alternatives are flat or tamped-down gravel. Neither produces the desired stability and in both cases the chances of rot are greater as the necessary vapor barrier is harder to create between a bumpy surface and the log.

The footing is 6" high and 14" wide and was poured directly on the leveled ground using a 1:5 mixture of cement to sand and gravel. Immediately following the pour we inserted pieces of ⅝" reinforcing rods protruding from the centerline of the footing, one in each corner and the others at approximately 4' intervals, which later served as anchors for the first course of logs. The height of these rods depended on the thickness of the first log. Steel bars or pipe can also be used as anchors; we happened to have some extra rods left over from another project.

After the concrete was poured it was dampened for three days and covered after each watering with feed bags to hold in the moisture. Since cement should cure four to five days before being built upon, we took the opportunity for a break and went camping. Once home, with renewed energy we recommenced work by removing the forms from the now dry cement and placed a strip of 50-pound roofing paper all along the top of the footing as a vapor barrier. This prevented the first course of logs from sitting directly on the cement, which would be constantly wet if in contact with moisture. Logs will rot faster if wet.

Our first course of logs proved our first major mistake. We took the two logs for the long walls and drilled holes to fit them over the rods sticking out of the footing. We then ripped a log in half lengthwise with the chain saw for the short walls, fitting them over their rods in the same manner. These logs were ripped to compensate for the displacement of height between the long walls and short, perpendicular walls. This half-log displacement is necessary for the notching process.

The rectangle of the first course was formed by butting the ends of the short logs against the sides of the long logs at the corners. Much smarter would have been to put down the short half-logs first and then notch the long logs to fit over them, thereby creating a more tied-together fit. These first logs are just sitting over the rods, which is sufficient anchorage as only lateral movement is possible. We did not have a drill long enough to go clear through the logs and so were unable to use thinner ¼" rods which would have been bent over the top of the log for a tighter anchor (13-34).

With the first course down we had reached the point of deciding how to make the door space. The front half-log would serve as the door sill. Fitting the outside door tightly and accurately is a necessity for good temperature control and much harder to achieve if the sill is cement, wood being easier to plane. We knew of two methods of making door spaces in log walls: If enough long logs are available, a

holes drilled in logs to correspond to rebar positions

building paper vapor barrier

end logs are butted up against side wall logs

toenailed

doorway

13-34 Placing the first course.

13-35 Cutting the door.

solid wall can be constructed and a door can be cut out later; or if there are only shorter logs, they can be notched into the structure at one end and later be tied together at the other end by a solid door frame. Since we had few long logs we chose the latter method and stacked the logs at random lengths that were each a bit longer than the beginning of the openings. Using a chalk line as the guide, the logs were later sawed, making straight vertical lines for the door frame (13-35).

The time had now arrived for our first notch; we could no longer procrastinate. The challenge must be met. Knowing ourselves to be the complete novices we really were, we

traded dinner with a more experienced friend for a lesson. It proved invaluable and boosted our confidence. If no one is around as an instructor, use an old log to practice on. It beats wasting a good building log.

We began each notching operation by examining the log for the two straightest, flattest, opposite surfaces and these became the top and bottom of the log as it fit into the wall. We secured the log in place for measuring the notch with a log dog at each end. Using a ruler we took an "eyeball" measurement of the distance between the log we were working with and the parallel one below; this would determine the depth of the notch. By "eyeball," I mean that I made sure my eye was parallel with either surface to be certain I was accurately at the low point of the upper log to be placed and the high point of the parallel one below. Once the depth of the notch was determined, I followed the contour of the end of the perpendicular log below with the ruler and transcribed a series of dots ⅛" shallower than the determined depth. I reasoned marking it ⅛" shallow to allow for miscalculation and overcutting. Be sure that the ruler is always straight up and down or the contour will not be accurate. Also, use a thick crayon when marking so you'll have a clear line to work with. When finished, a semicircle was drawn by connecting all the dots as in a child's game.

We later found an easier way to determine the depth of the notches. Using a scribe or an old compass you measure the distance between the log you are working on and the parallel one below. Open the scribe to that width and lock it there. Then place the scribe at the end of the perpendicular log you want to notch to and transcribe the contour onto both sides of the end you are working on. Repeat the process on the other end, it's as simple as that. Too bad we didn't know this when we were building (13-36).

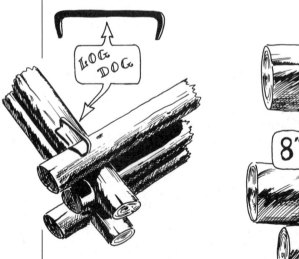
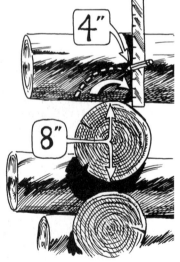

13-36 Determining the depth of notches.

Because so many of our logs were fairly narrow and we did not realize the importance of uniform thickness when they were cut, we sometimes came up against a space between the logs that was larger than ½ the diameter of the log at the notch. This means that if we cut the notch large enough so that the log sat directly on the one below we had to cut out much more than ½ the width of the log. This would weaken it. On the other hand, if we cut the notch to a depth that matched the radius measurement, the log did not sit on the one below but hung suspended. To compensate we had to shim in between some of the logs. This also occurs when the logs taper too much so that you are notching a very small top log over a rather large bottom butt. To avoid this, choose logs that are of uniform width or make a progression from widest to narrowest that is steady, and if possible cut your logs at the same time so they can be compared.

After we individually marked either end of the log, the log dogs were removed and the log was rolled to an upside-down position and was redogged for the chain-saw kerf cuts. The kerfs were then cut to the lines of the semicircle. Remember, for safety, when the walls get too high, take your logs off and do the cutting on the ground. Also, until you are an experienced notcher, and maybe even then, always cut out your notches smaller. It is easier to chisel out a little more to fit the curve than to deal with an oversized notch (13-37).

Using a hammer we knocked out the pieces of wood between the kerfs and chiseled a flat, accurate border on the edge of the notch as a guideline (13-38 and 13-39). With the nose of the chain saw we smoothed out the interior of the notch (13-40). It is wise to practice this step. We ruined a few good logs because of our inexperience.

Once or twice we did hit a perfect bull's-eye on the first try when the log was rolled back into place, but usually we had to chisel out several times to get a good fit.

13-37 Cut kerfs a little shallower than needed.

13-38 Knock out the wood between the kerfs.

13-39 Use a chisel to get an accurate edge.

13-40 Use the chain saw to smooth the notch.

13-41 *Leveling the bumps on the logs using the chain saw.*

Sometimes the notches proved satisfactory but bumps in either the top or bottom log where they met prevented a tight fit. To correct this we wedged up the top log at each end and, using the chain-saw blade laid flat, leveled the bumps (13-41). If done right the logs fell into place when the wedges were removed. When the fit was satisfactory we rolled the log away once more and laid down fiberglass insulation in between the two logs and at the notches. These 2" wide strips of insulation had been cut with a handsaw when the stuff was still tightly rolled.

We used fiberglass to insulate because it would be permanent. The backfilling would make re-chinking from the outside impossible. Once the fiberglass was laid we rolled the log to its final resting place and spiked it down at each notch and at several points along the log to ensure that there would be no movement when backfilling occurred. We used 6" spikes, but the size of the nails depends on the width of the logs. If you have spikes which are not long enough, a hole can be drilled partway through the top log and the spike punched down, using a long bolt as the punch (13-42).

13-42 *Preparing logs for spikes that are shorter than the width of the logs to the notch.*

2" x 8" DOOR FRAME

2" x 6" INSIDE FRAME

6" of fiberglass with paper backing to the outside

1" x 8" CEDAR SHEATHING

2" x 8" BOTTOM PLATE

8" WIDE CEMENT BASE

13-43 Building up an interior nonload-bearing wall.

With each succeeding course, the ends of the logs were alternated so that the butt end of the log above sat on the smaller end of the one below, thereby keeping the building level.

When our courses were completed, we were left with one tier lower, or two sides lower than the others. To compensate we nailed plates of dimension lumber to even out the final tier. Aesthetically, logs would have been preferable but our log supply was exhausted.

Once the log walls were up we poured an 8"-wide cement footing to accommodate the interior wall. This was not a bearing wall

(one carrying structural weight) so reinforcement was not necessary. This wall was framed with 2 × 6 material. Using a chain saw and chisel, a channel was notched in each log at the place where the frame wall met the logs. This provided a straight, flat surface for the end studs to be nailed to and created a snug fit for the wall with no air spaces. We stapled 3"-thick fiberglass insulation to both sides of the frame so that the paper backing of the insulation formed a vapor barrier; then we covered the wall with 1" cedar clapboards (13-43).

13-44 Rafters on 24" centers.

Planer shavings that are stuffed down between the walls are also adequate insulation. The shavings must be bone dry and well tamped when first put in, because they settle. If the wall is not properly filled, the settled shavings will create a space at the top resulting in heat loss.

Constructing the Rafters

By the time we reached the construction of the roof, harvest season was approaching and as an expedient we resorted to the use of dimension lumber for ceiling joists and roof rafters. We had been wrestling with the type of roof to build throughout the summer. Originally, we had decided on a flat-log roof covered with 2' or 3' of dirt. This was cheap, easy, quick, and in our ignorance we believed it to be a good insulator. But the same friend who discouraged our idea of cement walls destroyed this notion too. In our wet climate, he said, this type of roof is sure to leak and as we have rains in the fall often followed by a quick freeze before the snow, we could be left with a frozen mass of dirt covering our precious food. When it did finally fall, the snow would act as an insulator and the big ice cube over the root cellar would remain so until the spring thaw.

Once it was established that we would be building some sort of regular roof design, we had to decide if we wanted to make a functional space under such an exposed roof. Our neighbors had built a log root cellar with a hip roof high enough to allow for a storage area above a well-insulated ceiling. Other root cellars in the area have entire second stories built above them for use as workshops. In the end we chose a simple peaked roof with a 45-degree pitch, coming down to the backfilled ground level.

It was fairly economical; we didn't really need the storage or work space, and we were pressed for time. But most important we considered our root cellar to be aesthetically pleasing as is in its surroundings in the woods as a space exclusively for food. This may seem extravagant, a waste of a good foundation, but for us it was appropriate and resulted in a much lovelier building.

For the ceiling we used cedar 2 × 8s as joists and the random leftover 2" lumber for the ceiling boards. The two boards where the ceiling met the roof rafters were carefully notched to attain a good fit for better insulation. The roof rafters were also 2 × 8s on 24" centers (13-44). The roof had to be strong enough to hold the whole winter's snow load. There would be no interior heat coming up to melt the snow.

In order to determine the pitch of the roof we overlapped the ends of two pieces of lumber, leaving the nails loose so that the boards could move. One of us stood on the ceiling and held the sample rafter while the other stood away from the building and studied the effect of different pitches. We were aiming for a roof that blended the building with the slope of the hillside and whose pitch was steep enough to shed some of the winter's snow. We finally chose the 45-degree pitch.

The rafters were cut and butted at an angle at the top, then supported there with small 2 × 8 horizontal braces. We cut 2 × 8s as blocking for the space between the roof rafters and the ceiling joists and doubled them up to increase the insulative value of the wood (13-45).

The roof of the root cellar is shaked. The shakes (shingles) were split intermittently during construction as a change of pace. If shake bolts can be picked up in the woods, the

13-45 Detail of ceiling joists and top plate of wall.

shakes would be a very cheap, durable, and beautiful roofing material to use, especially in a building where no fire is to be laid.

Our shakes are far from perfect, but there is no leakage from the roof. We had gathered the bolts before knowing much about bolt quality. Western red cedar provides the best shake material, but in the west spruces, firs, and pine can also be used. We picked up our bolts on a Sunday from a logging operation site. They had been rejected because they came from decadent trees whose centers were beginning to rot out. We were most careless in our selection, lugging home many bolts good only for kindling, but we managed to get enough suitable ones to make the hard chore of gathering them worthwhile. Bolts should be straight grained, dry, clear of knots, and if possible from 20" to 30" long, though shakes down to 14" are adequate. The center should not be too rotten so that the shake is of sufficient width, at least 6". The larger the shakes the faster the roof goes on, the fewer nails are used, and the fewer cracks there are, minimizing the chance of leakage.

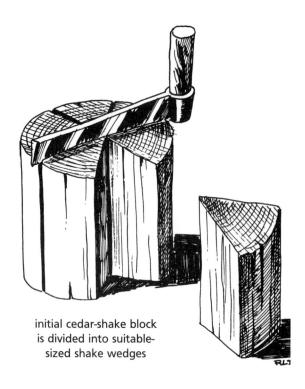

initial cedar-shake block
is divided into suitable-
sized shake wedges

13-46 *Dividing the block to make shakes.*

13-48 *Kathryn Woodward making shakes.*

The bolts were sectioned into a few easy-to-handle chunks and the shakes were split from them with a froe (frow) which was pounded with a birch mallet (13-46 and 13-47, and see pages 216 and 217). The heavier the mallet, the fewer whacks were required to sever the shake from the bolt. But by the laws of diminishing returns, if the mallet is so heavy you cannot lift it, it is of little use.

We tried to make our shakes ⅝" thick and always turned the bolt upside down before the next split for proper taper (13-48). With cedar shakes it is wise to cut the outer white cambium layer off with an ax. It rots much faster than the rest of the shake and will decrease the life of your roof (13-49).

The shakes were attached to 1" × 4" boards that had been nailed across the rafters. Because our shakes were so irregular in length, these purlins were put on separately as we were ready to add another row of shakes. The shakes were nailed in rows, thick end down, starting at the bottom of the roof. Two shakes were nailed down first, using two shake nails in the bottom and one at the top of each shake. Then a third one was nailed to cover the crack and to cover the nails of the shakes below. The distance between the first two shakes depends on the width of the one that is to be laid over the crack, but they must not be too close because

froe

TURN BOLT OVER

produces wedge shape

13-47 *Producing wedge shapes from the bolt.*

13-49 *Cutting off the outer cambium layer.*

13-51 *The shakes being applied to the roof.*

shakes will swell when wet. The next row of shakes was laid down in the same manner, overlapping the first row by 3" or so, and the shorter sides were butted directly against the longer one (13-50 and 13-51).

If your shakes are uniform in size, they can be nailed at regular intervals, eliminating the constant culling and juggling of shakes we were forced to do, and the purlins can also be put on in advance.

3"

COVER CRACKS IN
FIRST ROW

13-50 *Applying shakes to the 1 x 4 wood purlins.*

13-52 The front gable and the roof finished with cedar shakes.

Splitting the shakes and roofing with them was an incredibly satisfying experience. The rhythm of splitting is akin to creating music. And there we were, laying down a lovely, brown-red natural roof high enough up for a good view of the fall color explosion advancing down the mountain slope.

Because the roof looked so nice and shaking was such fun, we used the leftovers to cover the front gable which faces west and gets rained upon. The back gable, facing the mountain was left open for ventilation and to enable the addition of more insulation over the years as settling occurs (13-52).

(Note: there are several other ways to lay shakes on a roof. This is not the most popular way but it fit our needs. Choose one to fit yours.)

Once the roof was waterproof we drove to the site of a long abandoned mill and scraped off the top dry layer of planer shavings from several piles. We managed to accumulate enough for a measly 6" layer of insulation before the fall rains destroyed that source for another year. We were about to abandon shavings as our roof insulation material when a neighbor arrived with a pickup load of new shavings, explaining that she had overestimated her need. With hers we gathered enough for an insulation level of 18".

Prior to adding these shavings we cut a hole in the middle of the ceiling to insert a square box the width of 1" × 6" cedar boards, long enough to reach above the 18" of insulation over the ceiling and extend into the root cellar 2"—20" all together. The ends of the box were screened to deny entry to insects and small animals. This screen is a heavy-gauge stainless steel screen (13-53). This vent allows air circulation inside the root cellar's main chamber to prevent mildew. During very cold weather the vent can be closed to protect against freezing. Some vent boxes are built to almost touch the floor of the root cellar. They bring the low, cool air in. Since we have a ground-level entrance, the cool air can come through the low vents at the bottoms of the doors. Venting a root cellar is dependant upon climatic conditions and should be locally assessed.

To break the monotony of digging the backfill we finished the inside root cellar chamber. First, we chinked over the fiberglass insulation with 1¾" triangular surfaced strips which were cut on a table saw. They increased the insulative value of the walls by adding more wood to the thinnest. At first we tried stuffing the insulation back into the crack before nailing on the strips, but stopped for fear that hard-packed insulation does not work as well. Instead we just let the wood push the insulation as far back as was needed, leaving it fluffy (13-54).

13-53 *Insulating with wood shavings and adding a vent.*

We were now ready to furnish the root cellar. This is an entirely personal matter and depends on what is harvested and what is put up. The number of canning jars and what vegetables and other perishables are stored should determine the size during the initial planning. In our case we resorted to doing the best with

13-54 *Chinking the logs with fiberglass and wood strips.*

what we had to work with. We built a shelf area along the back wall which is 18" wide for the canning jars and divided it in half for the two families. This solid 2× divider acts as a brace to support the crossing shelves. Along the side walls we bolted shelves of varying dimensions to the ceiling joists. The 2× shelf braces hang from the joists so the shelves could suspend from them and not need to be supported from the valuable space below. The space below is a tall space for winter cabbage which is harvested with its roots. The narrower shelves are for storing tomatoes and other wrapped vegetables. Under these shelves are racks made of 2 × 4s to support bins filled with moist sand for storing root crops.

We wanted to experience a full year with the root cellar before building more permanent bins, so we temporarily stored the potatoes, carrots, and beets in small wooden boxes that are used to transport fruit from orchards. We have now decided that the permanent bins should be unattached boxes, larger than the fruit boxes but small enough to be carried out of the cellar in summer for cleaning, airing, and receiving a change of sand.

The life expectancy of a log root cellar is about 25 years if the logs are protected from ground moisture. There are several methods of waterproofing among which are: painting the logs with tar, burning them on the outside with a torch or covering them with a vapor barrier. We chose to cover the walls with building paper, stapling it around the contours of the side and back walls to avoid tearing when the building was backfilled. Once the paper was put on we began the tedious process of bringing the dirt up to the level of the top log in back and under the roof eaves on the sides for maximum insulation. The front was left open.

If a good machine operator exists in your area with a small front-end loader, you can eliminate this tiresome task. This summer we plan to hire this modern alternative to a shovel to push the remaining earth into a long, gentle slope at the sides. We will then build a retaining wall of logs to keep the dirt in place.

The entire floor of the root cellar is covered with a sand and light gravel mixture which can be turned over each summer when the building is aired out (a cement floor would have to be disinfected each year).

Now that we know the root cellar is satisfactory, we will be growing

Birch

Fir can also be used for shakes.

13-55 *The inner door.*

For the outside door a chalk line was drawn and the logs were chain-sawed to create the opening. 2 × 6s were nailed to the top and both sides of this opening to frame the 34" wide × 66" high door (refer to 13-35). It is made of 1 × 12 cedar boards nailed perpendicularly to 2 × 8 cedar with the same vapor barrier. The 2× side faces out. The nails come through the 1×s into the thicker outer board, hiding the nail heads from the visible surface of the door. The size of this door was determined by the need to bring animal carcasses in and out which would be hung in the small outer room. Beneath this door is a very shallow air space to supply the inner door air-intake holes. A stone step was added in front of this door as a finishing touch (13-56 and 13-57).

Our root cellar is now one year old and has proven itself. The only difficulty was the ventilation system was not properly equipped with

more storage crops; but the size is perfectly adequate for the two families, provided that we are careful to utilize the space efficiently. This past winter we were able even to offer some space to a neighbor.

The interior work was done prior to hanging the doors so that we had light, though it was still pretty dim and insufficient. If we had used a method other than hanging for attaching the shelves and if the autumn rains had not been rapidly approaching, it would have been easier to work inside before putting on the ceiling (refer to 13-31). As it was, Jim had just enough time to stand back and admire his handiwork of the newly hung inside door before he was shoved aside by the rest of us rushing to put jars and potatoes in. This inward opening door is 32" × 72" high (2" shorter than the tallest member of the family) and is made of two layers of cedar 2 × 8s nailed perpendicular with a vapor barrier of 50-pound roofing paper between the layers. There are stout handles on both sides of the door that are well secured with screws (13-55).

13-56 *The outer door, looking through the inner door.*

13-57 The finished root cellar.

a sufficient low cold-air intake. Mold developed on jars which had not been wiped clean enough and on the boxes storing the root crops. To allow more air into the inner chamber we drilled three holes at the bottom of the inside door. They were closed off with fiberglass insulation when the cold weather arrived. To eliminate using insulation—which can be eaten by mice—we will build a sliding panel over the holes.

Last winter was a mild one. An occasional nighttime temperature of minus 5 degrees F (minus 20 degrees C) was noted. If this winter is colder we can always leave a pan of coals from the fire to ward off freezing inside the building.

Gambrel-Roofed Root Cellar

A root cellar that was sufficient for two families with plenty of roof space for an out-of-the-way storage area was just what we needed. We didn't want this structure to be incorporated under the same roof as our house or any other building that is heated with wood because of the chance of fire. If it were under the same roof as the wood-heated house, a fire could wipe out our home, clothing, and entire winter food supply. I would never want my food supply to be in such a vulnerable spot. Besides, to have a sufficient cellar for two families we would need a large, accessible area that could be properly protected from the extreme weather. Such a site should have good drainage and preferably be into a hillside or mountain for protection against frost and direct exposure.

As long as we were building another space we might as well incorporate several uses for it. We needed space for wood storage to keep it dry and to allow it to season. We also required additional living quarters like a space for guests to crash or a meditation area away from the general order of things (13-58).

Siting the Root Cellar

We found the perfect site for this structure within the old rock slide to the east of our house. This slide area contained rock and gravel and didn't contain clay like the rest of our soil. Clay is not very porous; consequently a building constructed in this material would probably rot out within 15 years. A large hole over 10' in width was dug out in this slide with a backhoe and the floor area was made reasonably level. The first round of logs was then put around the 10' × 12' area and was lifted and leveled over hefty rock corner piers.

13-58 Our idea for the gambrel-roofed root cellar, showing the pole framing for the roof.

RIPPING LOGS
IN HALF

SNAP CHALK LINE

find center

13-59 *Ripping the logs where they fell.*

Cutting Logs for the Walls

Because we had only a few heavy logs, all much larger than we needed, we decided to rip them at the site where they were felled (13-59). All our material was 80' long, fire-killed snags which were dry as a bone and still standing. To rip these snags we dogged them in place on skids, raising them 16" off the ground at bottom so the chain saw wouldn't kiss the ground while cutting through. We found the top point at either end by holding up a level flush to the end. A chalk line was then snapped along the top of the log and the log was ripped down the center with a heavy-duty chain saw. No guide was used. The cuts were eyeballed, consequently they were not perfectly straight, but they were fine for our purposes. After the rip was made, each of the half-log tops and bottoms was flattened out to create 1½" shelves for strips of fiberglass insulation to rest on (see 13-60 at the top of the following page). This insulation sealed the spaces between the wall courses.

Since we had a flat surface to work with, it was easy to draw the outline for the notch rather than having to scribe it around a contoured surface. The notch used was a triangular one with a vertical inside line to keep the flat walls plumb.

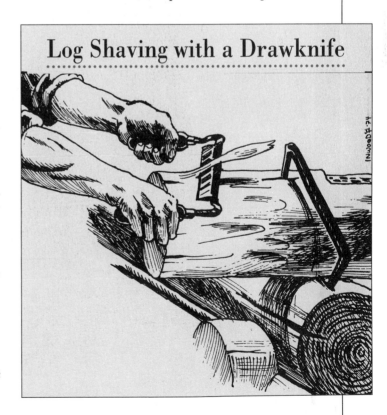

Log Shaving with a Drawknife

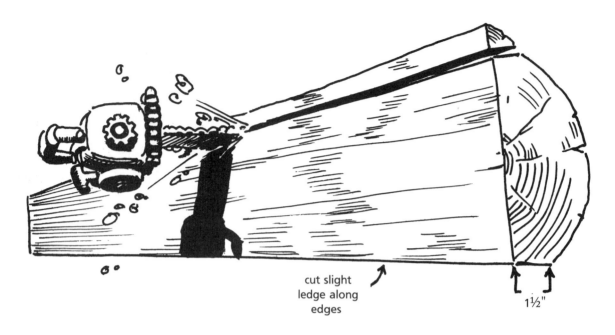

cut slight
ledge along
edges

1½"

13-60 *Cutting the tops and bottoms of ripped logs to allow for insulation.*

The outside line closest to the end was cut at about a 55- to 60-degree angle, making a sort of triangular tenon for the interlocking pieces from the shoulder to the end. The half-round shoulder is jammed against the notch so it can't shift out. For added reinforcement the ends were then spiked through the notch. A simple jig incorporating a straight vertical cut and the angle cut was made. The shape was transferred to the flat face of the log and the notch was cut out with the chain saw. The walls went up extremely fast with this method (13-61). Two simple cuts and the notch was done (13-62).

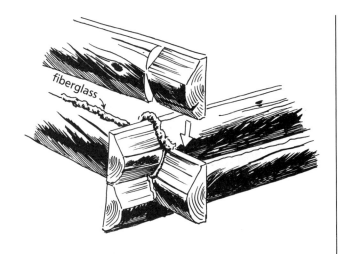

13-61 *How the walls go together so quickly.*

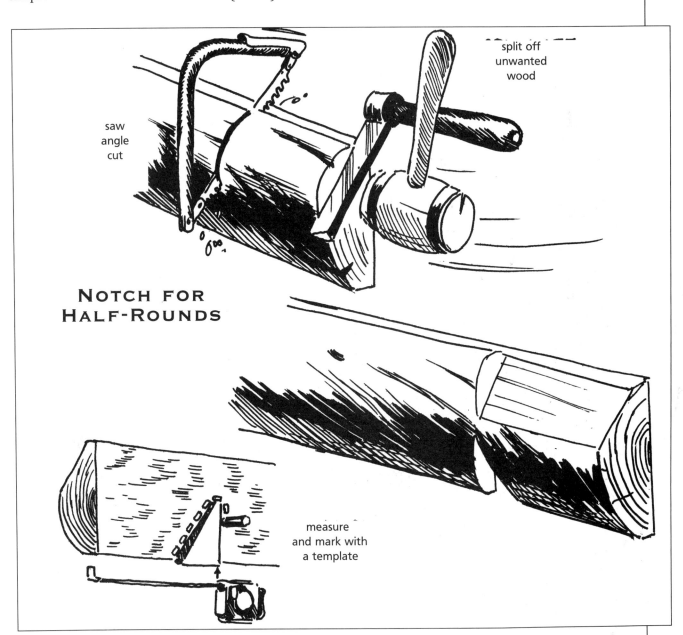

NOTCH FOR HALF-ROUNDS

saw angle cut

split off unwanted wood

measure and mark with a template

13-62 *Preparing the logs for building the walls.*

13-63 Half-round logs joined with a notch cut.

13-64 The corner showing the back of half-rounds.

Working with half-round logs provided a few additional structural benefits. The facing walls went up exactly at the same height each course, because we put one face of a ripped log opposite the other. This made it easier to deal with the ceiling and roof. The faces also provided a flat surface to hang shelves and fasten bins to (13-63, 13-64, and 13-65).

When constructing walls with logs that are stagger-notched you always end up with two sides higher than the other two. The side walls ended up 10" higher than the front and back walls. That 10" became our insulation space between the ceiling and the loft floor. Three 4" × 10" salvaged bridge timbers were notched into the bottom of the side-wall logs as ceiling joists to support the 1 × 6 cedar ceiling. These ceiling joists extend 1' beyond the side walls. The ceiling was nailed on. Two 10"-high logs were added to the top of the front and back walls to create a box over the ceiling. This box was filled with 2 × 10s on 24" centers and

10" of fiberglass insulation sprinkled heavily with lime. The lime is supposed to prevent rodents from eating through the fiberglass. It works well. Only one rodent has been able to do any damage, but he'll soon wish he never went in there.

13-65 The flat surface on the interior of the half-rounds makes adding shelves and bins simple.

13-66 *Angle braces, upright and crossing beam.*

13-67 *Front porch upright crossbeam and brace.*

The 1 × 6 cedar loft floor was then nailed in place. Once this platform was made we built two sets of braces. These are the uprights, crossbeams, and angle braces for the front and rear walls. The uprights extend at a slight inward angle up from the four corners of the building to create a slight slant for the lower sides of the gambrel roof. This slant complements the lines of the roof.

The crossing beams are notched over them and both are supported by angle braces. The side-wall beams were then notched across the frameworks (13-66 and 13-67).

To cantilever the lower roof sides over the side walls a 6" log was spiked over each of the ends of the exposed ceiling joists which extend beyond the side walls. These two poles serve as outer rail eave extensions for the 14" overhanging gambrel roof. This roof also extends 4' beyond the front and 2' past the rear of the building to protect it from direct precipitation.

13-68 Details of the lower part of the gambrel roof.

13-69 Side door with catilevered roof extension.

This lower roof consists of 7'-long rafters, 2 × 4 nailers for shakes, and shakes. The rafter tops were cut at an appropriate angle in a jig for uniformity and were nailed to the crossing side beams at 2' on center intervals. The bottoms were spiked to the eave extension rails at the same interval. The 2 × 4 nailers were nailed across the rafters at 12" on center for the finished roof shakes (13-68).

On the west side of the roof a doorway was constructed as a side entrance for wood. The gravel in front of that entrance was gradually sloped as a truck ramp so birch wood could be carried up for drying. The doorway is framed with 2 × 6s and the small gable roof extension above it is cantilevered on diagonal uprights (13-69 and 13-70).

The upper sections of the gambrel roof were dealt with next. First two 18" extensions were cut and were notched in over the front and rear crossbeams. They raised the loft area to a height of 7½'. A ridgepole was spiked in above the extensions. Rafters were then placed between the side-wall beams and the ridge-pole. The front rafters angle beyond the ends of the beams to outline a 5' overhang at the top.

13-70 The cantilevered roof extension joins the upper section of the gambrel roof.

13-71 *Gambrel roof overhang.*

13-72 *The upper section overlaps the lower section.*

Nailers were placed across the rafters and shakes were nailed above them in the same manner as the lower roof (13-71 and 13-72).

We have few buildings to store things in so it was important that we design the root cellar to contain as much usable space as possible. The gambrel roof on our root cellar almost goes straight up for the first 6' above the walls, the result being there is only about 6" of floor space on either side that doesn't have free head clearance. The inner area is more than sufficient to store the fresh fruits and vegetables and canned goods for two families. It is comprised of two sections. The 2' × 8' outer chamber is an insulating corridor leading to the inner chamber. The chambers are partitioned off by a frame-construction inner wall

with a door. The inner area is comprised of shelf space on the three walls and bins filled with sand on the floor. Some shelves are far enough apart for 2 quart jars to fit snugly on and some are for 1 quart jars. The distances between shelves were figured out accurately so there wouldn't be any wasted space (13-73).

The root bins are located along the bottoms of the walls. They are filled with sand so roots and root crops (carrots, beets, turnips, etc.) could be protected as if they were still in the earth (13-74). None of the bins were made with lids to separate potatoes, onions, and apples. We didn't feel this precaution was necessary. Our apples, potatoes, and onions were sitting on opposing shelves and they all did well. The apples lasted as late as July and were

13-73 *Shelf space covers three walls.*

13-74 *Root bins along the bottoms of the walls.*

13-75 *The root cellar needs proper ventilation.*

13-76 *The top of the outlet vent.*

still crisp and juicy. They did not have even the slightest taste of potato or onion. We ate every one that we stored without having any go bad. The potatoes and onions didn't have any peculiar tastes or odors either. They also kept very well. We attribute a lot of the success of our root cellar to proper ventilation.

A proper vent should have 1" on a side for every 1' along the wall of the root cellar. Thus an 8' × 8' cellar should have an 8" × 8" vent (13-75 and 13-76). We should have brought the vents up through the roof before putting on the shakes but we didn't do so. If the vent is extended beyond the roof, the air will circulate better—especially when the loft gets closed in and used for a room. We didn't want to have to leave a window open all year round for air circulation.

The front door construction of the cellar is unique, neat, and structurally sound. It protects against warpage and is really strong. The door is of laminated pine, planed down to a 2" thickness. It is reinforced with four 1½"-deep dovetailed fir splines. To cut the grooves for the splines I set the blade of the saw to what I

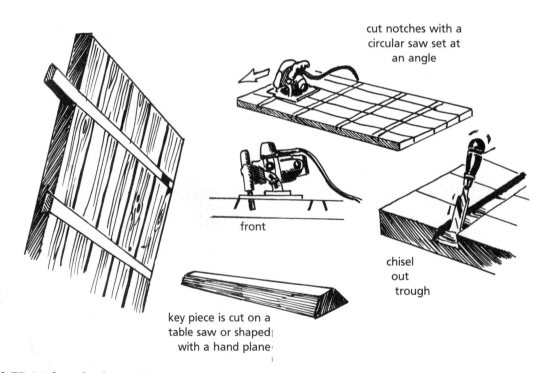

cut notches with a
circular saw set at
an angle

front

chisel
out
trough

key piece is cut on a
table saw or shaped
with a hand plane

13-77 *Making the dovetailed spline door.*

13-78 *Edge view of the dovetailed spline door.*

13-79 *The finished dovetailed spline door.*

the opposite direction. The piece between the cuts was chiseled out. The fir dovetailed splines were then cut out on a table saw and were driven into the slots (13-77, 13-78, and 13-79).

One other thing to note. Be sure to protect your root cellar from spring runoff, especially if it is built in clay or other nonporous types of soil. It should either have drain tile around its foundation or a length of drainpipe down the center to carry off the excess moisture. We have a length of 4" perforated plastic drainpipe just below ground level in the center of the gravel floor. It has helped to prevent moisture buildup and flooding.

thought would be a good angle and put a jig along the door so I could run the saw against it and keep the cut really straight. After that I cut from the other side, making the angle go

Metric Conversion

Metric Equivalents

inches	mm	cm
⅛	3	0.3
¼	6	0.6
⅜	10	1.0
½	13	1.3
⅝	16	1.6
¾	19	1.9
⅞	22	2.2
1	25	2.5
1¼	32	3.2
1½	38	3.8
1¾	44	4.4
2	51	5.1
2½	64	6.4
3	76	7.6
3½	89	8.9
4	102	10.2
4½	114	11.4
5	127	12.7
6	152	15.2
7	178	17.8
8	203	20.3
9	229	22.9
10	254	25.4
11	279	27.9
12	305	30.5

inches	mm	cm
13	330	33.0
14	356	35.6
15	381	38.1
16	406	40.6
17	432	43.2
18	457	45.7
19	483	48.3
20	508	50.8
21	533	53.3
22	559	55.9
23	584	58.4
24	610	61.0
25	635	63.5
26	660	66.0
27	686	68.6
28	711	71.1
29	737	73.7
30	762	76.2
31	787	78.7
32	813	81.3
33	838	83.8
34	864	86.4
35	889	88.9
36	914	91.4
37	940	94.0
38	965	96.5
39	991	99.1
40	1016	101.6

inches	mm	cm
41	1041	104.1
42	1067	106.7
43	1092	109.2
44	1118	111.8
45	1143	114.3
46	1168	116.8
47	1194	119.4
48	1219	121.9
49	1245	124.5
50	1270	127.0

inches	feet	m
12	1	0.305
24	2	0.610
36	3	0.914
48	4	1.22
60	5	1.52
72	6	1.83
84	7	2.13
96	8	2.44
108	9	2.74
120	10	3.05
180	15	4.57
240	20	6.10
300	25	7.62
360	30	9.15

Conversion Factors

1 mm	=	0.039 inch
1 m	=	3.28 feet
1 m²	=	10.8 square feet
1 kPa	=	20.88 psf
1 liter	=	0.26 gallons

1 inch	=	25.4 mm	= 0.025 m
1 foot	=	304.8 mm	= 0.305 m
1 square foot	=	0.09 m²	
1 psi	=	6.89 kPa	
1 psf	=	0.048 kPa	
1 gallon	=	3.8 liters	

mm	=	millimeter
cm	=	centimeter
m	=	meter
m²	=	square meter
kPa	=	kilopascal
psi	=	pounds per square inch
psf	=	pounds per square foot

Index

Addition, shed-roofed, 228
Adz, shipbuilder's, 181
Afterthoughts, 54, 55. *See also*
    Updates, site visit, *and specific*
    construction
Applewood door latch, 152–154

Barn
    with curved-pole roof. *See* Roof,
        curved-pole
    door construction, 152–154
    dovetail-notch logs, 140–157
        door construction, 152–154
        doorways, 148
        joist placement, 148
        lifting logs for, 148
        loft floor, 151
        notch cutting/fitting, 145–147
        retaining wall, 148
        roof covering, 151–152
        roof framing, 150–151
        site, 142
        window glazing, 154
    earthen floor, 144–145
    footings, layout for, 143–144
    hay-drying racks, 228–229
    hayloft, 229
    living in, 156
    planning, 142–143
    shed-roofed addition, 228
    site visit update, 157, 233
    stall building, 154–156
Basement construction, 122
Boards, ripping, 212–213, 275
Boom, swinging, 107–108
Bracing, wind, 202–203
Building site selection. *See* Site
    selection

Ceiling, for wood-frame house,
    75–76
Ceiling joists
    fitting, 215
    installing, 135–137
    placement, in dovetail-notch
        construction, 148
    root cellar, 265

Cellar. *See* Root cellar
Center post, 181–183
Chimney
    building, 34–35, 56, 116–117, 201
    cap installation, 46–47
    cleaning, 63–65
    completion, 56
    forms, 116–117
    foundation for, 34–35
    for sauna, 168
    for wood-burning heater, 63
Chinking, 8, 9, 156
Chisel, stone, 14
Clapboarding, 8, 9, 78, 136–137,
    184, 187–188
Clean up process, 47
Corbeling (splining), 38, 139
Corners, stone foundation, 15
Creosote, 62
Cripple, 73
Cutting dovetail notches, 146–148

Damper
    for fireplace, 40, 42
    for wood-burning heater, 59–60
Door
    construction, 152–154
    cutting openings for, 138
    Dutch, 239
    frame
        setting in a stone foundation,
            23–25
        splines, 138
    front, 219, 282–283
    latch, applewood, 152–154
    root cellar, 282–283
Doorway
    construction, 111–112, 148
    root cellar, 259–260
Dormer
    log framework, 136–137
    pole-framed, 114–115
    shed, 97–98
Dovetail-notches
    construction, 8–9, 140–157
    cutting, 145–148
    site visit update, 157

Drainage
    for log house, 87
    root cellar, 196, 283
    sauna, wood-fired, 166–167
Dutch door, 239
    stained glass, 239

Earthen floor, 144–145
Earth, rammed, 194
End log, 145–149, 259

Fence, 221–222
Fillets, 26
Fire clay, 38
Firebox, 35–36, 51–54
Fireplace
    afterthoughts, 54, 55
    air circulation, 36–37, 56
    basement space and, 56
    building, 138
    central, 49
    chimney, 34–35, 56, 116–117, 201
    chimney cap installation, 46–47
    clean up, 47
    damper, 40, 42
    firebox, 35–36, 51–54
    flue, 42, 53–54
    flue liner, 42–45
    hearth, 34, 51, 54
    heating with. *See* Heater, wood-
        burning
    iron lintel bar placement, 55–56
    materials for, 33–34
    pouring slab for, 50–51
    rock face, 54–55
    "Rumford," 36
    shaping firebox form, 38–40
    slab/footings, 71–72
    starting construction, 37–38
    stone facing, 45
    throat, 40, 42
Floor
    built-up, 210
    earthen, 144–145
    loft, 151
    root cellar, 196, 279
    split-level, 178–180

Floor joists
    chinkless or Swedish-style log
        house, 124
    joist hangers, 72
    saddle-notch log house, 105–106
    setting, 124, 178–180, 196
    vertical log house, 87–88
Flue
    installation, 53–54
    liner installation, 42–45
    proper, 62
Footbridge, 224
Footings
    fireplace, 71–72
    layout for, 143–144
    rammed earth, 194
    root cellar, 258–259
Forms
    firebox, 38–40
    problem with, 28
    removing, 30–33
Forts, log, 101–102
Foundation
    design, for saddle-notch log house,
        104–105
    layout, for log house, 85–86
    piers, 177–178
    posts, 209
    pouring, for sunken greenhouse,
        245–247
    slab. See Slab
    walls, 123, 162. See also Stone
        walls
Framing
    rafters, 186
    roof, 150–151
    walls, 237
    windows, 112–114

Gables, sauna, wood-fired, 167–168
Gin-pole device, 85, 175
Glass installation, for sunken green-
        house, 249–253
Glazing, window, 154
Granite, 12
Greenhouse
    sunken
        designing, 245
        framework, 247–248
        glass installation, 249–253
        heating system, 251–253
        pouring foundation for, 245–247

rafters, 249
site, 244–245
wood-frame, 235–236
    glass, 238–239
    growing in, 243
    hot box, 242
    interior space, 241
    rafter placement, 240–241
    site, 236–237
    venting, 241
    wall framing, 237
    window frames, 239–240

Half-timbering
    fill-in process, 199–201
    technique, 197
Hay-drying racks, 228–229
Hayloft, 229
Hearth, fireplace, 34, 51, 54
Heatalaters (heatforms), 35, 52, 53
Heater, wood-burning
    ashes, cleaning out, 65
    brick enclosure, 63
    chimney, 63
    damper installation, 59–60
    design, 58–59
    firing up, 65
    heat exchanger drum, 58, 61–63
    laying slab for, 59
    outdoor loading door, 65
Heatform, 35, 52, 53
Heating a sauna, 168–171
Hewing
    purposes, 110
    technique, 108–110, 181
Hillside, building on, 192
Hot box, for greenhouse, 242
House Building shock, 71
Houses. See Log house; Wood-frame
        construction

Insulation
    fiberglass, 262–263
    for log wall, 109
    planer shavings, 264, 268–269
    Styrofoam, 19–20, 25–26
Inverted taper, 182

Jack fence, 221–222
Joist hangers, 72
Joists. See Ceiling joists; Floor joists,
        Joist hangers

Kemwood, 111
Kindling cutter, 18

Lifting devices, 148, 175
Lintel bar placement, 55–56
Loft
    construction, 95–96
    creating space for, 184–185
    floor, 151
    hayloft, 229
    joists, 183
    roof slope and, 215, 218–219
Log house
    chinkless or Swedish-style, 121
        basement construction, 122
        building log walls, 124–134
        capping the walls, 123–124
        cutting door/window openings,
            138
        fireplace, 138
        foundation walls, 123
        pouring slab, 122–123
        roof, 135–137
        setting floor joists, 124
        site visit update, 139
        time frame for construction,
            126
    saddle-notch
        basic concept, 101–102
        chimney, 116–117
        closing-in the gables, 115
        construction costs, 119
        doorway, 111–112
        foundation design, 104–105
        hewing logs to fit, 108–110
        insulation, 109
        interior finishing, 117
        joist placement, 105–106
        lifting logs into place, 106–108
        pole-framed dormer, 114–115
        root cellar, 102–103
        shake roof, 115
        sill placement, 105–106
        site selection, 103
        site visit update, 118–119
        walls, 106
        window framing, 112–114
    vertical style
        building site, 83
        drainage system, 87
        foundation layout, 85–86
        interior finishing, 98

laying floor joists, 87–88
loft construction, 95–96
personal considerations, 81–82
redesign, 97
roof finishing, 98
scouting logs for, 84
shed dormers, 97–98
sill placement, 86
site visit update, 99
siting, 84–85
stairs, 98
top plate installation, 90–95
walls, 88–89
Logs
chinking, 156–157
cutting the groove, 128–130
half-round, 275–278
hewing to fit, 108–110
peeling, 84, 208
seating, 128
Lumber. *See also* Logs
ripping, 212–213, 275
scrap or salvage, 176–177

Masonry problem, 20
Moisture, excessive, 19
Mortar, 17, 41

Notches
depth of, 260–262
dovetail, 145–147
hidden shoulder, cutting of,
132–134
saddle
adjusting, 130
cutting, 125–127, 259–262
trial fit, 131–132

Parbuckle, 148
Pointing, 21
Pony wall, 184–185
Post-and-beam construction, 27
with curved-pole roof. *See* Roof,
curved-pole
footings, 194
with half-timbering, 197, 199–201
site visit update, 205
with hand-milled planks
building out walls, 214
design considerations, 209–210
fitting ceiling joists, 215
flooring, 210

front door, 219
interior finishing, 219
loft space, roof slope and, 215,
218–219
raising walls, 210–211, 214
site visit update, 224–225
with log and chordwood infill, 188
beam placement, 181–183
cordwood, 188
erecting posts for, 180
foundation, 177–178
framing the rafters, 186
loft space, 184–185
log & framed walls, 186–188
planning, 174, 176, 177
roofing, 186
setting floor joists, 178–180
sill placement, 178
site visit update, 189
stairway, 189
rafter spacing, 203
roofing, 203–204
structural integrity, 202–203
with stucco & masonry infill. *See*
Sauna

Rafters, 76
constructing, 264–265
double-rafter poles, 231–232
framing, 186
spacing, 203
for sunken greenhouse, 249
Rammed earth, 194
Retaining wall, 148
Ridgeboards, 76
Ridgepole
first, 184–185
second, 232
Ripping, 212–213, 275
Rock. *See* Stone
Roof
for Chinkless-style log house,
135–137
coverings, 151–152
curved-pole
bending poles for, 230–231
double–rafter poles, 231–232
framework, 229–230
second ridgepole, 232
site visit update, 233
finishing, 98
framing, 150–151, 162–164

gambrel, 279–281
Pagoda-style for well, 222–223
pitch determination, 265
shake, 115
slope, loft and, 215, 218–219
Roof pole, raising, 73–74
Roof shakes
attaching, 266–268
making, 216–217, 265–266
nailers, 232–233
Roofing, 186, 203–204
Root cellar, 102–103, 254–283
cedar log
backfilling, 269, 270
building materials, 256–258
ceiling joists, 265
depth of notches, 260–262
doors, 272
doorway, 259–260
first course of logs, 259
footings, 258–259
furnishing, 269–270
insulation, 262–264, 268–269
need for, 254–255
rafters, 264–265
roofing, 265–268
site, 255
ventilation, 272–273
design, 193
floors, 196
gambrel-roofed, 274
ceiling, 278
cutting logs for, 275–278
drainage, 283
floors, 279
front door, 282–283
roof construction, 279–281
root bins, 281–282
siting, 274
venting, 282
walls, 278
setting floor joists, 196
usage, 198
venting, 196
walls, 195
windows, 196
"Rumford" fireplace, 36

Saddle notch
adjusting, 130
cutting, 125–127, 259–262
trial fit, 131–132

Sauna, 159
    adding stucco, 165–166
    advantages, 161
    alternative uses, 170
    back wall, 166–167
    basic construction, 160, 162
    benches, 169–170
    cautions, 170
    drainage, 166–167
    foundation walls, 162
    front overhang support, 164–165
    front wall area, 166
    gables, 167–168
    heat-loss problem, 169
    heating system, 168
    interior finishing, 168
    roof framing, 162–164
    side wall finishing, 165
    site visit update, 171
    subroof, 164
Self-reliance, 224–225
Shelving, 56
Ship-lap, See Clapboarding
Shoulder notches, hidden, 132–134
Sill logs, for earthen floor, 144–145
Sill placement, 105–106, 178
Site selection, 12
    greenhouse, 236–237
    hillside, 192–193
    house, 103, 142, 174, 193, 209
    root cellar, 255
    sunken greenhouse, 244–245
    sunlight and, 83
Site visit updates, See Updates, site
        visit, and specific construction
Skylight, 203–204
Slab
    fireplace, 71–72
    pouring, 122–123
    for wood-burning heater, 59
Sledge hammer, 14
Solar greenhouse. See Greenhouse,
        wood-frame
Splining, 38, 139
Stairs, building, 98–99
Stairway, 189
Stiff leg, 107
Stone
    cutting, tools for, 14

    foundation, 12
    shapes and selection, 13
    working with, 12
Stone walls
    arched windows in, 29–31
    cleaning process, 20
    corners, 15
    dimensions, 16
    height of walls, 22–23
    last courses, 25–26
    mixing mortar for, 17
    planning, 15–16
    post-and-beam construction, 27
    reinforcement of corners, 21–22
    setting in door frames, 23–25
    starting first course, 16
    templates, 18
    vents, 22–23
    wall structure, 19–20
    working time, 15
Stove, oil-drum, 99
String guide system, 18
Stucco, 165–166
Styrofoam insulation, 19–20, 25–26
Subroof, 164, 203
Sunken greenhouse. See Greenhouse,
        sunken
Sunlight, seasonal, 174
Swedish-style log house. See Log
        house, chinkless or Swedish-
        style

Tools, for stone work, 14
Trusses, building, 74–75

Updates, site visit, 79, 99, 118–119,
        139, 157, 171, 189, 205,
        224–225, 233

Vents/venting
    fireplace, 36–37
    root cellar, 196, 272–273, 282
    solar greenhouse, 241
    stone foundation, 22–23

Walls
    building out, 214
    capping, 123–124
    cellar, 195

    finishing, 165
    foundation, 123, 162
    framing, 73, 237
    log, building of, 124–134
    log & framed, 186–188
    pony, 184–185
    raising, 210–211, 214
    retaining, 148
    saddle-notch log house, 106
    starting, 88-89
    stone. See Stone walls
    top plate installation, 90–95
Well
    boulder cribbing, 222
    roof, Pagoda-style, 222–223
Window frames, 30, 239–240
Windows
    arched, in stone wall, 29–31
    bay, 136–137
    framing, 112–114
    glazing, 154
    openings, cutting, 138
    root cellar, 196
    splines, 138
    stained glass, 239
Wood-frame construction, 66–79,
        234–243
    greenhouse. See Greenhouse,
        wood-frame
    house, 67
        ceiling, 75–76
        designing around budget,
            67–69
        fireplace slab/footings, 71–72
        interior finishing, 77
        living in, 77–79
        model, 70
        rafters/ridgeboards, 76
        roof pole raising, 73–74
        site selection, 69–70
        site visit update, 79
        starting construction, 70–71
        trusses, 74–75
        wall framing, 73
Wood lift, dumb-waiter style,
        117–118
Wood stove, for log house, 99
Working alone, problems with, 175,
        209